Psyche and Death

THE JUNGIAN CLASSICS SERIES

serves to make available again works of long-standing value in the tradition of C. G. Jung's psychology:

Aniela Jaffé
APPARITIONS
An Archetypal Approach to Death Dreams and Ghosts

James Hillman
INSEARCH
Psychology and Religion

Marie-Louise von Franz
THE PASSION OF PERPETUA

Victor White
GOD AND THE UNCONSCIOUS
A Priest Responds to Jung's Theology

Psyche and Death

Death-Demons in Folklore, Myths and Modern Dreams

by

EDGAR HERZOG

English translation by
David Cox and Eugene Rolfe

Spring Publications, Inc.
Dallas, Texas

© 1983 by Spring Publications, Inc.

This impression has been prepared from the edition printed in England by Hodder & Stoughton, Ltd., London, and the American edition published (1967) by G. P. Putnam's Sons, New York, for the C. G. Jung Foundation for Analytical Psychology of New York, by arrangement and with permission of the author's heirs.

Originally published in German under the title *Psyche und Tod* by Rascher Verlag, Zurich, as edited by the Curatorium of the C. G. Jung Institute of Zurich.

Printed in the United States of America by Braun-Brumfield, Inc., Ann Arbor, Mich. Published by Spring Publications, Inc., P. O. Box 222069, Dallas, .Texas 75222

International distributors:
Spring, Postfach, 8800 Thalwil, Switzerland
Japan Spring Sha, Inc.; 31, Shichiku-Momonomoto-Cho; Kitaku, Kyoto 603 Japan
Element Books, Ltd; The Old Brewery Tisbury Salisbury; Wiltshire SP3 6NH; England

Cover design by Heather Ryan Kelley from her charcoal drawing, ''Evening Light''

ISBN 0-88214-504-5
Library of Congress Catalog Number 82-063008

Contents

Foreword   *page* 9

PART ONE

Introduction   15

1   The Horror of Death   21

2   Killing   28

3   The Shrouding "Hider-Goddess"   38

4   The Death-Demon as Dog and Wolf   46

5   The Death-Demon as Snake and Bird   55

6   The Death-Demon as Horse—from Animal to Human Forms   66

7   Tools and Attributes: Characteristics and Manifestations of the
       Death-Demon in Human Form   75

8   The Food of the Shades and Communion with the Ancestors   84

9   The Death-Demon as Fate   93

10 The Death-Mother, Marriage with Death and Paternal Aspects   99

11 Frau Holle and Percht—a Late Return of the Death-Demon   114

continued

PART TWO

Introductory Note   135

12   Dreams 1: Repression of Death, Flight and Initial Acceptance   139

13   Dreams 2: Killing   149

14   Dreams 3: Archaic Forms of the Death-Demon   160

15   Dreams 4: The Kingdom of the Dead, Death; Procreation and Rebirth   177

16   Dreams 5: Dreams of Death as an Expression of the Process of Development   194

Bibliography   211

Index   215

Foreword

I must begin by putting on record my gratitude to my teacher and friend Professor Gustav Schmaltz, who died in 1959. It was more than twenty years ago that he introduced me to the psychology of C. G. Jung, and enabled me to appreciate its wide range. As a result I learnt a new method of working in ethnology, ethnic psychology and, in particular, mythology. This method is based on depth psychology, and it has been of decisive importance for my studies, both in my psychotherapeutic practice, and also with respect to the present work.

To anyone acquainted with the work of Jung the influence of his personality and ideas will be obvious, for he will come across Jung's basic concepts everywhere, even when they are not explicitly acknowledged. However, I am also under obligation to the other great teachers and masters of depth psychology—to Sigmund Freud, the pioneer whose example of methodical care continually forces me to make new appraisals; to Alfred Adler and Fritz Künkel, who have had a greater influence on contemporary psychology than is generally realized. My book is intended for all those who are interested in depth psychology, and particularly for psychotherapists, whatever their approach may be. Its subject—Death—concerns us all equally, to whatever "school" we may belong.

One might suppose that those who have been exposed to the imminent risk of death in one or both of the great wars of this century, and who have endured the even more moving experience of the actual *death of the other person*—brother, son, friend or comrade—at close quarters would feel with special poignancy that the ability to endure the presence of death in life is of decisive importance for human living. To open oneself to death is to accept the aspect of "becoming", that is, of transformation, which is the very stuff of life, and so, at length, to realize that the human condition transcends itself. On the other hand it is also true that the "excess of death" has produced a tendency in men and women to shut themselves off from this aspect of life by putting aside all thought of death. This leads to the inhibition of *real* becoming, and creates in its place an appearance of security which is, in fact, continually threatened by unconscious anxieties giving rise to *neuroses*. In my work I have found it enormously fruitful to understand neurosis in this existential way, that is, as a failure of the psyche to come to grips with "the basic conditions of human existence" —either because it dare not, or because it does not succeed in the attempt. One of the most important of these basic conditions is death. I have come to this approach as a result of the ideas expressed by my wife, Johanna Herzog-Dürck, in her numerous publications, and these ideas have been a continual stimulation in my work.

This book is based on lectures given at the Munich *Institut für Psychologische Forschung und Psychotherapie*, in 1948 and later. *In the first part*, I have tried to show how mankind has always attempted to express and come to terms with death by means of images, how such images are often of tremendous power and how, as always with true symbols,[1] they allow the aspect of becoming and of transformation of life to grow gradually clearer and clearer. *In the second part*, I have tried to show a similar process in the dream-life of contemporary man and to draw out its significance for psychic development and growth.

I started work in the field of ethnic psychology many years ago under Wilhelm Wundt, but I cannot claim the authority of an expert. On the other hand I hope that the points of view derived from depth psychology, and the more recent approaches to mythology which take account of the work of Rudolf Otto, Walter Otto and particularly Karl Kerényi, may be recognized as fruitful.

The dream material which I present was made available to me not only by the kindness of the dreamers themselves, but also by that of many probationers and junior colleagues at the Munich Institut.[2] I am extremely grateful to them all. They have not only let me use single dreams, but also parts of reports on treatment referred to me as

[1] A "symbol", as Jung uses the word, has two characteristics: (*a*) It is an image naturally produced as a living expression of the thing symbolized (i.e. it is quite different from an arbitrary sign); (*b*) it expresses both conscious and unconscious factors, and in doing so it unites them (*Trans.*).

[2] Where it has been necessary to give biographical details they have been disguised in such a way that the identity of the dreamer cannot be inferred.

instructor. This was particularly valuable because the Munich Institut has a "bi-partite" organization, and most of the probationers had a psycho-analytical[1] approach. This means that we can be sure that the dreams they brought to me were not even unconsciously induced in the dreamers by my own lines of thought, and I consider that this is extremely fortunate, since it creates a form of control. Finally I must thank Gustav Schmaltz for the valuable assistance he gave me by his participation in and criticism of my work, and by apt references to the relevant literature.

I am delighted that I have been asked to publish this work in "Studies from the C. G. Jung Institute, Zurich",[2] as in doing so I can express in explicit terms my veneration for its founder.

[1] Psycho-analysis is a technical term for the Freudian school of psycho-therapy (*Trans.*).

[2] A reference to the German edition (*Trans.*).

Part One

Introduction

THE myth of the death of Hainuwele is a deeply significant story which is still alive on Ceram, one of the Molucca Islands. The divine maiden Hainuwele was born from a tree, and appeared to the men of olden time. She had a store of marvellous riches from which she brought priceless gifts, and continually showered them on the people. At first they were delighted, but after a time they found the immense quantity of the presents disturbing to them, since it seemed likely to disrupt the balance and harmony of their life. At that time the people were divided into nine families, and they used to dance the Great Maro Dance. This took nine nights, and on each night they danced a ninefold spiral. On a certain occasion Mulua Hainuwele sat in the middle of the spiral and distributed presents to the dancers until, after the eighth dance, the people made a secret resolve to kill her. They dug a pit, and on the ninth night they thrust the maiden into it, and in the course of the dance stamped the earth down above her.

The following morning the maiden's father searched for her, found the pit and dug up her body. He dismembered the body and buried it, piece by piece, round the dancing floor. The buried pieces transformed themselves into things which had not previously existed on earth—particularly the bulbous fruits which have been the main food of the people ever since. Her father did not bury Hainuwele's arms; these he took to Mulua Satene, another divine maiden, who was at that time ruler over men.

Mulua Satene was angry with the people because of the murder. She built a great gate on the dancing floor in the shape of the ninefold spiral of the Maro Dance. She stood on the trunk of a banana-tree on one side of the gate, and called the people together on the other. She said, "I shall now leave you, but before I go you must come to me through this gate. *Only those who go through the gate will remain human.*" *Those who did not go through the gate became animals or spirits of the wood*, and this was how pigs, stags, birds, fishes and all kinds of spirits came into being. Mulua Satene held an arm of the dead Hainuwele in each hand, and as each person came through she touched him with one of the arms. Since then human beings have had to die and undertake a difficult "journey of the dead" in order to see Mulua Satene again. There is a supplementary myth which says that only since that time have human beings been able to marry—that is, that since death came into the world there have also been procreation and birth.

In this myth we can see a fourfold interpretation of the relation between death and human life. First, it seems as though man cannot endure the unending abundance which life gives; the very abundance is like *a sin, and by leading to murder it brings death into the world*. Secondly, this reveals one of the conditions of life—dead life transforms itself into food, and food is transformed back into life: what we have here is a faint adumbration of the fact that *life itself means transformation*. The third and crucial insight is contained in the statement made by the divine Mulua Satene, that only those who are prepared to go through the Gate of Death and to allow themselves to be touched by death remain or become human, in the new and true sense. *Man can and should encounter death "consciously", and this is what distinguishes man from the animals.* Fourthly, from this knowledge comes the awareness of a further aspect of existence, since consciousness of death reflects back upon and illuminates the other frontier of life, its beginning, birth. Thus life, with its beginning and end, is seen as being embedded in something mysteriously all-embracing, something which may yet be one, even though it shows two faces to life—the face of death, the robber, that stirs up fear and horror, and the friendly, generous face of birth.

The myth of Ceram strikes the chord of death and its significance for man; and this is the subject of our psychological investigation. The question with which we are concerned is "How does man relate to, and come to terms with death, which seems to stand in irreconcilable contrast to life and to all his experience of living things?" We are not concerned with man's intellectual response to his peculiar physical defencelessness, and the protective measures which he takes against death by the creation of tools and other means: our concern is with the way in which *man as a whole, in the centre of his being, feels touched by the inevitability of death.* We ask whether he is able to bring this fact into harmony with his feeling for life.

There is no doubt that whenever man has encountered and become aware of death he has been horrified in the depths of his being: whether it is his own impending death or the death of others which presents itself to his consciousness. How can he endure this horror? How respond to it? He is confronted by something wholly incomprehensible, something monstrous in its all-conquering, dark power—and he is helpless before it. Should he banish this incomprehensible horror, forget all about it in order to grasp the reality of life with its appearance of intelligibility? How can he, *when death remains a fact which cannot be denied*? Death cannot be eliminated! Should man, then, deny the reality of life, and try to understand and organize it in relation to death? Man can only find a way of uniting death and life, of bringing them into harmony, if he is prepared to transcend the limits of his existence. This task is only possible if man can see that part of himself reaches into the unknown, and that it is from the unknown that order and meaning are given to his life.

Our investigation has two points of departure. One determines the character of the first part of the book; the other that of the second part.

The starting-point for Part I might be called "ethnological—mythological". Our material is reports and traditions from all parts of the world, and we shall use it to investigate, describe in comparative terms and interpret man's collective behaviour when face to face with death. In this part our concern is with the psychological reaction of groups, tribes and peoples. We shall be concerned with fully-developed rites, mythological stories and late, attenuated folk customs which still survive within our own cultural sphere. The methods we use are derived, in particular, from the depth psychology of Jung and the mythological studies of W. F. Otto, and these methods give results which have a fair degree of probability. We aim to give a synoptic account of a possible psychological development, so that we can say: "In some such way as this man may have evolved and matured his view of the world and his consciousness of existence, as a result of his repeated encounters with death." From this starting-point of primitive myths and rites, which belong to man in collective associations, we shall trace the development to the point at which the great religions, on

the one hand, and philosophy, on the other, speak to men as individuals
—challenging them to make a personal decision by which to bring
life into relation with the reality of death.

The starting-point for the second part is the dreams of contemporary
men and women, since psychotherapists recognize that dreams express
in man the striving and activity of the great unconscious realm of the
psyche.

Part I is mainly concerned with "earlier" man, and the situation of
the civilized man of today is very different from his. Religion, culture
and civilization no longer provide for man collectively, but demand
personal and individual decisions and response—and modern man
expects these things from himself. This demand is of enormous
proportions and, since there are few people who are in any way equal
to it, the development going on today is fraught with danger. The
danger arises because of the overwhelming multitude of those who
claim "individuality" as their unquestioned right, but are wholly
unaware of the deep obligation which goes with it. Individuality
demands that a man should seek to determine his own life by his own
decision, and this can only be done by those who are willing to engage
in a personal struggle. This is sufficiently well known, and I shall not
go further into the dangers implicit in modern developments. Between
the two groups, of those who acknowledge the obligations which go
with individuality on the one hand and those who claim the right to
individuality with untroubled calm on the other, there are a considerable number of people who are disturbed in mind. Recognizing
that it is impossible for them to fall back into the collective psychic
life of early man they feel the call to shape their own life, but they do
not yet have the strength to follow this call to individuality. They
too withdraw, not into the general callousness of the majority, but
into neurotic sickness—which may have somatic symptoms or be
purely psychological, creating more or less severe disturbances of
character.

The neurotically sick person of today is one who feels the challenge
to live from his own resources in a most painful and distinct form,
because although he is aware of the challenge he knows that he cannot
fulfil it, and cannot fully understand it. Thus it is probably true that
psychotherapy always means that the patient must establish a piece of
his own being as a starting-point from which his individuality may

grow, in order that he may enter into the struggle to shape his own life.

In the background of many neuroses, however, the question of death lies unexpressed and generally unconscious, yet also unavoidable. It is often disguised by the problem of realizing sexuality, and this is especially true of patients in the first half of life. If we are able to see the wisdom of the myth of Ceram and of many puberty rites this will not surprise us; the myth says that procreation and birth have only existed since death came among men, and countless peoples begin their initiations with a deeply horrifying experience of death. Because of the existence of the problem of death (however unconscious it may be) the psychotherapist finds that the dreams of his patients express the effort to come to terms with death much more often than is generally supposed. Such dreams are often difficult to decipher because they tend to make use of images which express primitive ideas about death held by early peoples, and this suggests that the dreamers in question are either repressing their awareness of death entirely, or else evading its full reality. Like most modern people they have grasped only one side of reality, the side of life, but as a result of greater sensitivity they are constantly disturbed by the full reality of death at an unconscious level—a reality which also reveals new aspects of life.

As C. G. Jung would say, the archetype threateningly raises its head in their unconscious, and they have no alternative but to encounter it there, and retrace in their own inner life the path taken by humanity in its early stages of development. This path starts in pure horror, without name or form, and leads to the creation of (or the encounter with) inner images which portray death. At first the images only express the horror of death in its most frightful form, but once the form and essence of death have been "seen" it becomes possible to "perceive" it through feeling. The form makes possible a differentiation of the essence, so that new images arise which express other aspects of death. From time to time the demonic monsters evolve and transform themselves in such a way that they remind us of chthonic divinities of destiny, in which death and life are brought together in a primeval harmony. Modern man sometimes experiences such a mythological process in his dreams, and in this way he experiences his own existence as part of a world order which begins to reveal a meaning for life as well as death. This has a rough correspondence to the collective development of the human race in the past, which today is too often distorted by the one-sided development of the intellect so that it cannot be lived through in its various stages.

In the course of psychotherapeutic treatment the original collective development can often be followed as an *individual experience*, and brought close to consciousness through dreams. In this way the individual comes to a threshold and, standing there, he can make the personal effort to mobilize his own resources in a living way, in order to face the challenge of making a decision about his attitude to life and death. Such a decision is always a religious act.

The second part of our work is an attempt, often fragmentary and inadequate, to show how these developments (which are often very subtle) can be seen as processes of the development and maturation of modern man, in and through his dreams.

1. The Horror of Death

THERE is a most remarkable story in the Grimm Brothers' collection about a man who set out on a journey in order to learn to shudder: that is, to learn how to be afraid. The boy who cannot shudder is still living in an undifferentiated state of the world. He is a part of the world with no individual destiny of his own, so that like the animals he is an unthinking expression of life and existence: that is why he cannot experience fear. He is not horrified by the dead lying in the churchyard, nor the spectre in the church tower at midnight, because he has not become aware of the existence of "the other" as other than himself. He is the child who "can make no differentiation". Everything is part of the same thing, which is himself—he is "identical" with everything, and everything is "identical" with him. When he is confronted by a hanged man he has no fear because he does not feel him as other than and different from himself. Finding a dead man in a coffin in the castle he greets him, "Ha! ha! that is my little cousin, who only died a few days ago," and calling, "Come, little cousin, come!" he lifts him up without any revulsion, and takes him into his own bed to warm him. Nor is he disturbed when the dead man comes alive (a real, active "other") and behaves churlishly—he simply puts him back in the coffin like a naughty child who is shut up in a dark room.

From one point of view the boy's inability to differentiate his environment from himself is pleasantly childish, but it is also inhuman. That is why the boy is sent away from human beings into the unknown, without a name or any individuality. His father says, "Do not tell anyone where you came from or who is your father—I am ashamed of you." His father, the sexton, the carter and the innkeeper all seem to agree that in order to be human one must be able to experience horror, and the boy agrees as well, since he has vague longings which drive him out to "learn to shudder". The horror which is constantly presented to him in a vain attempt to evoke fear is horror in its original and immediate form—the horror of death.

It is always like this—one has to learn to shudder before one can really become human.[1] The capacity to feel horror at death is one of the most essential characteristics which distinguish man from the animals, and this horror is quite different from the instinctive fear of death which is, of course, a feature of animal life as well. Even though it is true that some animals seem to feel something which we tend to understand as grief at the death of a close member of their own species, this is probably more the dull sensation of a gap—an unpleasant alteration of the environment—which is felt by the animal as a diminution of its own life and vitality. The animal does not experience death as something which confronts it like an abyss and engenders immeasurable horror because it seems beyond all comprehension. The attitude of the boy in the story is *in*human because it is *pre*-human. It is only on the basis of horror that a man can develop an inner attitude to the fact of death, and only when he has done this can life itself emerge into consciousness.

The feeling of absolute horror as a primeval reaction to death can still be found among ourselves. For example, a sixteen-year-old boy who was involved in the final struggles of the last war formulated the feeling: "When I saw the dead lying there I felt nothing except a horror-struck revulsion. For God's sake don't look! Get away, just get away!—and if I could I would have run blindly away, as far as I could; but of course we were not allowed to." This feeling seems to lie behind, and to be the preliminary stage in the mythical formation of the world pictures which have evolved among different peoples in a great variety of ways; blind horror and panic revulsion in the face of death are found among the most primitive tribes we know, and these tribes may have neither rites nor formulated mythical conceptions, and so lack even the rudiments of a world picture. For example, it is

---

[1] In the story the young man finally learnt to shudder in the marriage bed, when his wife poured a bucketful of wriggling fishes over him while he slept. Humorous as this may appear the symbolism is deeply significant. The fishes make the young man experience horror at that which is intensely alive. In myths and dreams the fish is a symbol for sexuality and birth, and, as we shall see later, the "Divinity of Death" protects unborn children in the well or pond in which fishes live.

reported that until recently the Senoi (one of the group of Weddoids in the north-east of the Malayan Peninsula) knew no form of burial, but that when one of them died they left the body and fled from the place, never coming back to it if they could avoid doing so.

The Takkui are an unusually timid food-gathering people living in the forests of Laos on the Upper Mekong in North-East India: they too take to their heels in panic flight when one of their relatives dies, because the dead man inspires such revulsion. The same kind of thing is reported of the Kubu, another primitive Weddoid people in Southern Sumatra. These have been influenced by neighbouring tribes, and have developed various forms of "burial"[1] (exposure on a platform, and burial in hollow trees or the earth), and have even been settled as agricultural peasants by Europeans; yet even today when someone dies it is their custom to abandon the place of death (and their fields and settlements as well) for several months—not troubling about cultivation and harvest. Naturally we know very little about tribes who wander in the jungle and fearfully avoid meeting Europeans, but we do know that the Takkui, for instance, have no domestic animals, not even dogs, and that no traces of dances or other rituals have been found among the original Kubu.

It seems likely that the original and natural "human" response to the experience of the horrible is flight, and that the remote ancestors of more developed peoples reacted in this way. This is why it is important to have a right psychological understanding of the flight reaction. Wundt has made an intensive study of it, and he says, "The moment the human being dies the first impulse is to abandon him where he lies and to fly. . . . The flight from the corpse shows that man's chief terror is on his own account. If a living man remains by the dead he is involved in the danger of being overtaken by death himself . . .", because now "the dead man becomes a demon in the eyes of the living, i.e. a being which can invisibly catch, overpower, and kill man." This interpretation, however, does not do justice to the panic element which is clearly involved. Horror gets its special character from its incomprehensibility, its formlessness, and from the absence

[1] The English word "burial" has the specific meaning "earth burial", the German word used here means "disposal of a body" and there is no English equivalent. We have used "burial" in quotation marks when it has the more general meaning. (*Trans.*).

of any image, as well as from its invisibility. So long as the feeling of horror has no object *everything* becomes an object of terror, and (paradoxical as it may seem) both the terror and its object become unlimited. The "world" becomes uncanny, and man feels that his whole existence is threatened and called into question. In such moments it is not so much that a man fears for himself as that he experiences nameless horror because he is confronted by something nameless—he is not confronted by a demon (which he would have to name) into which the dead man has turned. The idea of the demon probably belongs to a later stage of psychological development, because when man can find an object for his terror he no longer flees in sheer panic horror, even though the object may be conceptual rather than actual. Having found an object man can take counter-measures, and if the object he "finds" is a demon these counter-measures will take the form of a magic spell; alternatively man may recognize a mysterious power in the demonic, before which he must bow in awe. Sheer flight neither represents a counter-measure nor expresses reverence. In itself the experience of horror does not have anything to do with the magical, but it contains the seeds of both the magical attitude and the attitude of reverence. Horror is probably "the earliest" human experience of a "tremendum"—of that which is "utterly unapproachable", as Rudolf Otto describes it: the decisive thing is that the experience of horror is clearly different from the purely instinctive terror of death when it threatens the life of the individual himself. We are concerned with *the death of the other person,* of the tribal or family comrade, and when man is gripped by terror and horror at the inexplicable change in his comrade it is because that which was living and comprehensible has suddenly changed into something different and incomprehensibly uncanny. Since he feels momentarily cut off from the known world his existence is threatened in a deeper sense than it is by the instinctive fear of death. Thus it is likely that the primary psychological aspect of the encounter with death is this being gripped by a "wholly other" which seems to open up strange dimensions, and so to call in question the secure and self-evident character of existence. Man encounters the tremendum and his first response to it is flight.

One can observe a more developed and differentiated attitude among some of the people who react by flight to the death of a member of their tribe. For example, the Mangyan (primitive Malays in Mindoro)

24

abandon a dying man, but come back after a time *to see whether death has taken place*, and this shows something more than the purely panic horror of the most primitive peoples. When a man has died the Mangyan let him lie in his hut, cover him with leaves or (probably at a later period) bury him in some other way, and only then desert the place for years—without any concern about the fields they have begun to cultivate. It is reported that the Dungans of North Turkestan abandon the dying in their dwellings and go right away. The Kirghizes and Kalmuks are nomads who carry the sick far away into the bush or the steppes and leave them there with a supply of food. We also find traces of the simple abandonment of the dying by African bush Negroes, but this seems to be due to necessity on their wanderings, and their usual custom is to bury a corpse, then hastily abandon the burial place and avoid it carefully afterwards. Yet when there is sickness they make a "pilgrimage" to the graves and talk to the dead. Burial and, even more, the consultation of the dead who are avoided in great fear at other times, suggest that a psychological development has brought about an attitude very different from the sheer horror of the Senoi, Kubu and Takkui.

Since the Mangyan still flee from the dying and from the place of burial they are still aware of the fearful quality of the tremendum, but their return to one who is expected to be dead and the act of burial shows that they have begun to accept as part of life the reality which roused the horror, and to realize that man must *adopt an attitude* to it. The return to the dead man is to some extent a realistic assertion of oneself in the presence of death: the act of "burial"—whether it is abandonment in the hut, covering the body with leaves, interment in the earth or the cave, or exposure on a platform—expresses a "recognition" of the final otherness of death. Eventually, when this "recognition" gives rise to a regular "burial" practice it also involves the recognition of death as the general destiny of man. Thus "for the first time", in spite of terror and horror, the tremendum is revered in a practical way through these early forms of burial.

The return to the dead and the practice of burial mark the stage in man's development at which he is able to assert himself and his reality in the presence of death; but the return from sheer horror brings about a change in man's awareness of life, since it can only be achieved by the inclusion of the fact of death in his attitude to life. It is only when this stage has been reached that man can make the attempt to include the secret of death (or, better, of the dead) in his conceptual thinking. Naturally it is inconceivable that life has simply disappeared:[1] it is not that life is seen to be extinguished by death, but that what was accepted as self-evident at an earlier stage is now seen as a mystery. Before he died the dead man presented no problem—he was simply accepted as he was—but through death he has become a mysteriously changed being. He has been transformed, and it is possible for the living to imagine that something of the tremendum, the incomprehensible, the wholly other, has been incorporated in him—or, rather, that he "is" the reality which has presented itself in the shape of death. Once the dead man is thought to share in the uncanny he can become a demon, and horror at the sight of his corpse becomes real fear for one's own actual life.

If this is a rough characterization of the psychological situation of the Mangyan, then their *second* flight (and the parallel among the African bushmen, the *final* avoidance of the place of the dead) takes on a different aspect. It appears as a security measure against the danger presented by the dead man who has become a demon, and it is at the same time both an expression of the primal horror, and the first stage of "magical" defence against it.

We have now seen two different tendencies directed towards the psychological assimilation of the experience of the tremendum. The return to the dead man and burial originally signify an inner *recognition* of death, and an actual partaking in the action of unfathomable fate. This is one of the earliest steps towards the "perception" of human experience. On the other hand, the flight *after the return* and the avoidance of the place of death is the first outward, magically-intended[2] counter-measure against death. In so far as one can speak of a

---

[1] The fact, mentioned by J. Maringer, that the men of the recent palaeolithic period often put ochre (which is the colour of blood) in the grave with their dead or poured it on the grave as a libation may be relevant here.

[2] "Magic" and "magical" are commonly used with many meanings and shades of meaning. We understand "magic" and "magical attitude" in contrast to a really religious attitude. The religious man seeks for a "comprehensive", "divine" order and recognizes and accepts it with voluntary reverence. "Magical man" endeavours to break through the divine order (which he implicitly presupposes) in his own interest, and to take the godhead into his service.

"recognition of death" in relation to this it is at most a reluctant recognition of the outer fact—a fact so monstrous and dangerous that man does all he can to avoid and eliminate it.

It should not need saying that both these tendencies operate simultaneously in the psyche, and influence human behaviour: yet human development always seems to lead to a point when one becomes more clearly differentiated and gains predominance over the other. The second trend (towards defence against death) suggests an assertion of the ego in its *adaptation to outer reality*; the first (the acceptance of fate) suggests a self-subordination to inner reality. One leads through magic to the domination of the physical order by means of natural science, the other leads to religion and the perception of being.

2. Killing

MAN first encountered death as "nameless horror", so that it is not surprising that he had to undergo a long process of development before he could accept the dreadful fact of death as something essentially related to life, and as an essential feature of the human condition. At first death must have seemed to be the absolute opposite of life, revoltingly alien. Yet man only becomes conscious of "dear life" (as Homer called it) in its familiar reality as a result of the contrast with death, and this contrast gives life a value of its own by providing a dark background to show it up more radiantly.

Because the encounter with death lies at the very beginning of consciousness of life, the many mythologems which speak of an original state of the world in which there was no death must be of great antiquity. The best known and most profound is the story of the Garden of Eden in Genesis, in which it is said that death came into the world when man ate from the tree of knowledge, and it is to be noticed that birth is said to have come into being at the same time. The story goes further, and it may seem strange that the first event related after the expulsion of man from the paradise of everlasting life is a murder: the killing of Abel by Cain. This story seems to sound the first distant notes of a mythological motif which is spread all over the world, according to which death originated from a murder among the first people. The myths of the nations say again and again that there has been death in the world since the first murder. A classic formulation is the myth of Hainuwele from the island of Ceram, recounted in the Introduction. In that story the divine maiden Hainuwele is actually murdered by the people among whom she lives in a kind of cultic ecstasy. Since the murder, the story goes on, men die—they must pass through the Gate of Death—and also there is procreation and birth among them. This maiden is ambiguous: on the one hand she is human and on the other hand she has characteristics which suggest both earth and moon deities. A related idea is found among aboriginal Khonds of North-East India[1] in the form of a dark tradition about the murder of the Earth-Mother, and the Vedas have the story of the slaying of Soma, god of life and death, who, as god of death, is also the moon. It is uncertain whether the motif of the murder of a primal father of the human race is reflected in the Egyptian myth of Osiris, but the dead were all called "Osiris" as children bear their father's name. Among the Witoto Indians of South America it is made explicit that the story of the first murder refers to the killing of the *primal father Moma*. This Moma was a moon-creature, a creator and the god of the underworld, and it is said in the Witoto myth, as in that of Ceram, that because of this first death all men afterwards had to die.

The corresponding mythologems of the Luiseño Indians of Southern California show some very remarkable details. For example, one story about the primal period runs as follows:

"At that time all the animals were still human, and the Earth-Mother sent her children into the four quarters of heaven. . . . In their wanderings the people came to a pond and stopped to play and swim in it. *Ouiot*, the primal father, was with them. *Wahawut*, the frog, was an attractive woman with long hair, and when she jumped into the pond Ouiot (to his surprise) saw that her body *had no flesh on its back*. He did not say anything, but he thought about it, and Wahawut read his thoughts and began to wonder how she could kill him. Her wish made Ouiot sick, and none of his people could heal him. The titmouse found out that Wahawut was trying to kill him by witchcraft, but Wahawut herself had disappeared in the mud and water because she had been consorting with evil thoughts, and she could not be seen." (There is another version which says, "When Ouiot grew old the eldest of his descendants decided to kill him with poison".) "As Ouiot grew more and more ill he told the people that he would have to die, and he also told the royal crested stork, *Chehemal*, that he would come back after his death . . . after three days Chehemal climbed to the roof of his house in the darkness, and everyone heard him sing, 'Ouiot, Ouiot is coming! he is coming! I am looking

[1] Fuller details in *The Golden Bough*, J. G. Frazer, v. Khond. See too references to related ideas among the Pawnee Indians and in West Africa (Lagos and Benin).

for him, watching the East. Ouiot is coming!'—then the new moon rose in the sky."

The Luiseños have other, supplementary legends. In one we read: "Before he died Ouiot called together the people of the primal period and told them it was he *who brought death*. Nobody had ever died before, but after he had died all would have to die. Before his death Ouiot said to the people, 'You have never killed anything; *now you are to kill the stag*' (i.e. as game for eating). . . . It was some time before they found the right means for killing the stag, but they did so in the end." A similar story is told of the *eagle* who was a "big man" in the primal period. They told him that they wanted to kill him to perform certain ceremonies, and he tried to flee from death like a stag; for "there was no death before this time": wherever he went he found death.

In individual cases it is difficult to establish whether or not mythologems of this kind preserve the memory of a custom of murdering parents practised in earlier periods, but as we shall show there are in fact many tribes who did do this. In any event the mythologems in themselves suggest that a specific stage of psychological development in man's attitude to and experience of death is brought about by the fact that he becomes *a killer himself*—or, rather, by the fact that he becomes conscious of it. This is an enormous development, a development from the earliest panic horror of and unthinking flight from death to the conscious act of killing undertaken by oneself. We have to consider how to interpret this process. It is clear that we must start by assuming that man has in fact killed from the earliest times, either in self-defence against wild animals, or in the course of hunting, or in internecine strife, but it seems that killing did not have the same meaning at all times. We have highly illuminating evidence about the behaviour of primitive "genuine hunting peoples", for when they had killed a wild animal they performed peculiar ceremonies of which the main object was to maintain that they had not actually killed: Adolf Jensen writes, "However keen they may be to assure the success in hunting which they desire, they are just as keen to pretend to the animal they have killed, to themselves and to all the world that *they* have not done the killing." For example, Palaeo-Asiatic tribes stand up the hide of a bear that they have killed and make a speech in front of it, explaining to the animal that it is not they but strangers who have murdered it: and moreover, they say, it is not really dead at all, it has only been liberated from its hide and is now entering as a god into the land of the gods.[1]

Primitives identify themselves with animals, and for them the transition from human to animal form, or from animal to human, is entirely natural;[2] when we remember this we see that the problem of killing is the same thing whether it is concerned with animals or human beings, hunting or war. The usual explanation of the hunting ceremonies which we have mentioned is that they are due to fear that the slain animal will revenge itself, but psychologically it is probable that the numinous horror of death lies behind this fear and that it is this horror which is allayed by the ceremonies. The ceremonies are *magic practices*, and their intention is to cancel out the event of death so that it is as though it had not happened, and this is done by denying the death of the animal—or, at any rate, the fact that one has killed it oneself. In other words, these hunting people anxiously avoid coming to terms with the tremendum, and deny its presence so that they can feast undisturbed and preserve their lives. This is why we are justified in regarding their attitude as in some way parallel to the second flight mentioned earlier, which is a magical practice aimed at avoiding death.

A touching folk-story of the Bena Lulua in the Congo Basin is recorded by Leo Frobenius;[3] and it confronts us with something quite

[1] Much evidence in *The Golden Bough*, J. G. Frazer, abridged edition 1950, pp. 509, 518–532. This contains reports on the Ainus, Gilyaks, Goldis of Kamchatka, the Ostyaks and Coryaks. There are further examples from Africa and Cambodia, where the small animals get similar speeches to those made to the terrifying large ones—in this connection some ancient sacrificial customs can also be explained as a psychological echo of the original primitive hunting culture: it is reported in *Opferritus und Voropfer der Griechen und Römer*, S. Eitrem, Oslo, 1915 (p. 76) that the agreement of the sacrificial animal was a necessary condition of the sacrifice from the psychological point of view. The fear of killing is even more clearly demonstrated by the very old (originally Ionian) cult of the Bouphonia, in which the participants transfer the guilt to the knife in exactly the same way as the Palaeo-Asiatics: cf. *Griechische Feste von Religiöser Bedeutung*, M. Nilsson, new ed., Darmstadt, 1957.

[2] This attitude is excellently reflected in Eskimo fairy-tales.

[3] According to Frobenius the Bena Lulua are a mixed people descended from Wemba—Luba tribes and pygmies—of which the latter, as is well known, are primitive food-gatherers and hunters.

new. The story tells that Fidi Mukullu (a kind of creator god) made a man and woman who had many children, and that all people are descended from them. One day Fidi Mukullu gave a "Mojo" (= life): he greeted all the plants, animals and birds, the water and the trees—and everything lived. When the woman wanted to fetch wood for the fire the wood said, "No, Fidi Mukullu has given us life!" When the woman wanted to fetch water the water said, "No, Fidi Mukullu has given us life!" When the man wanted to shoot a bird the bird said, "No, Fidi Mukullu has given us life!" One day Fidi Mukullu called "Mojo!" to the people again. The people were asleep, and did not answer. Fidi Mukullu called, "Mojo!" again, and again the people did not hear. Then Fidi Mukullu called, "All people die!"; at this the people nodded their heads and called, "He-e-e-e-e-e!", which means "yes!" and is a form of eager affirmation made with the head thrown back. Since then, the story concludes, the people die.

When the people were unable to kill they went to sleep: since they have had to die they are awake—and kill: for we can read out of this story the implicit sequel that since Fidi Mukullu's decree of death the people "kill" wood,[1] water and birds and take away their Mojo so that they may live before they finally die themselves. In this story we can feel something of the fear with which primitive hunting people must have become conscious of their own killing, at the same time as they felt that it was "really forbidden". But at the same time a completely new attitude appears: killing is not magically denied; rather its necessity is affirmed and recognized, and this affirmation requires a kind of self-assertion against the contradictoriness of the creator, coupled with the affirmation and acceptance of the antinomy; this antinomy is then resolved by the idea of the general destiny according to which all must die. There is even a certain ecstasy in the acceptance of death, because since men die they *live* through killing. Put another way, the explicit and conscious act of killing involves the affirmation of life (which is nourished by that which is killed), and together with this the acknowledgement that death itself belongs to life.

We have here a valuable indication of the way in which the signi-

[1] Similarly in the *Upper Palatinate* the woodcutters beg the pardon of the tree which they want to fell in the wood; "For trees, too, have life" (A. Wuttke). Traces of the same conception were to be found in *Switzerland* (L. A. Rocholz).

ficance of killing changes as the human psyche develops. It is first consciously permitted, but in more developed peoples it is affirmed as a necessity. Jensen goes so far as to speak of a "new spiritual orientation of the cultural peoples", and he goes on, "Because killing was recognized as such a decisive factor in the order of being . . . the killing of animals had of necessity to be integrated into this new perception of the world." Whereas the purely hunting peoples were anxious when they killed, it would seem that agricultural peoples believed that killing gives greater pleasure to the gods than any other act, so that they ranked killing as one of man's proudest deeds and gave the killer all kinds of decorations—these decorations having importance and significance for the journey of the dead, and acting as passes which had to be presented to the god of the underworld. It is a fact that when we compare the customs of the original, purely hunting peoples who dare not admit their own killing with the myths and stories (some of which we have quoted) from later stages of development we see the deep gulf between them. A change has taken place in man's whole psychological attitude to death.

Certain customs found among various tribes enable us to offer a tentative account of the way in which the new psychological attitude was developed. These are the customs, found all over the world, of killing the old or the dying before death comes to them naturally. This is a custom which modern man finds difficult to understand emotionally but (when it is rightly understood) it provides a key to the psychological understanding of the later attitude to death.

It is reported that members of the Abipones (a tribe of Chaco Indians, probably very primitive) used to hasten the death of the dying by suffocating them under a heavy hide, and it is reasonable to suppose that they also used to abandon their dwellings after death and burial and form a new settlement some miles away, since this is still done by the Lingua who are their cultural relatives. We are not here concerned how far mythical conceptions of the demonic power of the souls of the dead play their part in this custom,[1] for the immediate horror of the incomprehensible can be clearly discerned in the Abipones' attitude. This horror is combined with a practice, *an act* by which man explicitly

[1] According to H. Dobrizhoffer, the Abipones think that death is due to spirits, either because they are evil or because they have been adjured by magicians.

33

carries out what the tremendum meant and demanded, and what is clearly recognized as the destiny of man. The practice which we have already mentioned of the Kalmuks and Kirghizes of exposing their dying on the steppes or in the bush can be understood in a similar way, the only difference being that the actual killing is not done overtly but is, as it were, carried out clandestinely. Other tribes, on the other hand, have customs in which the act of killing the dying is open and explicit. For instance "Among the Buryats the old are killed with special solemnity. The men and women who are advanced in age are dressed in their best clothes and conducted to the seat of honour, then after a wild drinking bout they are put to death by strangulation." The Yakuts actually consider it "as a disgrace" if their aged parents die a natural death (for they believe that if this happens the evil spirit eats the soul of the deceased), and elderly parents are buried alive or abandoned to death by hunger to the accompaniment of festivities and ceremonies.[1]

These customs are complemented by the mythologems of the first murder which we described above: the two belong together psychologically, and by bringing them together it is possible for us to enter emotionally into an attitude to death and killing which is alien to our feelings.

The dissimulation of the primitive hunting peoples whereby they attempt to deny the fact that they have killed shows how killing (combined with a new aspect of death) strives to emerge from the unconscious against an inner resistance. The rites involved were explicitly "dams and walls to keep back the dangers of the unconscious, 'the perils of the soul' ".[2] The act of killing, previously unconscious, is becoming conscious and so arouses anxiety, because as man begins to perceive what he is doing he also perceives that he is crossing a border in a way that is somehow "forbidden". The primitive hunters attempt to exorcize this anxiety by means of their cultic magic ceremonies

[1] Even German legend preserves isolated memory traces of similar ritual killings of the old. According to a legend from the Rhineland the heathen stayed at the Löwenburg hunting lodge, and there they buried their old women alive. As they did this they said: "Bend down, old woman, you can't live any longer!" and gave them a number of rolls to take into the grave with them. ("Bergische Sagen", O. Schell, Elberfeld 1897, p. 506.)

[2] C. G. Jung, Collected Works, Vol. 9, Pt. 1, *Archetypes of the Collective Unconscious*, p. 25.

before the slain animal. At the same time the rites, followed by a banquet, also seem to contain an element of intoxication, and this element is probably related to killing as such—whether the killing by the hunter or the warrior, by the man tempestuously angry or possessed by jealousy, or even ritual killing. Such intoxication gets its specific colouring from the indissoluble mixture of lust for power and excess of ultimate horror. It is possible that what occurs is a kind of enthusiastic approach to the tremendum, a kind of union with it in fear and trembling.

The great change in attitude which comes about consists precisely in the fact that at a later stage the killer carries out the act by which he approaches the tremendum with conscious affirmation. Acting in horror and at the same time despite that horror the killer actively enters into the execution of destiny: he acts both as a tool and as an agent in his own right, and in this way he reaches out into the transcendental sphere—transcending, as it were, his own limits. He has to transcend those limits in order to assert himself, and in order to be able to live. It is life at the cost of one's own death, as was hinted in the fairy-tale of the Bena Lulua.

The mystery of the fate of death seems to be given into man's hand, so that he becomes, as it were, a partner in its execution. In some such way as this we might understand the psychological attitude involved in assisting the death of the dying by active participation, even though if this is the meaning it is expressed in symbolic action and not in words. In a similar way we can enter emotionally into the sacral aspects of war and hunting, and also into the elaboration of various forms of torturing and killing prisoners, head-hunting and the bloody sacrifice of men and animals. What we have said is not contradicted even if we accept the view of John Koty that the killing of the old and sick (particularly among nomadic people) was primarily due to anxiety caused by lack of food and the hardships of nomadic life. Even though this may be true it would still be the case that the survivors were themselves the agents of the destiny which they recognized as being inevitable.

Among certain peoples, for example the ancient Medes, the Caspians and the Tibetans, there is another aspect to killing the dying, because the fear that the dead man will return as a ghost plays a part. There are certain Tibetan tribes in which the dying man is asked whether he intends to return after he is dead, and if he says, "Yes!" then he is throttled by his relatives. Such behaviour clearly shows that death is still experienced as an impenetrable mystery and that it still gives rise to impotent horror, but the counter-movement to this horror is not simply an execution of the ineluctable destiny by man (as it is in the case of the Yakuts and Buryats), since the survivors take in hand the execution of fate for "their own purposes", as though they were trying to correct it in order to protect themselves and their own lives against the danger of death—and this is an essentially magic attitude. It is not that men are unhinged by the monstrosity of death, nor that they enter into the execution of the terrible thing with ecstatic exuberance; it is rather that an "ego-assuring" fear for their own life transforms the whole action into a rigidly observed magic ritual of supposed, though illusory, effect.

These considerations bring out the clear distinction between two opposed and equally extreme attitudes. On the one side there is the horrified feeling of being utterly overwhelmed by death, and on the other side a self-assertion which only affirms life. The magical attitude only appears to be an acceptance of death; what actually happens is that through fear man attempts an *absolute* assertion of himself. In apparent confidence he tries to take power over death and destiny so that he may hold them at a distance from himself, and this is the whole purpose of his magical practices.

This claim to power gives rise to the belief which is widespread among primitive peoples, and occasionally found among contemporary Europeans, that death never occurs naturally, but is always "murder" in that it is the result of the evil will of personal enemies, and that it is brought about by a magician or by magic. If this were the case man would have complete control of death.

Records of magical practices of this kind have been brought from all parts of the world. The medicine-man gets hair, finger-nail clippings, faeces or a fragment of clothing from his victim, or else makes a picture of him so as to bring him into his power, and then he pierces, dismembers, buries or kills in some other way the "accessory of the personality":[1] the result is that the victim inevitably dies, unless he sets to work a counter-spell which wards

[1] Compare the comprehensive psychological expositions of G. Schmaltz in *Komplexe Psychologie und Körperliches Symptom*, pp. 44 ff.

off the evil and, if strong enough, turns it back on the originator.[1]

It is a strange paradox! When men reject the all-powerful predominance of death and try to take away the horror of the incomprehensible by an illusory assumption of power over it, then they are delivered into a bewildering anxiety—the constant fear of countless and equally unknown enemies who threaten life. By magic man supposes that he has won power over destiny—he can kill, or allow to live—but the result is that destiny has become as petty as man himself.

On the other hand the genuine killing of which we have spoken is psychologically a way of accepting death which is partly ecstatic and which brings about something like a union with the tremendum. Through killing of this kind there begins to appear the first consciousness of the fact that man extends beyond his own limits into an unknown something which envelops him, and to which he is unconditionally delivered up.[2]

---

[1] Exhaustive account of her own observations in *Sex and Temperament in the Primitive Society*, M. Mead. Numerous further examples in *Die geistige Welt der Primitiven*, L. Lévy-Bruhl, pp. 20 ff., and also *Die Seele der Primitiven*.

[2] Very instructive from the psychological point of view are numerous ethnological examples of behaviour towards the dying and those who are bound to die quoted by Lévy-Bruhl, *Die geistige Welt der Primitiven*, pp. 270–287. Man is obliged to execute what the power of death wills or has fated. Yet how deeply potent the horror of such an immediate encounter with the tremendum has been through all ages, and still is even in modern man, we learn from Hans von Hentig's far-ranging study *Vom Ursprung der Henkersmahlzeit*; cf., for example, p. 124, Note 1.

3. The Shrouding "Hider-Goddess"

BOTH the conscious experience of killing and the related idea of sacrificing living beings can be seen as attempts to understand the unknown killer, and to determine its place in the scheme of things. To kill and to know that one kills is, from a primitive point of view, an identification of oneself with the unknown being that brings death. Lévy-Bruhl has shown that such identification and participation are probably best understood as an early primitive way of understanding another person or thing. In the conscious act of killing the primitive must to some extent feel the existence of a being which is a killer, and with which he identifies himself, but at first that being remains formless—"uncanny" and nothing else. The formation of an inner conception (that is, an image) of such a being would be a kind of liberation, however frightful the image were, because such a conception is to some extent comprehendable. When the Killer-Being takes shape as an image in the mind then that image expresses something of its essence and action.

It is difficult to find out when and in what way man first formed an image of the Killer-Being, but it seems certain that from the beginning this image was one of unfathomable strangeness and that it could only be thought of as the image of a being working *from the hidden*, and *in the hidden*. No one knows when or where such a being may appear, and even when it appears it remains unrecognizable, shrouded from human eyes. This shrouding not only expresses the mystery and hiddenness of death as the Killer; it also reflects the actual appearance of the dead: the dead man is both there and not there, and it is as though he were shrouded behind a rigid mask. It seems that an uncanny "someone" has shrouded the being of the dead so that one who was near and familiar has suddenly become distant and strange.

In the following chapters we shall come across images of the Death-Being in the traditions which we consider, and when we do we need to think or feel this specifically numinous character into them: the element of incomprehensibility is a decisive and indispensable element of them all, and this particular quality of feeling can be shown to have occurred in the earliest period, at the first beginnings of our own cultural development. The evidence for this is available in the penetrating and sensitive investigations of the Indo-Germanist Hermann Güntert into the history of language and meaning. Güntert has established the *name* of the Death-Demon for the earliest Indo-Germanic (and even for the pre-Indo-Germanic) period, and the name is also a characteristic epithet. It is one of those rare cases in which the history of language has lit up the prehistoric depths with certainty, and the name which percolates through from pre-Indo-Germanic times means "hider"—in either masculine or feminine form. By means of extensive linguistic material (not all Indo-Germanic) Güntert shows that the mysterious hiding and shrouding has been experienced as the first essential character-trait of the numinous, hidden power of death from early times, and that this was the general rule in our particular cultural sphere. All language depends upon a relation between emotion and inner images, and this appears so clearly from Güntert's investigations that it is well worth while describing them in more detail.

Güntert starts with "Calypso", the nymph who encountered Odysseus, and he shows that her name, her nature and her attributes all indicate that she is an embodiment of death. The name comes from the Greek καλύπτιεν, which means, "hide in the earth", "bury", so that Calypso is "she who hides". In the pre-Greek Indo-Germanic period the verbal stem -*kel(u) meant "to cover with earth", "to hide in the earth", and the following words (among others) belong to the same context:[1] Lat. *celo, occulo* (to hide); O.Ir. *celid* (concealed); O.H.G. *helan* (to conceal, hide). That the root expressly relates to hiding in or under the earth is shown by noun-forms in the most

---

[1] In what follows we use the customary philological abbreviations with minor modifications. I.G. =Indo-Germanic; Lat., Gk., Germ., Goth. =Latin, Greek, Germanic, Gothic; O.Ir. =Old Irish; Kelt. =Celtic; O.H.G., M.H.G., N.H.G. =Old, Middle and Modern High German; O.S. =Old Saxon; O.Fris. =Old Frisian; A.S. =Anglo-Saxon; O.Ice. =Old Icelandic, etc.; * before a word means that its existence is inferred on the basis of linguistic laws although it is not found in the sources.

diverse Indo-Germanic languages, for example, O.H.G. *holî*; Eng. *hole*; Lat. *cella* (subterranean storeroom); O.Ir. *cuile* (cellar), so that it is not surprising to find O.Ir. *cel* (from **kelo*) meaning "death"; Goth. *halja* meaning "Hades", "hell"; O.Ice. *hel* meaning "kingdom of the dead", "underworld"; and A.S. *hell*; O.Fris. *helle*; O.S. and O.H.G. *hella*; N.H.G. *Hölle*, all meaning "hell".

In the Greek legend of Calypso there are still traces which contradict her superficially harmless nature and link her to the dark divinity of death. In the *Odyssey* she appears as a sister of the Hesperides,[1] and in other sources these are regarded as sisters of the gods of death.[2] In the Homeric "Hymn to Demeter" she is named as a companion of Persephone; in *Cassius Dio*[3] (a late work) it is said that a Calypso was worshipped with a cult of her own on Lake Avernus in the Alban Hills—which had been thought of from ancient times as the entrance to the underworld, the place where the Sibyl dwelt and the dark grove of Hecate. Finally, when we consider more closely the island of Ogygia, the home of Homer's Calypso, we see that it has the characteristics of a garden of death, however enchantingly lovely it may be. The meadows are adorned with ivy and violets, the sepulchural plants of antiquity, the nymph herself lives in a cave (!), and her grotto is surrounded by the trees of the underworld—black alders, dark poplars and cypress: it is not at all far-fetched to see in this a parallel to "the dark mysteries of the hill of the grave and the house of the dead", called *Hel* by the Scandinavians. This word, of course, is directly related to Germ. *helan* (conceal), and *Hel* (Germ. **halja*; I.G. *koli̯o*) is rightly translated "concealer" or "shrouder" (in the feminine). The female demon of the grave "hides" or "shrouds" the corpse from the eyes of the living, and the original Germanic belief was that all who died fell victim to Hel, not only those who died a "Stroh-death" (i.e. died in their beds).

The Greek Calypso and Germanic Hel are related in that their names have the same origin, and that they both mean "hider" or "shrouder": that is, they were originally thought of as those who shroud the living by bringing death—in other words, as killers. It is to be borne in mind that whereas καλύπτειν, *celare*, *helan* point to the primal phenomenon of the tremendum—that which is hidden and shrouded, and which is the incomprehensible mystery—the shrouder

[1] *Odyssey* VII, 245. [2] Hesiod, *Theogony*, 215. [3] 48, 50.

is the mysterious *power* already partly conceptualized and so partly comprehensible.

The names Calypso and Hel have specific reference to hiding *in the depths of the earth*, and in later times the Greek word became the technical term for earth-burial when that was no longer a matter of course, and this leads to further considerations. First, it sets the psychological significance in a clearer light. In the early period earth-burial was the custom of all Indo-Germanic people, but as ethnology has shown, it was by no means the only form of "burial".[1] Corpses have been left exposed, buried in leaves, "buried" in the hut in which the living man dwelt; exposed to be eaten by wolves, dogs, hyenas or birds, "buried" on platforms; they have been dried and smoked, "buried" in trees or caves, drowned in water and burnt by fire. Most of these forms of "burial" are no longer practised, but this does not mean that they all express a primitive mentality as we can see from the fact that the Parsees still expose their dead on "Towers of Silence". Earth-burial is not the earliest form of "burial", but it was certainly a very early form, and it is likely that it originated from the observation of what happens when a dead body is left to lie on the ground—something which modern Europeans have been able to observe in recent wars. If the unburied corpse does not become the spoil of beasts of prey it is almost visibly drawn into the earth in the course of time as it is grown over, enveloped and grown through by plants and vegetation until it becomes part of the earth kingdom—"In the sweat of thy face shalt thou eat bread, till thou return unto the ground; for out of it wast thou taken."[2] Such a sight is deeply impressive, and it is as though the earth opens to take the dead man into it, to hide and shroud him in itself.

The deliberate disposal of the corpse—particularly, the very expressive act of burial in the earth—appears to have the same kind of significance as killing the dying; that is it seems to represent a deliberate participation in the inevitable event of death, but to do so at a more differentiated level. So long as man thinks in visual images it is probable that he does not think that another man is "really dead" until that man's body has wholly disappeared and become decomposed. This idea crops up in the beliefs and customs of many people and is, for instance, the basis of the widespread practice of holding a second

[1] See note, p. 23.   [2] Gen. 3, 19.

funeral solemnity—usually about a year after the first; such a solemnity marks the final departure of the dead man from his family circle, and his translation into another realm of existence. Burial in the earth, however, means that the dead man is already swallowed by the earth and hidden in its belly; he has disappeared, and can be regarded as truly dead. It is as though the earth "wills" to take the "slain" into itself, and despite his horror man obeys its "will" when he buries the dead in the earth, as though voluntarily "giving to the earth what belongs to the earth".

The practice of the South American Abipones of suffocating their dying in an ox-hide and the ceremonial suffocations of the Buryats (which we have already mentioned) are also "shroudings" and have the same motif as earth-burial, but man's execution of the "will" of the devouring earth is more vividly expressed by the Schoschones of California and the Yakuts, who bury the dying alive in the earth.[1] This idea that burial helps the earth to gather in its own easily leads to the idea of the earth as an enormous and frightful monster, opening hungry jaws which will, sooner or later, swallow and engulf the living; and it is a fact that in all parts of the world gorges and fissures in the earth are regarded—both in mythology and popular belief—as the gaping jaws of earth, the entrance to the underworld and the place of the dead. As late as the Middle Ages the jaws of earth were displayed in many mystery plays before shuddering audiences, reinterpreted as the jaws of *hell*—and in the end they were still the ancient "Jaws of Hel".

These considerations make it possible to picture an early starting-point from which the crysallization of the formless horror of death into the image of a Death-Being began, although one cannot tell whether the image took shape before, after or at the same time as the name Hider (either male or female) came into use. The name is certainly very old, because we come across it just where philology penetrates furthest into prehistory. One can confidently postulate the existence of an Indo-Germanic *kol̦jo, from which Hel and Calypso are derived, and it occurs as *Koljo* (with exactly the same sound) among all Finno-Ugrian peoples, living in widely scattered groups from the Baltic to the Yenisei River. This means that there is no possibility of later borrowing after encounters with North-Germanic peoples, as is the

[1] Cf. Chapter 2, p. 33 above.

case with many words which only occur in Finnish and not over the whole ethnic group. Nor does the primitive form of the word make such borrowing likely. If it is a case of borrowing and not of original relatedness, then that borrowing must have taken place in a period lying far behind any historical evidence, when the two primitive groups must have lived in close proximity.

The Finno-Ugrian demon or god Koljo is an earth-being represented with a fearful and terrifying appearance, and often thought of as gigantic, and in Vagilsk, for example, he is thought to devour the corpses of the dead. To the Finns he is giant son of the cold; to the Estonians he is a bugbear to whom (until very recent times) a jug of beer known as "Koli-anna" (Kol's gift) had to be sacrificed by being *poured out on the earth* when a corpse was carried out; to the Syrjanians he is a devil, an evil water-spirit; to the Wotyaks an evil spirit living in hollow places and sending severe sickness; finally, to the Woguls he is the master of the underworld who kills and visits men with sickness.

It may be mentioned that similar ideas are found among the Palaeo-Asiatics, some of whom (the Yenisians) are still settled close by the Ugrian Ostjakes. The Koryaks believe that the "Kalau" (plural of Kala) are death-demons who "dwell in the West", and appear as "regular cannibals" eating men; they also believe that they are bearers of sickness and are devouring Death. In one Koryakian story a Kala appears as a man-faced dog who kills all the inhabitants of the village saying, "The old people (i.e. the dead) send me to kill the young." The Chukchee call these death-demons "Ke'let", the Yukaghir call them "Ku-kul".

The corpse-devourer is given names which associate it with manifestly ancient Indo-Germanic conceptions of the divinity of Death. In Greek Hades himself is called παντοφάγος (all-devourer) or σαρκοφάγος (eater of raw meat or corpses); the same name is given to Hecate, and even Demeter is called ἀδηφάγος (voracious to satiety); and above all, ὠλοφάγος (devouring raw meat) is applied to Cerberus, the hound of hell. According to tradition the Germanic Hel still possesses characteristics like those of the Finno-Ugrian Koljo; it is well known that she is descended from a tribe of huge wolves, and her brother is the Fenris-wolf who with the pack he leads (Skoll, Hati and Managarmr) will devour the sun and the moon at the end of the world. At the gate of Hel's kingdom there lurks Garmr, the hound of hell, in the cave of Gnitahellir. Garmr means "devourer", and the figure of this hound is evidence for the antiquity of the conception of the bestial, greedy, swallowing death-demon known as the "corpse-eater". This conception lies behind the four-eyed dog of the ancient Indians,[1] and the two hell-hounds of the Iranians (spoken of in the Avesta) as well as behind the Greek Cerberus.[2] It is often a wolf instead of a dog and Odin, for instance, has two wolves for companions. In the later poetry of the Scalds Hel is still described behaving like a beast of prey pouncing on the corpses. The *Gislisaga* says: "The annihilator of the Scots fed the steed of the giantess (Hel); Nar's sister (Hel) tramped (*sc*. like a wolf or hound) *"on the eagle's nightly feast"*. The *Hofuðlied* says: "Hel *has her pleasure* on Dyggvi's corpse, for the sister of Ulf (the wolf) and Narvi was to choose the king, Loki's daughter (Hel) has beguiled the ruler of Yngvi's host." In these descriptions one can feel the more than bestial, demonic lust of Hel upon the corpses.

Hel is related to the Fenris-wolf, and her own behaviour is also vulpine, so that one may well suppose that at first she herself was conceived of as a wolf or hound. In *Greek myth* we find similar ways of picturing the demons of death and the underworld. It is well known that the guardian of the underworld was the three-headed dog Cerberus, but Hecate, the old, dark goddess, was also thought to be a corpse-devourer in the shape of a hound,[3] and the dog-headed Scylla was her daughter. The Echidna-serpent, dwelling "in the lap of holy earth, in a cave, in a vault of rocks" and devouring raw meat was the mother not only of Cerberus but also of the fearful hound Orthros. This dog is also a creature of the dark depths of the earth, and a strange relationship is established between Artemis and Dionysos by the fact that this dark epithet is given to both of them.

We can now turn back from these later ideas to the *pre*-Indo-Germanic period in which the Death-Being began to be called Hider and the first beginnings of its crystallization into a figure or image became apparent. The killer is the earth itself, figured as a huge animal which suddenly and greedily thrusts open its fearful jaws, like the fearful jaws of a wolf, to devour the living. Psychologically this

[1] See *Rigveda*, 10, 14. 11.   [2] Hesiod, *Theogony*, 311.
[3] Hesiod, *Theogony*, 297 ff.

crystallization into an image is a tremendous step in human development: at first man could only kill in a blind self-identification with an unknown, though active, being, which could only be grasped at all in and through man's own killing. The idea of the "Hider" (Hel-Calypso), and the closely connected image of the gigantic but formless Earth-Demon with gaping jaws provided an inner image which man could confront, thereby confronting the active Death-Being through the image. It is because of the "independent nature and autonomous power of the human image-world" that the existence of such an image enables man to "comprehend his own world as an essential reality contrasted with his environment". The enigmatic "otherness" opened up by the imagination is a transcending power in experience which "is the pre-condition for the fact that man, in contrast to the animals, wakes up to himself".

The works of Jung have taught us that the inner images have a double nature. Although they rise up out of the psyche of man they also confront man as a copy of "the other". The images arise as a response to the world, and serve as a means of understanding the world, so that what Jung calls "archetypes" appear as creative, primal responses of the individual human soul to the "basic conditions of existence" which, of course, are the same for all men—that is, the "archetypes" which occur in individuals are in themselves "collective".[1]

At first man is only dimly aware of his psychic existence, and this means that his psychic existence itself remains unformed, and that is why it is of immense importance (both in human history and in individual life) when it begins to take form and is articulated in an image of the "other". It is in this way that consciousness begins to dawn, and that consciousness is kindled by the encounter with the Other. When this begins to happen man enters the world of myth. As we shall see the inner images are not fixed and rigid but change and develop like living things, and this is a characteristic that we must keep in mind as we encounter different forms of the Death-Demon—the root of each is the same, it is "the Hider".

[1] See esp. Jung, *Archetypes of the Collective Unconscious*, Collected works, Vol. 9, Part 1, "The Archetypes and the Collective Unconscious".

4. The Death-Demon as Dog and Wolf

IT must be understood that the process of development which we have outlined has only been inferred, but at the same time the model of an historical development serves to simplify the material. Having made this reservation we can say that a Death-Demon has existed[1] ever since the event of death was regarded as the work of a "being" which had a name—"Shrouder" or "Hider". This Demon is first experienced as formless on the one hand, and as devouring ($\pi\alpha\nu\tau o\phi\acute{a}\gamma os$) on the other, but it strains towards a form, or, rather, an adequate image strives to take form in the psyche. As we have seen from a first look at Indo-Germanic and Finno-Ugrian mythology, it is the idea of greedy, devouring jaws which seems to be the starting-point from which the images crystallize out. It seems likely that one of the earliest, primeval, barbaric images of death that we encounter is *kolio, the male or female "Hider", represented as a greedy, corpse-devouring wolf or a carrion-eating dog. This image (or, sometimes, that of some other, similar beast of prey) is found in the customs and stories of primitive peoples of all races up to the present day, and we find unmistakable traces of a Death-Demon in the form of wolf or dog in the myths of the oldest civilized peoples as well as in the popular myth-like legends of modern Europe.

The *Italmens* of the Chukchee peninsula give their dead to be eaten by dogs, and picture the "Lord of the Underworld" wearing a dog-skin, and riding a sleigh drawn by strong dogs. Nicolai von Prschewalski observed among the *Mongolians* that: "At the burial

---

[1] Strictly it is the *image of a Death-Demon* which is in question here, but if we were to use this phrase in the text it would tend to weaken the author's sense of an image as a living, objective entity. In dealing with images which arise from or in the psyche there is always the same ambiguity. The Death-Demon, for example, does not exist except as an image, and in a very real sense the image is the Demon (*Trans.*).

place close to Urga ... the corpses are ... thrown directly to the dogs and birds of prey to be eaten. Such a place makes an horrifying impression; it is covered with heaps of bones among which packs of dogs, living entirely on human flesh, wander like shadows. Directly a corpse is thrown down these dogs, together with crows and hawks, begin to pull it to pieces, and within two hours there is nothing left ... The dogs of Urga are so accustomed to this food that they always follow the relatives of the dead as they carry the corpse through the streets of the town." Sven Heden tells us that in Tibet the corpses of all those who are not religious dignitaries are "put in a remote spot, preferably an exposed hillock, and left to the birds of the air and the beasts of the wilderness, especially the wolves. In Lhasa and other towns and temples special dogs are kept, and they destroy the dead bodies with astounding appetite. In many temples the corpse-eating dogs are regarded as holy, and a man acquires merit by allowing his dead body to be eaten by them."

Freda Kretschmar points out that such corpse-eating dogs are very different from European dogs.[1] "In this case," she says, "we do better to imagine those half-domesticated wolves who attach themselves to man because they could always hope for prey near human settlements." Hedin also describes troops of roaming, wild, often wolf-like dogs who follow caravans today. From the *Avesta* we learn that Iranian dogs often inter-bred with wolves, and that wolves instead of dogs are described as corpse-buriers. Dogs, in fact, play an important role in the extremely comprehensive corpse-ritual of the *Avesta* and Herodotus and other ancient writers said that such West Iranian and Caspian peoples as the Medes exposed corpses (and sometime the dying) to be destroyed by dogs.

As a matter of fact there is evidence everywhere in Asia that wolves and dogs were representatives, or at least attendants, of the demons of death and the underworld. For instance, the two Chinese dogs of the underworld still have to guard the books which record the good and evil deeds of the dead, and we have already mentioned the dog-forms of the Kalau and Ke'let who are the demons of misfortune and death among the Koryaks and the Chukchee. The ritual of the dead among

[1] There are important references to the mythological relationship between the dog and death in Jung, Collected Works, Vol. 5, *Symbols of Transformation*, pp. 369 ff.

the Samoyeds shows the peculiar connection between dog, wolf and death very clearly. According to a myth told among the members of this tribe Ngaa lured away the dog who had the job of guarding the first man, and then ate the man; today when a man dies a dog is sacrificed by the Shaman, and then an image of a wolf is carved. The Shaman addresses the image, saying, "My old friend Ngaa!"—showing that Ngaa, devouring death, was originally wolf or dog himself.

We find traces of the Death-Demon as wolf or dog in Europe as well; the material is very full and only a few instances can be given. In the Finnish epic, *Kalevala*, it is told that Ilmarinen the Smith must chain the wolf of the kingdom of the dead before he can win the maiden he seeks: the Lapps frequently offer sacrifices of dogs to the dead: the Estonians, Lavonians and the Courlanders believe that dogs can see spectres and "churchyard people", and also that such spectres and the dead appear in the form of dogs: the Slovenes and Croats used to believe that the plague appeared in the shape of a dog: in Hungary it was thought that certain dead people appeared as "wolf-beggars" or "dog-beggars" which persecuted perjurers.

Some of the countless death-hound and death-wolf legends from the Germano-Teutonic cultural area—to which we shall return in more detail below—may be cited. For example we read in the Edda:

> "*A hall I saw, Far from the sun*
> *On the shore of the dead . . .*
> *. . . The Nidhögg*[1] *sucked*
> *Lifeless bodies, The wolf tore corpses.*
> *Know ye still more?*"

In contrast with this sombre picture the German legends, which represent a much more recent form of the tradition, seem faded; yet in the ubiquitous stories of the "Wild Hunt" (which is of course the hunt of the host of the dead) we can still feel the shudder which came over men when they heard the baying of the demonic death-hounds.

Even in the late local legends, which are usually recounted very soberly, the horrible power of the early conceptions is often very clear. For example, in the district of Rochlitz in Saxony it is said that a dog with a glowing chain appears at the Helloch at night, and the name of the place shows that it is (or was) thought of as a place of entry into

[1] The "hostile biter".

the underworld. It is also said that a black dog lives in a certain place near Bockau (also in Saxony), and that anyone who sees it will be stricken with severe illness. The vivid way in which the primeval idea of the Death-Demon lives on is shown by one legend, among others, from Freiberg (Saxony again): this legend is given an historical date, and it is said that in 1654 a spectral hound kept night-long vigil outside the burgomaster's house for three months, and that although the night watchman kept chasing it away no one could catch it: when this visitation ended the burgomaster died.

A legend from the Bergisches Land also shows a connection between the hound of death and the devouring jaws of earth. It is said that in Schladern an old man saw a black dog trotting along ahead of him and after he had been watching it for some time it changed into a black coffin—then the earth opened and swallowed it up. The legend makes special point of the reality of what took place, because it goes on to say that the old man told his neighbour what had happened and that the neighbour would not believe him, but that not long afterwards the very same thing at the very same place befell the neighbour himself. A dog legend from Terlan in the South Tyrol brings out the horrifying, pagan and primitive element even more strongly. One evening a poor man heard a hunting dog barking outside his cottage; he said, "Dear little dog, bring me some of your prey." The next morning he found the half of a human body hanging on his door, and nothing he could do could get it off. He appealed to the parish priest, and it was only by means of his help and the use of consecrated objects that he eventually persuaded the dog to take the corpse away. It is clear that the legend shows the dog as a killer of men and eater of corpses.

Similar ideas are found all over the world. For instance, the Aztec calendar shows the close connection between dog and death: "The sign of the tenth day of Tonalamatl was named 'dog' . . . the Regent of this sign is Miktlantekutli, the god of the dead." This god and his wife fed on the hands and feet of human corpses. Among the Aztecs and among some tribes of Southern Central America a red dog is supposed to escort the dead, and this is an idea found almost everywhere. In Mexico the god Tepeyollotli ("heart of the mountains") is said to be embodied in the jaguar, "the devouring animal *par excellence* which was also regarded as a symbol of the earth". The coyote also has the role of death-animal, but more among North American Indians than in Mexico. The California Indians have many legends to the effect that the coyote introduced death out of malice after man had been created. In this connection the coyote is often coupled with the wolf, and the wolf appears as Lord of Death very impressively in the mythological stories of the Kwakiutl and the related Nutka of North-West America.

Among the Kwakiutl the Hamatsa Dance appears to have been originally a wolf-dance during the course of which those to be initiated into the cannibalistic Hamatsa society are engulfed by a gigantic wolf's jaw. The Nutka also have a secret society, Tlocoa'la, and a legend with deep symbolic meaning describes its formation—by wolves. The brave son of a chief disguised himself in a seal-skin and smuggled himself among the wolves, who carried him away. The chief wolf ordered that the "seal" should be slit open, and when a man leapt out many of the wolves were afraid. The chief wolf called a meeting of all the wolves and other animals at his house, and the young man was set in the centre and asked what he was seeking. The wolves showed him many tempting magic charms, but he made no answer until they showed him the Arrow of Death and said, "If you point this at a man he will die at once": then the man said, "Yes, I came for that." The wolves gave him the arrow, but when he touched it he fell into a swoon, and only at the fourth attempt could he keep hold of it. Then the wolves taught him to sing the Tlocoa'la song, while they danced the associated dances . . . Then the wolves dragged in a dead man wrapped in a wolf's hide and laid him by the fire in the middle of the circle. They sang, beating time with their thighs, until the dead man got up; at first he tottered about and then slowly, under the influence of the song, he changed *into a wolf*. The chief wolf said: "Now you see what happens to the dead—*we make them into wolves* . . . and" (he went on) "Know that this is the Tlocoa'la! When you get home teach the dance to men . . ." The wolves carried the chief's son home and he explained to his friends what had happened, and taught them the ritual saying, "The wolves gave all this to me, and it is to be passed on to my daughters (!) and their husbands."

This legend tells us something about man's courageous search to learn more about the origin and nature of death, and it is properly "religious". This is shown by the fact that there is no suggestion that the chief's son tried to gain power over the Arrow of Death so that he could work magic with it: his exclamation, "I came to get this!" must be understood in the sense, "I came to experience this!" We may also notice that the changing of the dead man into a wolf echoes the idea of the Wild Hunt, since the dogs of the hunt are really dead people, and likenesses of the Death-Demon himself. In fact the dogs are identical with the Death-Demon and this is in accord with the general, popular Teutonic conception that the spirits of the dead are "shrouded ones" representing the shrouded Demon of Death. The Nootka myth also contains the idea that death and transformation are recurrent events in life, and this idea is symbolized by the fact that the Lord of Death recalls the dead man to life and transforms him—and since the Tlococa'la dance is a ritual which repeats the process it brings this idea nearer to consciousness.

A reanimation of the dead is also carried out by the psychopomp of the Aztecs mentioned before—Xolotl, the red hound of the dead—who breathes on the bones of the corpses in the kingdom of the dead, and brings them back to life. Parallel ideas are found in the cultural spheres of Egypt and Babylon. For example, Anubis is the Lord of the Grave in ancient Egypt, and he is represented as a dog- or jackal-headed god. Since he is mentioned in the oldest authenticated grave-formula as patron of burial it is not surprising to find that the jackal-headed one (usually painted in black) appears in almost all Egyptian pictures of the dead. The cult-legends of Osiris and Isis centre on death and the life after death, and the two gods are commonly represented in the company of dogs. In Mesopotamia the dog is also thought of as an animal belonging to the underworld. Clay images of dogs were devoted to Labartu, a demon hostile to men bringing sickness and death, while Gula, a healer of the sick from very early times and consort of the god of boundaries, Ninib, reveals affinities with death and is represented with dogs—showing that in Babylon the image of one Lord (or Mistress) of Death-and-Life was split into the demon of sickness and death (Labartu) and the healing goddess (Gula), while the dog remains a symbol connecting them, and can be thought of as the primeval form from which the two have developed.

The figure of the Indian god Shiva (together with his female mani-festation Shakti-Durgha) is probably the most powerful expression of the horrifying antithesis of death and life brought together in one figure. Shiva is worshipped as the procreative god of fecund nature under the symbol of the phallus, but at the same time he is the destroying, world-anihilating power of death[1]—and this second aspect has been emphasized from earliest times. Shiva is the "Lord of Dogs", and in Benares it was only in the temples of Shiva that dogs could freely pass in and out. At Benares again he is pictured in dark, blue-black with a dog behind him, and on this dog he is said to ride; another mighty dog is carved on the gate of the temple, and pilgrims offer small sugar dogs to the god. Shiva's favourite place is the burial-ground, "full of hairs, bones, skulls and flesh, polluted with blood and fat, swarming with vultures and echoing to the howl of jackals",[2] and this description reminds us of the graveyard of Urga:[3] it clearly describes the dwelling-place of greedy, devouring death "lusting for corpses", and the accompanying dog or jackal is the reminder that the original idea is that the god of death himself devours the dead. In a cave temple Shiva is represented as a skeleton (the Death-Demon in the shape of a dead man) with a girdle and necklace of snakes, sitting on two corpses which are gnawed by a ravening wolf. Moreover, Shakti-Durgha is described as wolf-faced in the Mahabharata, and is worshipped as a jackal.

There are some Teutonic-Roman votive tablets dedicated to the Batavian goddess Nehalennia, and there is some reason to think that she expresses the same horror of the united opposites death and life—not with the dramatic quality of the Indian god and goddess, but by holding the opposition in a sustained equilibrium. It is likely that she is the goddess whom Tacitus[4] identifies with Isis. Güntert made possible a real understanding of this goddess by deriving her name from *neh* and *halennia*: *neh* is cognate with the Greek νηκύς (dead man), and Latin *nec*-are (to kill), and the Teutonic *helan* (to which we have referred above) is a constituent of *halennia*, so that Nehalennia may be understood to be a corpse-hiding goddess. Her name also seems to connect her directly with Hel, and the Frisian goddess Hludana who was also worshipped in the Romano-Germanic period.[5]

---

[1] Cf. the story of *Kalidasa* which tells of the conception and birth of Shiva's son Kumara, the saviour of the world—see *The Hero with a Thousand Faces*, J. Campbell.

[2] See *Mahabharata*, XIII, 141.   [3] See pp. 46–7 above.   [4] *Germania*, IX.

[5] Cf. Hloðyn, the mother of Thor, who is easily recognized as an earth-goddess.

The best preserved of the tablets (which can be seen in the Museum of Antiquity at Nymwegen) shows Nehalennia throned on a chair, wearing a *capa* (hooded cloak), with a basket of apples on one side and a wolf-hound on the other. The dog is probably the fearsome Garmr, the hound of death, "the wolf who rends corpses" of Nordic mythology, and although as the result of Roman influence the significance may have been lost to those who dedicated the tablet it can be assumed that the attributes of the goddess were rooted in the old ideas and that these ideas were still closely linked with her worship.

The figure has no great excellence from the craftsman's point of view, but by allowing the image of Nehalennia as it appears on the tablet to work on us we can first experience the calm of the figure of the woman hidden (i.e. shrouded) in her capa; then the powerful dog sitting up on one side and the basket of apples on the other hint at something which we can understand but hardly express—something which expresses the essence of the woman. One might say that there is a dangerous menace on one side and nourishing goodness on the other. Servius, a late Latin commentator on Virgil's *Aeneid*, says of Cerberus, "*Cerberus* terra *est et consumptrix omnium corporum*" (Cerberus is the earth and devours all living things), and this might well apply to Nehalennia: the polar contrast between devouring and bestowing fruit (new growth) enriches and deepens the idea which is personified and made alive by the mysterious, concealed and concealing goddess.

This image of the divinity of death holds the opposites death and life in a living balance, and it is more mature and developed than one which expresses nothing but panic fear and horror: at the same time it has not become a "flat" image of the kindly mother-earth giving only blessings which occurs in later times. On the contrary, the shrouding brings out the majestic and uncanny quality which is the essence of this feminine deity who is destroyer and giver of seed at one and the same time.

Through the rites, legends and mythological images which we have considered in this chapter we have tried to gain insight into man's struggle to come to terms with the experience of death. It is clear that in all parts of the world the earliest image which arises in the course of this struggle is that of the demon who mysteriously snatches away that which dies and hides it from view, and this image is embodied in the figure of a greedy, devouring, carrion-eating beast of prey—usually a wolf-hound or wolf. Yet most of our illustrations show that once this figure has taken shape it seems to develop of itself: it enriches itself with new features, until the need to "recognize" the nature of death demands new images—even though the validity of the old images remains.

5. The Death-Demon as Snake and Bird

It is noticeable that one people may express the idea of the "Terror-Consumptrix" (the gigantic, devouring earth) by means of the images of several different, voracious beasts of prey. It is true that the beasts of prey are alike in many ways, but each hints at different aspects of preying and devouring. The wolf, dog, coyote, jaguar (Mexico) or leopard (Upper Lomani, Congo) stress different aspects from those implicit in the hyena (upper part of the White Nile), and the lioness (Ancient Egypt) stresses yet other features, different from the rest. The fact is that all these images arise out of the shock and terror called forth by man's encounter with the incomprehensible tremendum, and in the end this terror is quite different from the terror caused by a real beast of prey so that it cannot be comprehended in a single, unequivocal image of such a beast. It is for this reason, for example, that the Death-Demon of the Greeks is not represented as a dog but as the dog-shaped monster, Cerberus, with three (or even fifty) heads or as the closely connected figure of Orthros, a dog with two heads, seven snake-heads, and often a snake-tail as well.

In this connection the death ceremonial of the Juaneño Indians is very impressive. A fellow-tribesman dressed as a coyote breaks into the funeral procession in order to devour raw a piece of the corpse, and he is hailed by names meaning not only "thief" (*sc.* of life) and "man-eater", but also "meteor" and "globular lightning": he is also called "man-eating monster"—which can hardly be understood in terms of the coyote's rather small natural figure—and he is even described as "the sea-serpent". It is clear that the names used in the ritual come from an ancient tradition, and express the feelings of the living when they are confronted by the death of one of their number. The various names clearly show the way in which the human psyche has struggled to express the numinous experience of death in adequate images even though the experience itself lies beyond direct

55

comprehension—and this is true despite the fact that among the Juaneños of the later historical period the man who impersonates the coyote is not consciously thought of as a personification of the Death-Demon.

The images of voracious animals of prey give expression to one aspect of death. In so far as the Death-Demon is comprehended by means of such images it is seen to be *horrible* because of the fear which man experiences when confronted by its devouring aspect, but once images have begun to form, the underlying *numinosity* and the uncanny character of the Death-Demon come to the fore again. This aspect is well expressed by the *snake*, since the snake cleaves to the darkness of the earth. By its nature the snake appears more alien to man than does any other creature, for the snake is uncanny both because of the way it moves and because it appears suddenly and unexpectedly and disappears, with equal suddenness, into dark holes, clefts and caves. Man's encounter with the snake is almost identical with his encounter with that which is ultimately strange, and ultimately at enmity with him, and it is for this reason that the snake appears so often, and it seems so very early, as a form of the Death-Demon.[1]

This image gives rise to an enormous number of new associations. The snake figure does not appear at first as the sole representative of the Death-Demon, but seems to have been added to the wolf-figure. The wolf-figure represents only the preying and devouring aspects of death and when the snake is added the new totality reflects in a far more impressive way the horror of man when he is confronted by death.

The new complex is the dragon: the dragon opens its hellish mouth to devour and crush living creatures, and even as it does so it can hurl them to earth with its terrible scourging tail, or strangle them in a deathly embrace; moreover, its bite is poisonous like that of a snake. The horror increases, but the threat itself alters: instead of the indefatigable speed of a murderous wolf or dog there is the secret lurking of a creature hidden in a cave of the rocks, ready to dart out

[1] Jung describes the snake as an anxiety symbol, and he stresses its power by referring to the Midgard Serpent and to the Snake in Rubens' *Last Judgement* which is emasculating one of the damned: he also gives an illuminating illustration of the Midgard Serpent with the wolf's head (Fenris-Wolf!). See *Symbols of Transformation*, pp. 349, 438.

with lightning speed or, lazily malicious, to paralyze with a look. The "Earth-Dragon" dwells in darkness.

Both Greek and Teutonic myths indicate that the snake-form intensifies the horror of the Death-Demon, and in both the wolf and snake aspects are frequently represented as brother and sister. As we have already pointed out the Midgard Serpent, the Fenris-Wolf and the Managarmr (moon-eater) are among the brothers and sisters of Hel, and Hel herself is wolf-like. Hesiod says that Cerberus sprang from a brood of snakes;[1] the Lernaean Hydra and the Chimera were his sisters and his mother was the snake-shaped, "wild divine Echidna, dreadful, horrifying and gigantic, brightly coloured and voracious, dwelling in the depth of the earth"—clearly a Death-Demon. The consort of Echidna was the snake-like monster Typhon, the son of Gaia (earth) and Tartarus, who fought against the gods and threatened the world with fire and destruction: a fearful battle, not unlike the Teutonic Ragnarök (the twilight of the gods) in the future, when the Fenris-Wolf and the Midgard Serpent will destroy the world. Yet the Midgard Serpent was thought to embrace the world already and this symbol is found in many mythologies; it evolved out of the image of the snake of death and has deep significance.[2]

As the mother of Typhon Gaia must necessarily have something snake-like in herself, and the Aztec earth-goddess Couatlicue[3] is represented as a being built up out of huge, knotted snakes. The Greek Hecate, the goddess of chthonic darkness who dwells in caves, has snake's feet, and this idea seems to endure since it occurs in representations of the element earth in Romanesque Churches—for instance, on the Schottentor at Regensburg, built about AD 1180. Representations of cult images from Ur and Uruk show the great (Earth-) Mother with a snake's head. The Erinyes belong to the same psychological context; they are not snake-headed but snakes curl round them like hair, and it is as clear of them that they were originally Death-Demons as it is of Medusa, the Gorgon.

[1] *Theogony*, 311 ff.

[2] For the mythological significance of the encircling snake (the Uroborus), see especially Erich Neumann, *The Origins and History of Consciousness*. Neumann's extensive exposition starts from the primal bearing and procreative aspect: the death aspect referred to here provides an important complement.

[3] See below, p. 71.

The image of Demeter in the cave of Phigalia is even more impressive: according to Pausanias[1] her head is "surrounded by snakes", and this shows that the memory of the snake-headed Earth-Mother still survived when the image was made. In later times the snake is still a companion of Demeter and a snake was kept in her temple at Eleusis—although it must be admitted that it was supposed to be the embodiment of a chthonic hero. At the Thesmophoria at Athens the women sacrificed to Demeter by throwing pine-cones[2] and young pigs into the subterranean chamber (the Megaron) in which the goddess lived in the form of a snake. The subterranean gods of the Greeks were imaged as snakes for a long time: this is true, for example, of Zeus Eubuleus, the Boeotian Trophonios, Amphiaraos and, most important, Aesculapius—all of whom had special connection with Death. The death-bringing aspect of the serpent in Paradise is clearly brought out in the Old Testament, and the brazen serpent raised up before the children of Israel in the desert is not only associated with Death but, like the serpent of Aesculapius, has a *healing* significance as well. The snake of death brings life when it is worshipped by men— that is, when it is accepted as a divine reality.

The healing significance of the snake is probably associated with its primary phallic symbolism and its peculiarly mysterious nature. We need do no more than mention the fact that when a phallic symbol is included in the image of Death that image becomes, as it were, "transparent", and opens upon life. That killing Death is also and at the same time an expression of procreating life is a deep wisdom, known at some inner, emotional and intuitive level which remains unconscious and yet touches upon the mystery of the world. Thus snakes themselves are supposed to possess the equivalent of hidden wisdom and of knowledge of the hidden,[3] whether it is that they are thought of as the souls of the dead guarding hidden treasure, or that they are thought to watch over an enchanted (i.e. hidden) maiden, or that they themselves are thought to be enchanted girls, or whether it is believed that since they dwell in secret depths they are in contact with the water of life, hidden wisdom and healing counsel.

[1] 1 Pausanias, VIII, 25. [2] Phallic symbols.
[3] I.e. the unacknowledged awareness of a hidden knowledge *in man* is projected upon the symbol which, at the same time (symbolically) represents the knowledge itself (*Trans.*).

The Witoto Indians and Cameroon Pangwe Negroes make use of another aspect of the snake symbol, that of the circling snake. They represent the Death-Demon as a gigantic, man-eating snake coiled round a tree which is worshipped in cult ceremonies and is the central point of their ritual dances. This introduces us to the motif of the spiral which constantly returns to the same place at a new level, and which opens up a further aspect of death to which we shall return in Chapter 9.

In the *Epic of Gilgamesh* there is an episode which presents the symbolism of the snake with great beauty and depth. Gilgamesh encounters the destiny of Death through the death of his blood-brother Enkidu, and driven by despair he has sought for the herb of life in the depth of the sea of Death, and brought it up with his last ounce of strength. On the way back to Uruk he bathes in a pool when a snake rises out of the water, seizes the herb which Gilgamesh has left on the bank and "hurrying away leaves only its old skin behind". It is indeed the case that man is not permitted to wrest immortality from the Snake of Death, but this story teaches us that another possibility is open to him—he may slough off the old skin, renew and transform himself. Gilgamesh understood the significance of his adventure and, although tears "flowed like brooks from his face", he put aside *hubris*, defiance and despair and turned back to his work as a new man.

The snake is often combined with other animals in a peculiar way to form a terrifying image. We have already referred to the wolf- or earth-dragon and the feathered or winged snake; the bird- or air-dragon, is just as common. For example, the favourite name for the Mexican god Quetzalcoatl (a god who dies, and who brings salvation) is "the plumed serpent". Birds in themselves belong to the heavenly, spiritual, "light" side of things, but when bird-characteristics are combined with those of the "dark" chthonic snake the image which results is just as terrifying as that of wholly chthonic snakes and earth-dragons.

It would seem that in the process of renewing its images of death the psyche can only free itself from the specially alien and numinous character of the snake with great difficulty. A chief mark of the numinous is that it holds together in tension opposites between which no bridge can be built, and one can hardly imagine a greater contrast than that between the bird, free-flying in the air, and the snake, bound close to the surface of the earth. Since it is likely that knowledge of these things exists in the depths of the psyche we have some right to assume that in seizing upon an image which is the polar opposite of the snake the psyche is taking a further step in the unfolding of consciousness, and this assumption provides a clue which can help us understand the *appearance of the Death-Demon in the form of a bird.*

Having said this we must also acknowledge that some birds do have a direct association with death—in particular, birds of prey like eagles and vultures, and carrion-eating ravens or crows. Although man does not experience such birds as a menace to his own life they can be seen to carry the event of death onward through corruption to dissolution, and we have considered the meaning of this as it appears to primitive thought above.[1] Vultures (in particular) are regarded by Asiatic people as holy disposers of corpses, and they play a part in their rites and customs[2]—generally in addition to dogs and wolves. As we pointed out before, the Death-Demon in its original form was both the devourer and the burier: the disembodying of the dead which men can perceive directly is also perceived as the visible concrete act of the Demon, and this side of its uncanny activity is brought sharply to consciousness by the image of the carrion-bird. At the same time this image takes up and transforms the idea of the hidden and mysterious nature of Death which was expressed with straightforward naïvety in the image of the "Hider" (*koljo), and of the "darkness of the earth". The image of the bird tends to "spiritualize" the mysteriousness of the Death-Demon, and it does this to such an extent that in later German ballads and fairy-tales it appears in the form of three doves, thought of as birds and nothing more, who reveal secret knowledge of coming death.

In Greek myth the Harpies retain elements of the vulture-form and function of the Death-Demon, although in an attenuated way. There can be no doubt that the Harpies were originally a very old form of Death-Demon and as late as Apollonius Rhodius (born 265 BC) they were still called "the *Hounds* of Zeus". According to the general

[1] See p. 41.
[2] Compare the rites for the disposal of corpses in the *Zend Avesta*, and the Towers of Silence among the modern Parsees and the reference to Urga above pp. 46–7.

tradition they were winged, and often had vultures' bodies with brazen claws at the end of human arms and legs, but with human heads with the faces of beautiful girls; their function was to snatch away swiftly and suddenly. Their essential nature (i.e. as Death-Demons) was not consciously known in later times, but the full horror of death appears in relation to them in Apollonius Rhodius' description:

> "The Harpies hastened thither,
> Swift as lightning and whirlwind.
> Sudden as a storm they fell from the clouds
> Shrieking their greed for food.
> Loud cried the heroes standing near,
> Shouting aloud when they saw them appear . . ."[1]

and as true Demons that feed on corpses they left behind a foul smell. Their names are equally illuminating: according to Homer ῞Αρπυαι means "storms that snatch away, robbers, spirits whirling in the storm-wind,"[2] which recalls the spirits of storm and death which form the Wild Hunt. One Harpy is Aello, which means "tearing wind"; another is Okypete, "the swift flier";[3] and there is Keleino, "the dark one," whose name indicates her character as Death. On the other hand there is mention in the *Iliad* of a Harpy called Podarge, which means "swift of foot", who "pastured" on the strand of Oceanus and, impregnated by Zephyrus, became the mother of the two immortal and soothsaying steeds of Achilles:[4] in this case name and character point to a relationship with the horse-form of the Death-Demon. The Sirens also have a bird-form and, according to Sophocles, they sing "the melodies of Hades":[5] they are thought to be daughters of the snake-bodied Achelous, or else of Gaia, which connects them with the dragon-form of the Demon. They were companions of Persephone before she was abducted by Hades, and afterwards they were sent out as servants and messengers of their mistress from the kingdom of the dead.[6] Like the Harpies they are represented as birds with charming and seductive faces. In later times (e.g. on Attic tombstones) they were presented in softer form showing a quiet loveliness, but as late as the *Odyssey* the dominant idea is that of the horror which they inspire,

---

[1] *Argonauts*, II, 266 ff.   [2] *Odyssey*, I, 241.   [3] Hesiod, *Theogony*, 267.
[4] *Iliad*, XVI, 150 f.   [5] Sophocles, *Fragment*, 777B.
[6] Apollonius Rhodius, *The Argonauts*, IV, 895, 897: Euripedes, *Helena*, 168.

and their dwelling-place is said to be a meadow on which human bones lie dried and bleaching as they do round the eyrie of a bird of prey.[1] On a Corinthian vase of the sixth century the Sirens and the ship of Odysseus are represented, and above the ship crouch two huge birds of prey who seem to be waiting to plunge upon the tiny human beings.

The Gorgon with her golden wings is even more impressive, and her gruesome appearance has a paralysing effect. She is represented as a human being with terrible features—"with bared fangs in her opened mouth, crowned and girded with clustered snakes".[2] Kerényi stresses the fact that the Gorgon represents the terrifying side of the sublime Persephone,[3] and Aeschylus says, "At the sight of her the breath dies in every man."[4]

There are bird-demons which can be seen to originate from the Death-Demon in the Teutonic sphere as well. Although the two ravens of Odin do not sing the beguiling songs of the Sirens they do have the same secret wisdom. Freya has a raiment of birds' feathers, and the fact that it is called "Valhjamr" (shroud) suggests that she is somehow connected with a bird of the dead. It is even more clear that the Valkyries were originally winged Death-Demons, and in Anglo-Saxon they are linguistically connected with the raven—the Anglo-Saxon word for "raven" is *waelceasig* which is identical to *waelcurge* (Valkyrie). In the Nordic *Wölsungensage* Odin's Valkyrie, Hliod, takes the form of a crow, and another Valkyrie is Walðogn, which means "receiver and consumer of corpses". "Küren", "kiesen"—the second part of "Valkyrie" is cognate with N.H.G. *kosten*, Lat. *gustare*, Gk. γεύειν, which emphasizes her original character as a corpse-eating (winged) Death-Demon.

Rasmussen recently recorded a number of Eskimo fairy-tales, and in these both eagle and raven still retain the characteristics of Death-Demons, even though their significance is not brought out. In the same tales there is a winged monster which in the form of a demonic nursling is a bloodthirsty divinity of Death, and then as a winged youth a bestower of life and strength. The Kwakiutl Indians of Vancouver Island have a cult-legend in which the raven is unequivoc-

---

[1] *Odyssey*, XII, 45. [2] Hesiod, *Shield of Heracles*, 224 ff.
[3] Cf. *Odyssey*, XI, 635. [4] *Prometheus*, 800.

ably associated with the Death-Demon. The account given to explain the origin of the winter Hamatsa cult[1] runs as follows:

"Once upon a time Chief Nauwaqawe sent his four sons to hunt mountain goats. He said: 'Do not go into the house where the smoke is red like blood. If you go in you will never come home again. It is the house of Baxbakualanu Xsiwae.' The second day the young men came to a house where the smoke was red like blood: the door was open and despite their father's warning they went in. The raven Qoaxqoaxualanu Xsiwae sat by the door, and there was a woman rooted in the floor. The woman said: 'This is Baxbakualanu's house, but I will help you. Dig a deep hole in that corner! Make stones red hot in the fire and put them in the hole! Cover the hole with boards!' The young men did as she said and as they finished there was a loud whistling outside and Baxbakualanu came through the door. *The body of Baxbakualanu was completely covered with mouths;* he put on the Hamatsa mask and danced round the fire with the raven [*author's italics*]. As the evil spirit danced over the pit the eldest brother pulled away the boards and Baxbakualanu fell on the red hot stones and was burnt to death. The young men took the Hamatsa Mask, the Raven Mask and the rest of the dancing-gear, and the woman taught them the proper songs and the Mask Dance. She sang the 'Hamatsa Mask of the forehead', the 'Hamatsa Mask of the Whole World' and the 'Beautiful Hamatsa Mask of Baxbakualanu Xsiwae'—and then she sang the same songs of the Raven Mask. She said to the young men: 'Establish a winter dance when you get home, and let the eldest of you be Hamatsa!' She taught them all that was necessary."

There is no doubt that this winter cult-dance symbolizes the defeat of Death the all-devourer by identifying with him and by means of the help of the feminine earth. The Earth-Woman clearly represents the "other side" of the devouring Death-Demon—the life-giving, birth aspect. In this story the raven has only a subsidiary role and its exact connection with Baxbakualanu can only be guessed. It would be of great interest to trace the way in which the raven, which is here the companion of the Death-Demon, became the bringer of life and a culture-hero who procured the light of the sun among neighbouring Indian and Eskimo tribes.

There is a Mexican myth known as *The Descent into Hell*, in which

[1] Cf. Chapter 4, p. 50.

63

it is said that the four "*dismembering* animals"—bat, jaguar, Quetzal-bird and eagle—stand at the four entrances to the south region of the underworld, and the "disc of the moon" stands in the middle: the moon is the "perpetually self-renewed", and so refers to rising again. We have already come across the idea of dismemberment and re-birth in the myth of Ceram[1] where, it will be remembered, it involved a complete destruction which led to the transformation of the victim (into life-giving food).[2]

The winged bird-like demons of death play roles which contrast with those of the tearing wolf or all-devouring Hell-Hound. It is true that like these other monsters they are terrifying, horrible, greedy and insatiable, and that the corpse-like character, the greed and the irresistibility of the Harpies, for example, add nothing to the earlier forms, but in other respects the bird-demons play a new part. Like Odin's ravens, the Valkyries, the Sirens and the raven of the Kwakiutl myth, the birds often appear as helpers or messengers of the real Death-Demon who remains *hidden* and *remote*, so that the mediating bird-form emphasizes the mysterious "otherness" of the Demon as well as revealing new sides of its nature. One new aspect is the alluring element found, for instance, in the Sirens and the Valkyries. Again, the vulture-form brings out the lightning-swift appearance of death out of the unknown and its equally sudden disappearance, and also the final taking possession of the dead, leaving nothing but scattered bones. In this way new light is thrown on the ideas of dismemberment, renewal and transformation. The idea of dismemberment is like that of the sloughing of the snake's skin in the Galgamesh epic, but it stresses more clearly that transformation requires a painful and complete sacrifice of the existing form.[3] The winged Gorgon, Medusa, was dismembered and Chrysaor and the winged horse Pegasus sprang from her blood as transformed embodiments of her nature. Perseus who slays the Gorgon is given wings by Hermes (the psychopomp) and is able to rescue the maiden (Andromeda) from the devouring

[1] See Introduction, *et al.*

[2] C. G. Jung discusses the meaning of dismemberment in *Symbols of Transformation* (Collected Works, Vol. 5, paras. 354 ff., 556), and *Psychology and Alchemy* (Collected Works, Vol. 12—see Index).

[3] Cf. on the level of the speculative use of images, the "alchemical process": see in particular C. G. Jung *Psychology and Alchemy*.

dragon of the sea (symbolically, of the underworld), and join with her in marriage. The bird-form shrouds the Death-Demon in the mystery of distance, and yet lifts a corner of the shroud, since through it man experiences the fact that annihilation is not merely destruction but also transformation—and this is why the birds of death have hidden knowledge like the ravens of Odin and the Sirens who sing of the wisdom of Hades.

It seems that we should be right to follow Jung's lead and see in the bird-form of the Death-Demon the beginning of a process of spiritualization, the early development of a spiritual symbol. The earliest images of the Death-Demon expresses the mystery of death by their monstrosity, and in so far as their most marked feature is a hugeness which can be neither formulated nor conceived they may be said to be "*quantitative*"; as the images develop they are transformed into that which is *qualitatively* beyond comprehension, something which is infinitely distant and yet immediate and near at the same time. The qualitative has far richer potentialities and possibilities of differentiation than the quantitative, and the spiritual development leads to the formulation of a mythological conception of the world as a whole, and the attempt to comprehend that which can never be wholly comprehensible to man.

6. The Death-Demon as Horse—from Animal to Human Forms

CONSIDERATION of the bird-form of the Death-Demon brings out the way in which the psychic standpoint alters. It is clear that in his actual experience of nature man is rarely threatened with death by even the largest birds of prey. A magnificent eagle or vulture may evoke a kind of reverence and give rise to some anxiety, but men soon learn that they have little or no cause to fear it—and ravens and crows are not a source of danger at all. The victims of the winged robbers are *other* and smaller living beings or the corpses of other, *dead* men.

When we considered the earliest, primitive reaction of panic flight from the presence of death we saw that man's first horror does not arise from fear for his own life, but is instinctively evoked when he is confronted by the death of the *other*. This is implicit in the primeval name of the Death-Demon, Kolịo, "the Hider", since it is obvious that it is not the man who pronounces the name who is hidden, but that the *other*, the one who has died, is shrouded from his sight. When, however, death is expressed in the image of wolf or snake we may assume that the sense of a *threat to one's own life* has come into greater prominence, and this is a step which brings man to what Vetter calls the "basic condition for achieving spiritual independence". The bird-image represents a "suspension" of the direct development of this motif, which recedes into the background to allow a more precise and more mature reconsideration of the destiny of the *other*—first, of other living creatures, and then of living beings in general. The other as "thou" is more strongly emphasized, and by holding before his eyes both the death of the "thou" and his own death man becomes aware of Death itself. This theme runs as an undertone through the story of Odysseus and the Sirens, for Odysseus is concerned that death may come to his companions and they that it may come to him, and each knows that the death of the other would lead to death for himself.[1]

If the threat to oneself has to some extent receded into the background when the Death-Demon has the form of a bird, it is even less noticeable in relation to the Death-Demon in the form of a horse. Yet the horse-form is extremely common, at least in the Indo-Germanic area, so that we need to ask what psychological idea this image expresses. Although the power and the dangerous aspect of a horse snorting in anger makes a deep impression the general sense of danger involved has not enough specific content to offer an adequate explanation of the significance of the horse, and in fact this particular image plays little part in the mythological accounts. Elucidation must come from a study of the accounts themselves.

In both Greek and Teutonic myths the bird- and horse-shaped demons are closely connected, and the same individual may appear in both forms. The Harpies provide good examples: one Harpy is Okypete and this word, which means "the swift flyer", is used again and again in the *Iliad* as an adjective applied to horses;[2] another Harpy is Pordarge, and not only does Pordargos, the name of Menelaus' horse,[3] seem to be another form of the same word, but Pordarge herself was generally thought of as a pasturing mare and became the mother of the two immortal steeds of Achilles. The winged Gorgon was sometimes thought of as a horse and gave birth to the winged horse Pegasus. In Teutonic mythology the Valkyries have a bird-form, but came to be thought of primarily as riders on horses.

We also come across the horse-form of the Death-Demon in the legends of the Wild Hunt and the Host of the Dead, and especially in the Bavarian description of the Wild Huntsman as Rosswoderer.[4] In legends of the Allgau we hear of a horse which carries men off in a mysterious way and has other features of the Death-Demon. In Germany the bier was called *St Michael's Horse* in the Middle Ages and in

[1] *Odyssey*, XII, 154–157.   [2] Cf. *Iliad*, VIII, 42 and XIII, 24.
[3] *Iliad*, XXIII, 295.

[4] No literal translation is possible. "Ross" is horse. "Woderer" is a verbal noun which includes the root belonging to "Wotan" related to the sanskrit word for "storm", and also the root found in German words meaning "Strong excitement", "anger". The author writes, "Woderer may be a reminder of Wotan riding at the head of the army of the dead" (*Trans.*).

modern Persia the word for a coffin means "wooden horse", and these two echoes of the ancient idea of the Death-Demon in the form of a horse bring home, in a most impressive way, the symbolic significance of the horse as that which carries man into the realm of the "beyond".

It seems that the main feature which makes the horse an appropriate image of the Death-Demon is speed—a feature which it shares with birds, and which is often thought of as a swiftness like that of the wind. By means of their speed both horse and bird can appear from "nowhere" and disappear as suddenly as they come, and we have seen that such appearances from the unknown and disappearances into it are important aspects of the Death-Demon in all its forms. The horse-form of the Demon gives rise to further complications, because it is usually associated with the idea of a (visible or invisible) rider, and it is in fact the rider rather than the horse who is thought to seize and carry of, as Hades carried off Persephone at her play and the Valkyries carried off warriors slain in battle. It may be further remarked that the steeds of the Valkyries seemed to have a double meaning: in that they fly through the air they are birdlike and so share with the birds the attribute *waelceasig*—corpse-tasting; in that they are the mounts of the Valkyries they partake in their function of carrying off the dead to the world of the Lord of the Dead, a world which is hidden and secret from living human beings. Odin, who is the *Val-god* (i.e. god of the dead), is always associated with, and partly characterized by his eight-footed steed Sleipnir which is swift as the wind; Hel's steed is also mentioned in the myths, and it seems that the bestially-devouring and hideous element which belongs to the earliest horror of death cannot be separated from Hel, since her steed is fed on the victims of the bloody spear.[1] In Danish popular belief the image of this steed lingered until recent times in the idea of a ghastly, three-legged horse. We may also notice the North German legend of the rider on the white horse, and a story by Theodor Storm about a demonic steed which comes from distant and mysterious lands, plays a fateful role which fulfils life with a remarkable intensity and then disappears (together with its rider) as mysteriously as it came.[2] In this story the

[1] *Hofuðlied*, 10.

[2] In *Psyche* (9th Ed., p. 242) Erwin Rhode mentions that a horse is frequently shown on Greek graves, even when the dead man had had no special connection with a horse or horses. He suggests that the horse is a symbol of death

writer has penetrated deep into popular beliefs, using great imaginative insight.

There are other ways in which the horse is associated with ancient images of the Death-Demon. For example, in many countries the last ears of corn that are cut are dedicated to the divinity of Death[1]—such as the Rye-Wolf or the Rye-Aunt in Germany—and this Demon represents the death of the corn: in some places in England, France and Germany it is thought to take the form of a horse.[2] Again both horses and birds are often supposed to bring the mysterious, intoxicating liquor which is thought to be the Water of Life and the Water of Death: this appears from many fairy-tales, and also from the fact that old drinking vessels often have the shape of a horse.

The connection between the horse and intoxicating drink is particularly marked in the older Vedic religion of India. At the height of their power victorious rulers offered the great Horse Sacrifice, and this was associated with a three-day Festival of Soma, the intoxicating and life-giving drink of the gods. During the festival the consecrated horse was suffocated with robes, and this recalls the rites of death and killing which have had a sacred content from earliest times which we discussed in Chapter 2. After the horse was killed the chief wife of the king lay down beside the dead horse and took its generative organ in her lap, and this reminds one of the impregnation of Isis by the dead Osiris and shows that the sacrificial horse had characteristics of a fertility spirit—that is, that the sacrifice expressed the idea that death gives rise to new life.

There was also a horse sacrifice in ancient Rome. The sacrificed animal was called the "October-Horse", and the sacrifice took place after a chariot race on the Campus Martius. Wilhelm Mannhardt has shown that this was certainly a fertility rite, and the association between fertility and a chariot race is of special interest. The irresistible circling of the horses symbolizes both the circular course of the year and the all-conquering power of fate. The horses symbolize irresistible instinct and fertility on the one hand, and irresistible destiny and death on the

but is unable to elucidate the connection. Our investigations would seem to help clarify this. It may also be noted that Death has been shown as a horse-rider by Albrecht Dürer, Alfred Rethel, Arnold Boecklin and others.

[1] See below, pp. 128 f. and p. 140.
[2] *The Golden Bough*, J. G. Frazer (Vol. 2, pp. 24–26).

other. It may well be that Goethe felt the force of this when in the character of Egmont he broke out at the end of *Dichtung und Wahrheit*: "Child! Child! No further! The sun-horses of time stampede with the fragile chariot of our destiny, as though whipped by invisible spirits; nothing is left to us but to summon our courage, hold fast to the reins and guide the wheels now right, now left, clearing a rock on this side, avoiding a fall on that. Who knows where he is going? After all, he hardly remembers where he came from."[1]

It may help at this point to take note of our modern experience and understanding of dream-symbols. Jung and others have shown that the symbols in dreams are not clearly defined, unambiguous images which have a one-to-one correspondence with the things they symbolize; and Jung stresses that as a rule the peculiar character of a dream-symbol depends upon the fact that it combines polar opposites in a single image. Thus if a galloping horse is the symbol of abduction by some frenetic power, it may refer to being carried away to the world beyond, on the one hand, and to being carried away by the ecstatic emotion associated with impregnation and procreation on the other: moreover, the horse is also a symbol of maternity, usually representing its dangerous aspect. Since we have seen that the bird-form of the Death-Demon may have reference to maternity and renewal (transformation by new birth) it may well be that the motif of the maternal, although not at first specific, plays a part in the horse as an image of death. Some confirmation of this is provided by the statue of Demeter at Phigalia which shows the (mother-) goddess with a horse's head surrounded by serpents, and by the associated cult legend that as she mourned the loss (death) of her daughter, mad with indignation, she took the form of a mare and had to submit to impregnation by Poseidon. The connection of the Death-Demon with the mother-goddess appears very strange to rational thought, and we shall return to it below.

The Demeter of Phigalia is one of the ancient mixed images of gods and goddesses, part-human, part-animal, of which classical Greek mythology contains very few traces—although certain features or special attributes and epithets of a Greek divinity often point to an older image of mixed or animal form. In other mythologies, for example that of Ancient Egypt, gods and demons of this kind play a prominent part, and some of them express the connection between

[1] *Egmont*, II, 2.

death and the maternal in a horrifying and grandiose way. Toeris is an Egyptian mother-goddess whose cult goes back to prehistoric times, and she is represented as a pregnant monster, part-hippopotamus, part-crocodile, with lion's paws and human hands, standing upright like a human being—and the total effect is horrible, like the most terrifying forms of the devouring Death-Demon. An almost identical figure, Amam or Am-mit, who retains her demonic character, has a place in Osiris' tribunal of the dead. *The Book of the Dead* says: "Her front is like a crocodile, her back like a hippopotamus and her middle part like a lion." Since, in later myth, this creature devours the dead who have not passed the tribunal it is safe to assume that it is an original form of the Death-Demon itself. Even if no historical connection were found it is psychologically easy to understand the inner relationship between the Death-Demon Amam and (in Neumann's phrase) "the Terrible Mother" Toeris.

The goddess Hathor is sometimes represented as a cow and sometimes as a hippopotamus, and she too, unites the maternal with the devouring killer. She was worshipped, particularly by women, as the mother of the sun and the goddess of love and destiny, but she was also the goddess of war, and a bloodthirsty destroyer of men. She is represented as saying, "As I live, I have made myself master of men, and it refreshed my heart;" and it was said that she always thirsted for human blood, even though she had already drunk streams of it, so that in the end the other gods had to protect men from her by a ruse.

Despite marked differences the figure of the Aztec earth-goddess Couatlicue gives the same general impression as that of Toeris. Couatlicue is also represented in a horrifying way: her broad figure rests heavily on two enormous jaguar paws; huge serpents coil from her neck and the stumps of her arms to form a kind of ghastly gorgon face with gigantic fangs on her neck; there is a chain of human hearts and heads about her neck, and her girdle is decorated with a human skull. The inscription "*Terra consumptrix omnium corporum*" would be entirely appropriate. Despite the gruesome appearance and the lack of human characteristics the statue gives the sense of a human being—not of an animal as do images of Cerberus, for example. She expresses perfectly the dynamic quality of death, but just as clearly she is a goddess, and the result is that the ghastly is raised to the divine.

These composite god-figures of Egypt and Mexico, and the Demeter of Phigalia raise the question how we should understand the human form of the Death-Demon from a psychological point of view, and set it in its place in the process of development. The compilation of the images from separated parts of a variety of death-bringing, devouring or constricting animals seems to have a clear enough meaning: it expresses something of the complex nature of the Death-Demon. The Death-Demon may be swift as a lion, it may lie lazily in wait like a hippopotamus, it may be maliciously greedy and disguise itself like the crocodile, and so on—and yet it seems that this is not enough. Its whole nature is not expressed by any one animal's form, nor in a combination of many; something else is needed, and this is provided by the overall *humanness* of the figure. The human form adds an element which makes the total figure closer and more familiar and yet, at the same time, more remote and uncanny, fundamentally mysterious.

These basically human figures rise out of the human psyche as if the hidden Death who drives the abducting steeds, or their previously invisible rider, had suddenly appeared before man, and this causes (or is caused by) a significant change in man's attitude to death. So long as the Death-Demon is imaged in a form which is predominantly feral, its activity is understood as unthinking, blind and instinctive, but when the form is predominantly anthropoid death is no longer conceived as blindly fortuitous acting without plan, but as directed and intended. The figure which is human but incomprehensible and which remains somehow shrouded and hidden embodies plan and intention, meaning and secret knowledge. No doubt just as the figure remains shrouded so do the plan and intention, but though these are hidden from him man recognizes that they must fulfil *some* meaning, however uncomprehended and incomprehensible it may be.

When the Death-Demon is presented in human form a basic psychological development has taken place. At first the metaphysical character of death was felt vaguely, as a numinous horror, in the image of the huge wolf's jaws; then as a mysterious "otherness", hidden and remote, in the images of serpent, bird and horse; in the human image it is less remote, and yet more deeply shrouded in darkness as a spiritual secret.[1] We may say that the Death-Demon has begun to become the God of Death.

[1] In *Natur und Person* A. Vetter shows that with this step something took place which was highly significant for man's understanding of himself.

It should not be supposed that the development can be pictured as a straight, steadily ascending line. The representation of death in human form occurred here and there before it became established, and purely demonic aspects of death can also be represented anthropomorphically. Impressive witness to this is provided by figures of the Death-Demon in Teutonic lands. In the "Wild Hunt" it is usually only the leader who has human form and his retinue is made up of animal-like demons, but there also grew up the idea of a multitude of anthropomorphic demons called "the Shrouded Ones"—their very name showing their affinity with Hel. In Nordic they are the *Huldren*—Nor. *huldre*, M.Ice. *huldufolk*, Swed. *huldra*—and the name is derived from *helan* which we have met before, and which is the feminine past participle of *huldi*, meaning "the Shrouded Ones". The name implies that the Huldren are the Shrouded Ones, and the victims of Hel, that is the dead themselves. The (Un-) Holden and Frau Holda of German legend belong to the same context and their names have no connection with the N.H.G. *hold* (gracious, favourable).

From extensive evidence Güntert shows that these creatures which dwell underground (in Hel) have the same form and function as Hel herself, as well as being in some sense her manifestations and executive servants. They usually appear in human form, but at times they change back into the well-known animal figures of the Death-Demon. It is possible that animistic ideas have had something to do with turning the dead into demons of death, but it is hardly possible to define exactly the extent of their contribution: our present concern is simply to point out that the "Shrouded Ones" are identified with the realm and figure of Hel to which they belong.

As the importance of the "Shrouded Ones" increases Hel herself seems to recede into the background, into an even deeper obscurity, and yet at the same time to retain her anthropomorphic, that is "spiritual", character. The Huldren or Holden dwell in the depths of the earth, or else in a mountain, and they nearly always wear something which indicates their shrouded nature. It is they who stir up sickness; if they strike a man's heart he becomes a corpse within three days; if they breathe upon a man their corpse-like breath brings pestilence and death. The *mares* or nightmares belong to the same class of being, and their name is derived from the Indo-Germanic base *mer, which means "pulverise", or "crush", and which has clear affinities with

73

Lat. *mors* (death), N.H.G. *morsch*, Nor. *morken* meaning "decayed with rottenness". It may be noted that in Westphalia, Oldenburg and East Frisia the mares are described as *Walriderske*, so that here we meet once again the Valkyries, the mounted maidens of Hel—the female servants who probably share the characteristics of their mistress since, as we have seen, Hel herself rides a steed which she feeds with corpses.

7. Tools and Attributes: Characteristics and Manifestations of the Death-Demon in Human Form

THE various forms of the Death-Demon which we have examined are the externalization of inner images by means of which the human psyche expresses its reaction to the experience of death, and when we look back over them they bring to mind something which psychotherapists have noticed about dreams. Dreams can often be seen to form a series, sometimes continuous, sometimes interrupted by long intervals, and such a series of dreams frequently circles with apparent monotony around a single theme—that is, the same problem is presented by the unconscious in a number of different images. Actually there is a "working over" of the theme, because if we look carefully we always find that the later images are not mere repetitions of those that have gone before but express new aspects of the central theme, new insights into the nature of the problem and new possibilities inherent in it. In fact, it often turns out that the later dreams differentiate and make explicit what was already germinally present in the earlier.[1]

Since a dream series can be regarded as the unfolding of unconscious images we may treat it as an analogy of the unfolding of the image of Death, and if we do this we find that we gain fuller insight into the process which we have been illustrating. The devouring wolf, the serpent, the bird, the horse clearly represent something beyond themselves. They represent, in fact the inner crystallization of a numinous experience into an image, and the human form (which is only explicitly developed later) is secretly contained within them. We can see this from the mythical stories about them, which endow them with human characteristics and attribute human behaviour to them. At the same time the human form of the Death-Demon is also serpent or wolf.

[1] Cf., for instance, the "working over" of the mandala image in the impressive dream series given by Jung in *Psychology and Alchemy*.

Even though, in the course of time, the human-like Death-Demon (or God of Death) is considerably changed, it is frequently the case that some animal is recognized as his companion or provides an epithet for him, or that he is liable to change into an animal, and from this we can infer his earlier origins. Nevertheless, it is not until the Death-Demon becomes explicitly anthropomorphic that the full richness of the incomprehensible event Death begins to emerge, even though it can never be wholly contained in an image. When it is given human form the nature of the Death-Demon is enriched and deepened and related to the totality of the universe, the individual and life in a succession of new ways.

At first the new elements of death which are brought to consciousness when the Death-Demon is given human form are expressed in external traits although, at the same time, these traits have symbolic meanings which point to the essential character of the demon. In particular they are represented by *tools* which the demon uses. Thus the Harpies had *brazen claws*, with which they lacerated and dragged away their victims, and Percht had an *iron claw hand* and an *iron shoe*, a blow from which would strike a man with mortal sickness. The *Wassermann*[1] ("*Hakemann*" in North Germany) has an iron hook with which he maliciously drags a man from his home and family and drags him down into the hidden depths, and Agathe Schmidt tells of the Death-Demon Mabu among the Nsei (the Cameroons) which is represented as an anthropomorphic mask of wood dressed in feathers, carrying a large knife and with a *trident* in its hands. The Nordic *Ran* is said to drag men into her kingdom with *nets*, and Frau Holle is supposed to capture the dead of the coming year in a net made from flax spun during the Twelve Nights.[2] This net motif occurs among people altogether separated; for example, the Witoto in the jungles of Columbia speak of a mythical being (undoubtedly a Death-Demon) called Husiniamui who has a strange *net* with which he knocks off his enemies' heads! The Ke'lets, the death-demons of the Chukchee to which we have already referred, hunt men with dogs and in the darkness of the night they creep into tents and use *nets* to drag souls from the protection of their dwelling into the open, where they can dismember and eat them. Similar ideas may lie behind the use of *basket-nets* by the Luiseño Indians and the Nsei of West Africa in the

[1] A character in German folk-lore.   [2] From Christmas to Epiphany.

rites with which they bury their dead at night. According to Carinthian legend, if the Wild Hunter throws one raw haunches of men or horses one must preserve them in a *hempen net*, so that one may get rid of them without harm after a year and a day—in other words, by doing what the Death-Demon does (holding the corpse in a net) man can preserve himself from that Demon's anger.

The *rope* is a tool of the Death-Demon as well as the net, and it may well be that the rope is the earlier form. Hel is thought of as having a rope; and Yama, the Indian god of death, has either a net or a *noose of rope* with which he captures souls. In the *Pretakalpa* the messengers of the god of death are described: "Now the two fearful messengers advance, carrying noose and stick, naked, black as ravens, grinding their teeth, and armed with claws." The killer Kali (Durgha) is represented with a noose, and in the murdering sect of the Thugs[1] a noose of rope is both tool and emblem. One could multiply examples, but the Sirens deserve particular mention, for Güntert argues convincingly that their name is derived from the Greek σειρά or σειρή which means "rope", "noose" or "lasso". It may be that the rope of the Labyrinthine Geranos Dance which Theseus danced at Delos with those whom he had rescued from death is connected with the same circle of ideas, and if so it would mean that the dancers clinging to him were characterized as denizens of the underworld, "entangled ones".[2] One should also notice the Old Testament phrase "the bonds (i.e. nooses) of death", and vernacular German expressions like "death has him on the rope".

Rope bindings were a feature of the cult of the Spartan Aphrodite Morpho, and occur in a legend connected with the cultic shrine of the Attic Aphrodite Kolias (to whom, incidentally, dogs were sacrificed!) and these facts open up far-reaching perspectives. "Morpho" and "Kolias" link the Goddess of Love with the dark, enveloping depths of the earth, and "Kolias" seems to carry the meaning that she is actually the Hider of the Dead—i.e. *kolio.

The Wassermann's hook and the rope clearly stress the idea of "snatching away" as an aspect of death, and they also carry a suggestion of surprise and suddenness, and even of treachery and malicious, secret triumph. On the other hand, the net seems to express the collective

[1] The "Thugs" are actually "the hidden, shrouded ones"!
[2] But see *Labyrinthstudien* by Kerényi for another interpretation.

aspect of death, for a net does not catch one individual alone and in the end *all* the dead lie in the net together: there is the sense that the destiny of death is common to all men. Hook, rope and net reiterate the idea that the dead man is snatched away into darkness and obscurity, so that it is not surprising that we often find explicit references to the hiding and shrouding character of the Death-Demon in connection with these instruments. As we have said the Huldren in Norse realms and the Holde in German are the "hidden (shrouded) ones", and the earth-spirits and dwarfs which are known by many names in German legend belong among them.

The idea of shrouding is most clearly expressed by the *cap of invisibility* or the *hat of Hel* which is often worn by dwarfs and which occurs, for example, in the legends of the strong dwarf Alberich and of King Laurin. Laurin (as his name implies)[1] lurks invisibly in a rose garden which is bounded by a "thread"—that is, a rope. There is a story from Lower Germany about a peasant who swings a long rod through the air a little above the earth and by doing so knocks off the dwarfs' caps of invisibility and sees the Invisible Ones who are harvesting his field. The hat of Hel is like the cape and cloak which, as we have seen, characterize Nehalennia on the Roman-Batavian votive stone,[2] and dwarfs are still commonly represented with pointed caps and little cloaks. In "Heliand" the Devil, who, of course, dwells in Hell, is said to be "concealed in a helmet of Hel", and it is probable that the cloud-hat and -cloak of the Val-god Odin once had the same meaning of concealment. The Greeks spoke of the *cap of Hades* which, as can be seen from illustrations, was made from the head of a wolf or dog and which was also a cap of invisibility: for instance, we read, "Athene put on the helm of Hades so that she might not be seen by the mighty Ares",[3] and a well-known statue (called "Athena Albani") shows her wearing a dog-skin cap. The Demon of Death who shrouds the dead is himself one who is shrouded and, as we have seen, the dead, the shrouded ones, merge into the being of the Demon—which is probably the reason why the Demon is often represented with corpse-like traits: deathly pallor or a dark colour, corpse(big)-teeth and even empty eye sockets. It is clear that many characteristics which

[1] Laurin belongs to the M.H.G. verb "luren"; modern German "lauern" —cf. "lure", "lurk", "lower", all words connected with hiding.
[2] See Chapter 4.   [3] *Iliad*, V, 849.

are taken up into the image of the Death-Demon arise out of the experience of seeing human corpses.

It will be remembered that Shiva-Durgha is represented in Indian temples as being blue-black in colour, and even as a skeleton. Very often when the dwellers in the underworld are not represented as entirely dark they have a dark band round their eyes, or the skin about their eyes and on forehead and temples is blue or black: this suggests a mask, and it may well be that the feeling that a man who has just become rigid in death is a man wearing a mask makes an even deeper impression on the observer than the later change of colour. It is as though the man who had been alive is still there but is now shrouded behind a mask of mysteriously unapproachable rigidity. Small children are almost always frightened by masks, especially when they are put on by people near to them, and this can give us some idea of the horror with which primitive man saw the rigid mask of death. It is because of this horror that a horrifying mask is so often a main feature of the Death-Demon, since this mask gives expression to man's immediate feeling about those who have just died: a feeling which is associated with the apparent nearness of the dead man and his extreme distance from us, the visible presence of the body and the deepest concealment of the person.

Güntert points out that *Larve* (Ger. mask) is etymologically connected with the hidden spirits of the Kingdom of the Dead, the *Lares* (Lat.), and that their name is cognate with *la-tere* (to be hidden or to keep oneself hidden) and Latona, the goddess of death (*Lato* or *Leto* in Greek). Such etymological considerations enable philologists to deduce that many characters in myths and legends were once Death-Demons. *Grim*hildr in the Nordic "Sigurlied" is the "muffled, disguised or masked warrior-maiden": Lohengrin is derived from "Lorangrime" which means "the darkly disguised elf"; *Loran* is related to *Laurin* and *Lor*elei, "Grime" to the English word spelt the same, and to a Frisian word, also spelt the same, which means "a dark spot on the face". Moreover, since Indo-Germanic words for "blind" are used in two senses meaning "not being seen" as well as "not seeing" Odin's one-eyedness (blindness) may well have originated as a mark of the invisibility of the God of the Dead.

The cultic use of masks occurs all over the world, and from folk-lore and ethnology it can be collected that the mask was a means of representing the dead or the Death-Demon. This appears to be true of the use of a great variety of masks by the Polynesians and by many African tribes, and the Nsei in the Cameroons use masks which they say represent the spirits of the dead and which are brought out immediately after a death for the mourning ceremony, and then again at the later feast of the dead, the second funeral celebration. It is particularly interesting that these same masks are also worn at the beginning and end of the great corn-festival Nsiä, because such festivals centre upon the idea that life passes into death and death into life.

There is a Russian-Rusinian Christmas custom still in use which preserves the death-mask in an early form. From ancient times the winter solstice was the occasion for memorials of the dead, and the custom was for men dressed in wolf-masks and wolf-skins to run through the streets teasing and tormenting anyone they could catch. Wolf-masks were also used in South Germany in the medieval Schembartlaufen, and the "Schembart books" have illustrations of figures dressed in wolf-skins and carrying dolls—excellent images of the original conception of death as the one who steals and devours.[1] Similarly, in Greece the faces of the Gorgon and of Hecate are often represented as masks, and Dionysos (who is closely connected with death and partly identified with Hades, king of the dead) was worshipped in the cult under the image of the mask.

The idea of a mask combined with the corpse-like character of the Death-Demon gives rise to another image common in Teutonic lands —the image of one whose back is wholly different from his appearance in front. The Nordic *Huldren* are said to be hollow at the back like a kneading trough, and in Styrian and Carinthian legend the Devil, the Lord of Hell, appears as a captivating lover and is only recognized by his hollowed-out back. Frau Holle and the "Women of the Woods" are described in a similar way—they are beautiful and enchanting in front, but are hollow behind like a trough or rotten tree-trunk. The Luiseño Indians say that Wahawut who killed the primal father Ouiot "was at that time a pretty woman with long hair—but no flesh on her back".[2]

Female demons with beautiful, seductive faces and horrible backs can be compared and contrasted with the Sirens and Harpies of Greek

[1] Cf. the Masks of Percht below—pp. 120–1.   [2] See p. 29 above.

myth. The horrible aspect of the Harpies is expressed directly by fearsome animal appearance, that of the seductive demons by their corpselike backs. The corpse-like back masked by the lovely, young face is a specific characteristic of death-demons, and it serves to remind a man of his personal destiny, arousing anxiety as he contemplates his own, inevitable future. Medieval Christian ideology seized on this idea, and combined moral motifs with it. Frou Werlte[1] (Lady World) was presented as a beautiful woman with a seductive figure when seen from the front, but with a hollow back eaten by adders, toads and snakes—there are representations of her on the gate of Basle Minster, and she is described in the poems of Walter von der Vogelweide.

According to the view of medieval Christianity death is not an essential aspect of life and an ineluctable destiny, but an unfortunate and accidental incident. *Perfect Man* would not die, and we die only because of the fall—"the wages of sin is death". The result is that Frou Werlte is not explicitly a Death-Demon, and her conception is confined by the moral allegory; nevertheless one can feel the hidden meaning which comes from the fact that she is a successor to the old corpse-demon, Hel.

Hel prepared the throne for Baldur and the dead heroes, and welcomed them with a draught from her goblet: in Walter's poem "The Barmaid" (of the Tavern of Helle) Frou Werlte seduces the frivolous man to evil, and presents him with the terrible account at the end. A later poem, by *"Der Guotaere"*, in which Frou Werlte can be seen through all the moral disguise as kin to the horrible snake-like Hel, may come even closer to popular feeling; selections from it will show what is meant:

> "*Once there lay a lusty knight,*
> *Mortal sick upon his bed.*
> *A fair lady came to him . . .*
> *. . . fair as he had ever seen.*
> *She stood before him there and said,*
> '*Tell me, good Knight, if I do please thee now?*
> *Full well thou has served me all thy days,*
> *Now am I come to thee, and after thou art dead*
> *I will reward thee . . .*'

[1] In M.H.G. Frou is a higher title than Frau, corresponding to Latin Domina (*Trans.*).

"Then spake the Knight and answered,
'Lady who art thou?'
She said, 'I am the World! Look now
upon my back, and see the wage I bring.'
He looked and saw her back, hollow it was sans flesh,
all full of toads, crawling with worms and stinking
like a putrifying dog. He wept and said,
'Alas, that thou didst ever know my service!'

. . .

"Werlt takes from him wife and children,
his friends, and all that he did once possess.
She sends him naked, save for one thin cloth,
unto his grave: Then to the buried Knight doth come
to give the wages he had glimpsed on earth—
the toads and worms in very truth
devour him, bones and skin and flesh.
Attend the word! Go to the graveyard now
and know who 'tis you call your friend and kin:
where now are wealth and beauty?
Werlt laid the poor wight's bones before the rich man's teeth."

The last line has a hint of the idea that the dead themselves become *waelceasig*, that is, corpse-eating demons.

Like Frou Werlte the Sirens of Romanesque church sculpture hint that the old Death-Demon (or rather the feelings associated with it) was a felt presence when they were created. Honorius Augustodunensis, who died about AD 1150, said of them, "*Corda hominum ad vitia molliunt et in somnium mortis ducunt*"—"They soften men's hearts to vice, and lead them to the sleep (dream, deception) of death".[1] No doubt this is intended as a metaphor, but the choice of metaphor points to the close association of the Sirens with ancient demons of death.

The legend of Tannhäuser appeared in the fourteenth century, and

[1] According to the plausible argument of Richard Wirbel, the Siren to the right of the carving on the ancient "Schottentor" at Regensburg is the direct representation of the *lacus*, the pit of death, the subterranean Hel (Hell). Like the poem of Guotaere this helps to show that the old deep image of the Death-Demon lay at that time just below the surface of the more abstract Christian way of thinking—and it may still lie today in the unconscious of modern men and women.

it can be regarded both as a continuation of the idea of Frou Werlte, and also as a Christian re-shaping of an old story of the elves. The legend is about a lady and her maidens living in a mountain who captivate heroes with their beauty, and welcome them with a love potion: the oldest version (1391) is Italian and the lady is the Sibyl; in the Swiss version she is Frau Vrene, in the High German, Frau Venusinne. In both the Italian and Swiss versions the association with the mythological figure of the Death-Demon is clear in that on a certain day of each week the lady and her maidens secretly change into otters and snakes.

We have seen that there is a sense in which the ancient, demonic and monstrous *Kolio—the gaping jaws of Hel, the earth and the grave— lie hidden behind the Christian figures of "the World", Venus and the Sirens. The "moral", Christian idea is that the worm of death is concealed behind the seductive attractions of Frou Werlte and Frau Venus, but the same images also point to the opposite, compensating idea that Venus is the other side of death.[1] Thus these images show a deep and hidden knowledge of the polarity of death and life—of the fact that death is not only darkness, decline and ending but also light, ascent, fulfilment and blessing of life.

There are traces of the awareness of this polarity from earliest times —in the classical figures of the Sirens, in the original connection between Aphrodite and Persephone and in dark myths of Hel or Freya receiving dead heroes as lovers. Again and again the polarity seems to be on the point of being made clear in the mythological images of death, but in the end it would seem to be one of those secrets of which man can only become aware for brief moments—and that when he does the revelation is so deeply disturbing that it cannot be grasped and permanently held.

[1] Cf. pp. 6, 29, 70, above—*et al.*

8. The Food of the Shades and Communion with the Ancestors

As it expresses itself in mythology human fantasy has continually been preoccupied with the question of what food is eaten by the Shades or the dwellers in "the Beyond". The idea of such food is a symbol which brings into conscious awareness the mystery of the relationship of the living to the world of the Shades.

The Wild Huntsman of German legend was said to throw pieces of meat to passers-by (particularly the impertinent and inquisitive) and to invite them to eat: a horn-call sounded and the cry went up, "You have helped to hunt it—help to eat it!" If any ate, then the next time the Wild Hunt came by he was torn to pieces, and a woman who ate meat thrown in through her window became the wife of the Wild Huntsman. In other words, those who ate food offered by the Demon of Death became his victims; this idea is widespread, with many remarkable variations.

We have already mentioned that Hel prepares a feast for her guests and welcomes them with a horn of mead ("Balders Traum", 7). There is a late Danish legend of a knight who rested on the hill of the elves. An elf woman appeared and offered him a delicious drink in a silver tankard, but the knight's sister (who had already been trapped by the elves) cried out, "Pour the drink into your bosom! It is evil to dwell in the deep mountain with the women of the elves!" In the Middle Irish legend of Condla a fairy threw Condla an apple to lure him into the "Lands of the Living", where there is "neither Death nor Sin": "We feast all the time," she says, "without having to prepare food; there is good company, and no strife." Condla ate the perilous apple and he forgot all human nourishment and burned with longing so that when the fairy came back a month later he sailed with her in her glass ship to the Isle of the Blessed *in the West*—and was never heard of again. We notice that in this legend the food of death gives *Eternal Life* as well.

84

We find the same polarity in the food which Calypso offered to Odysseus: she offered him nectar and ambrosia to make him immortal *and* to bind him on her hidden island for ever. This double meaning is most often associated with an apple.[1] Hel's apples are referred to in the Icelandic sagas and according to Lüneburg legend there is an apple tree at the entrance to the Underworld. Nehalennia, the Roman-Batavian goddess who "hides the dead", was flanked by a dog on one side and a basket of apples on the other. Apples occur in German mythology in connection with Freyr, Idun and Freya as a source of eternal youth and of posterity. The fruit[2] in the Old Testament account of the Garden of Eden, which is offered by the snake-shaped Demon of Death, is also ambiguous and stands in a deeper and more mysterious relation to Life and Death than appears at first sight. On the one hand, "In the day that thou eatest of the fruit . . . thou shalt surely die," but on the other hand it is only from that time that children are conceived or that man "recognizes" himself, his wife and his existence in the world. In Greek mythology the apples of the Hesperides in the West are apples of the Land of Death, and there is the Apple of Eris which lets loose disaster. In the "Rape of Persephone" the "apple" or pomegranate plays an important and symbolic part because the Kore (Persephone) is irrevocably bound to the world of Hades by eating it and at the same time is changed from "Maiden" first to δέσποινα, Mistress and Queen, and finally to the Mother. In the fairy-story of Snow White the apple plays a very similar role. The unexpected relationship between the Demon of Death to the most ecstatic moments of life is also illuminated by the fact that the apple and the quince were particularly holy to Aphrodite—the apple appears as a symbol embodying both death and renewal.[3]

[1] The idea is certainly very old. Reinhardt says that the apple tree is the oldest fruit tree found all over Europe: "Central Europeans of the late Stone Age," he writes, "already cultivated at least one species of fruit tree. This was the apple tree, and fossils of its small fruits, almost all core with little . . . flesh, are found in the remains of pile villages on the banks of the Swiss lakes . . . The apple is the only fruit whose name is handed down from the indigenous tribes, and not borrowed from Latin. In O.H.G. it is *apful*; Nord. *appel*; O.Celt. *aball*; O.Slav. *jabluko*."

[2] The common assumption that the fruit was an apple is an indication of the numinous associations to the apple (*Trans.*).

[3] In Classical times Greek women carried a quince dedicated to Aphrodite

85

Before we discuss these relationships further we should notice another side to the idea of death which cropped up in the legend of Condla. The elf woman lures the knight into lands where he joins "gay company, feasting all the time without having to prepare food". The idea is that there is a *Land of Souls* which is like the world of men, and this idea is very widespread—often enough the world of the dead is imagined as more delectable than this present life. The account which Tesmann gives of the Baja of the Middle Sudan provides an example. Tesmann tells us that when a sick man had a vivid dream of the dead they say, "His bodily soul has gone into the Land of Souls." The dead place food before the man's bodily soul, and if he refuses to take any of it he will get well: if he eats, he will die. When a person is severely ill they frequently say that his bodily soul has been forcibly abducted by the souls of the dead, who say to it, "You are so withered up that you cannot remain in the body! Come with us, and we will give you proper food to feed you up! *It's simply marvellous among the souls!*" If the bodily soul goes with them it comes to a place where it meets the souls of its parents: the souls of the parents (particularly that of the mother) often send it back again, saying: "Who called you, then? We don't want you here; you should be looking after things in the village (i.e. seeing to the bringing up of children). Go back at once; what do you want here?" Then the bodily soul flies back and the man who seemed to be dead comes alive again.

The ideas of the Baja include both sides. Like the legend of the Danish knight and his sister they bring out the dangerous character of the Food of the Dead, and include a warning about it; at the same time the hospitable character of the world of the ancestors is brought out even more clearly than in the legend of Condla. A classic expression of this idea is found in India: according to the Vedas Yama was the first man to die, and he became the God of the Dead ruling over the "World of the Fathers" which was originally under the earth, but was later transplanted to the divine realm where Yama "revels with the gods beneath a luxuriant and beautiful tree", and where "the Blessed

at their wedding as a pledge of a happy marriage. The woman brought the quince indoors to her husband as a sign that she was now devoted to the service of Aphrodite. This was part of the official marriage rite from the time of Solon, and is believed to have survived to the present time.

(the Dead) live in bliss."[1] Hades, the dark God of the Kingdom of the Dead among the Greeks, is called πολύξενος, "the hospitable one", so that he and his realm are brought into some kind of relationship with Elysium and the distant "Isles of the Blessed". Hel is also "hospitable", but the most impressive image of the "Land of the Fathers" is Valhalla: there the dead warriors live a life of supreme happiness in the Hall of Odin—eating, drinking and fighting. At the same time the life of the dead Norseman was thought to be concerned with the preservation of the world.

Similar ideas can be found among other peoples, and some late formulations from German lands are particularly interesting. These concern the earthly, underground *Nobiskrug* (L.G. *Naberskrōch*) on the one hand, and the spiritual-celestial "heavenly Tavern" on the other. The *Nobis Host* of the Nobiskrug is really the "Host of Helle".[2] In the Inn before the Gates of Hell the dead dice and play at cards. There is a popular Bavarian belief which is much the same: there is a pitch-black bar lit by lights of wood shavings where the dead "drink beer and schnapps, take snuff, smoke Dreikönig tobacco, play cards and dice; they cheat, scuffle and brawl; they make friends again, wrestle, chaff one another and sing extempore songs . . .", the rolling of skittle balls is heard, and the fall of all nine together. If one imagines that this Inn of the Dead is above the heavens and that the weather god lives there and sends forth his thunderstorms, then one sees that this image is nothing else than a peasant's Valhalla. We also find the same ideas echoed in spiritual folk songs, for example:

> "*In heavenly realms they pour the Cyprus wine*
> *And noble souls are drunk with love.*
> *The virgins sit at table, the angels sing so fair,*
> *The Holy Ghost is butler and Mary waitress there . . .*"[3]

---

[1] *Rigveda*, X, 135; IX, 113, 11.

[2] Cf. The poem "Frou Werlte" of Walther von der Vogelweide.

[3] *Volkslieder*, L. Uhland, 881. In *The Nuns' Drinking Song* we find that same idea that the mystical union with the Divine is alike here and after death—

> "*Let us sing and be merry*
> *among the roses.*
> *Let us joy with Jesus and those we love,*
> *For we do not know how long we shall be here*

This song represents a further development of the ideas associated with the food and drink of the elves. In the legends of the elves the enticement and the horror are brought together in such a way that further meanings are hinted, and at first sight it might be thought that the images (ranging from the idea of Elysium to that of the Nobiskrug) of life in the realm of the gods which we have just considered were nothing more than an imaginative fulfilment of earthly wishes, either crudely material or more spiritual: that is, it might seem that the only purpose of the images was to take the horror out of death by offering rather cheap consolation in a better world beyond it. Such an interpretation would not really do justice to the images—it is too glib. More careful consideration of the mythological accounts brings to light a more serious motif, which is also suggested by some of the dreams which will be described below. As well as the hope of consolation, these images express a "first *affirmation* of death", and the nature of this affirmation is suggested by the description of the realm of Yama as "the World of the Fathers"—whether it is imagined to be under the earth or in the divine realm. The essential feature of all the images is the *Community* of the Dead,[1] and we have seen that this idea is already implicit in the archaic and animistic images of the Baja and Nsei. It would seem that according to the Nsei the ancestors fetched the souls of the dead in order to receive them into their community, and it would appear that from death to the time of the second funeral celebration the soul of the dead man hovers near the place in which he lived

> among the roses.
> The wine of Jesus is already poured
> among the roses:
> We must go there one and all,
> That we may know full joy of heart
> among the roses:
> He will pour us Cyprus wine
> among the roses
> We must all be drunken then,
> Drunken of His own sweet love
> among the roses."

[1] There is a well-known story that a Frisian chief was about to receive Christian baptism when he said to the missionary, "Shall I find my Fathers in the Christian beyond?" The missionary said, "No", and the chief strode away saying, "I would rather go where my Fathers are!"

until, after some kind of development and maturation has taken place, he is ready to enter the land and community of his ancestors. It is likely enough that there were similar ideas among the people of the oldest Aegean culture since finds in graves suggest that their grave chambers represented an assembly of ancestors, and it may well be that the "bone-chambers" in many Bavarian village cemeteries did the same. Nor is the idea that the spirits of the ancestors are concerned to influence the world of the living found only among the Baja and Nsei: it is an idea common to many primitive peoples, and it should be noticed that it is the ancestors as a community rather than as individuals who are thought to watch over and guide the living.[1]

That the dead ancestors form a community and that this community is active in the realm of the living are crystallizations of ideas which were probably implicit in the numinous horror of death as it was felt in earlier times. They are developments of the idea that it is through awareness of death that man comes to feel that he transcends the limits of his earthly existence. Among the Baja and Nsei this idea of transcendence is given form in the belief that the Community of the Dead has some kind of joint responsibility with the Community of the Living,[2] and this gives rise to an incipient feeling for "history": the individual dies but the race or tribe lives on, and the departed enter into its life through the activity of the Community of the Dead.[3]

The idea of Valhalla and that contained in the folk-song given above represent a further development of the same theme, because they imply that death brings the individual into union with the divine meaning of the world. The warriors in Odin's hall prepare themselves for the battle of the last days against the powers that will destroy the world and the gods, and the revellers of the folk-song do not only live in heaven but have an emotional awareness of their union with

[1] See pp. 86 f. above.

[2] It may be that the responsibility for everything which is done by the tribe, or which happens to it, is projected on the ancestors.

[3] According to the accounts of Tesmann the "feeling for existence" among the Baja only goes one generation back: according to Schmidt the Nsei remember several generations and include them in their cult ceremonies. This can be understood in accordance with what we have said.

the Divine—they are drunk "from love", that is, in unity of meaning.

What is probably the most fruitful way of describing the psychic core of "images of Elysium" is to say that they point to death as a gateway into unity, either with those already dead, or with higher, divine beings. Although the *Nobiskrug* and the Bavarian "Inn of Hell" stress the uncanniness of death more than any other aspect, they also hint at the idea of a great community in the world beyond death. The community to which these images point has positive qualities—when one rests and feeds in the Inn one is not enticed into an alien world, and there is nothing of the horror which is connected with the "Food of the Elves". The Inn is a place which the dead man accepts and within which he fashions his life to the best of his ability, just as one may accept life in the world of the living.

The idea of the Community of the Dead is clearly expressed in the *Feasts of the Dead* and *Feasts of All Souls* which take places in one form or another in all parts of the world, and which usually feature a meal shared with the departed. The customs which are associated with these feasts bring out further aspects of the symbolic significance of the Food of the Dead.

"The Anthisteria" was celebrated in Attica during the spring, and on the third day[1] of the feast seeds were cooked and set in earthern pots for Hermes. Hermes was the Psychopomp who led away the souls of the dead, but the original intention was to provide for the souls themselves, as can be seen from many pointers. The day on which this was done was called "the Day of the Chytroi", that is, the Day of the Earthern Pots, and at the end of the feast a cry went up, "θύραξε κῆρες, οὐκέτι, 'Ανθιστήρια"—"Go forth, Keres (i.e. Spirits of the Dead)! The Anthisteria are done!" The Persians celebrated a similar feast called the Feast of the Fravashis (the good ancestral spirits) in March. Many ancient customs have survived in Russia into modern times, and Feasts of Souls are very important both on days of special significance to the family, and also on days generally kept as memorials to the dead which usually occur in the spring. At these feasts the meal consists mainly of seeds, and at the end the host or hostess sends away the souls with a formal farewell, for example:

[1] According to Sam Wide and Martin Nilsson all three days were originally solely concerned with the dead.

> *"Holy Fathers who have flown to us,*
> *Ye have eaten and drunk.*
> *Now fly hence again.*
> *Say if you have further need,*
> *But better you fly to Heaven—*
> *Hush! Hush!"*

In Germanic lands Feasts of the Dead were usually kept during the twelve days after Christmas, and usually the meals for the departed souls consisted of seeds. At Thuringia in Orlagau, and in Vogtland they prepare a meal of *Polse* (a mush of meal and water) or *Zemmede* for Frau Holle or Frau Percht: at Zips they ate poppy-seed cake "with Frau Holda" on Christmas Eve: in Bavaria and many other places the feasts are celebrated on All Souls Day at the beginning of November, and even today the *Seelenspitz* (a small pointed loaf of rye and caraway seeds), or "All Souls Bread" (of buckwheat flour) or *Hallerknäckerl* are baked "for the poor souls". In the Upper Palatine pieces of bread in consecrated water or milk are put out for the souls, and in Southern Bavaria they use a "souls basin" in which they put "souls flour". The old belief is that those who give the food must not eat it nor distribute it to the living poor until the "poor souls" have taken their part, and it is thought that anyone who breaks the embargo will die during the year. This echoes and recalls the earlier horror of the food of the Shades or the Elves which also brings death, but there is this difference that this food is only lethal to those who through carelessness or greed transgress the holy laws which bind the world of the living to the world of the dead. There can be no doubt that the custom of providing food for the dead is a last, lingering relic of an older sacred meal through which the living proclaimed and confirmed their fellowship with the dead. Through such a meal the living entered into the *holy fellowship* of the feast which unites the dead in Elysium, Valhalla, beneath Yama's tree—or even in the Nobiskrug.

It is to be noted that seeds or a mush of flour and milk are regular features of these meals, and this should be linked with the fact that the apple (or pomegranate), which is the food of the Elves, is marked by its large number of pips—especially in its precultivated form. The seeds are the living symbol. It is not only the actual partaking of the meal which has symbolic meaning; the food eaten is also significant.

The partaking of the meal gives shape to the imaged idea of the communion of the dead with each other and of the living with the dead, and this is an affirmation of death, an acceptance of the fact that human existence extends beyond itself. This is already felt, in germ, as a duty. The food, whether apples or seeds, takes the affirmation further, for in the symbol of the *seed* is contained the first spark of a new light, a sense that out of the mystery of death there will unfold, like the unfolding of a bud, the *mystery of transformation*—a continual, recurrent process which is the essence of life. The grain must die that it may be transformed into new life. Among the Australian aborigines and other primitive people it is thought that in certain circumstances the souls of the ancestors come back as children of the tribe and it is this idea, modified and tremendously compressed, which is contained in the symbol of apple or seed. This symbol expresses the idea that death is return, and yet not return and nothing more: it is rather a continuous transformation occurring within life. It is not just *re*-birth, but the birth of that which is new and yet the same, which has passed through decay and destruction that it may enter into life renewed.

9. The Death-Demon as Fate

DEPTH psychology owes much to Kerényi for his elucidation and interpretation of the psychic symbols found in myths, and he has shown that the ancient spirals and mazes which are found all over the world are early attempts to give form to the idea of the underworld. The spiral is both a dynamic-topographical map of the underworld, and also a symbol of the meaning of the underworld—that is, the fact of Death itself. The symbolism of the spiral is closely connected with that of the seeds as the food of the Elves and of the dead, because it represents an unending circular movement. The circular movement of the spiral leads into the centre (which is also down into the depths) but at the centre the movement is "transformed" so that it returns to the periphery that it may return once more to the centre. The double spiral and the continuous meander-band give an even stronger sense of a continuing and unending process, and this process can be applied both to the life of humanity as a whole and also to that of the individual. It might be said that symbols of this kind express "death-and-becoming".

The double significance of death is implicit in a prehistoric statue found in Thrace. This statue is presumably that of a mother-goddess, she is presented as heavy, massive and naked, and a distinguishing mark is a double spiral cut upon her lap. Thus we could argue that this goddess does not express only birth and reproduction, but also the counter-pole which is related to it, the withering of life and the passage to the underworld. The spirals scratched on the so-called "soul stones" and rattles (Churingas) of Australian aboriginal tribes clearly have this meaning, because the stones are thought to enclose the souls of the dead ancestors, and a woman who touches one receives the germ of a child from the ancestor who dwells in it, and becomes pregnant. Contact with the realm of the dead makes new life possible and the new life

93

takes shape by a reversal, as it were, of the movement of the spiral. It will be remembered that this was the meaning of the Maro-Dance on the island of Ceram, which involved a ninefold spiral. As we saw, this was explicitly associated with the first death, and it was from the limbs of the murdered Hainuwele that the life-giving food plants were thought to have grown. After the first death all men had to tread the ninefold spiral path which was the Gate of Death,[1]

Ancient stones set in spirals are found all over Northern Europe and probably have a similar meaning. Swedish peasants in Finland called them *Jungfrudans* and the custom was for young men to run through them to a girl sitting at the centre—but according to another custom it was a stone coffer grave which was set at the mid-point. In England old mazes are found cut in turf, and similar customs are associated with them; moreover, they are usually near old burial grounds. Kerényi argues that the Geranos (Crane) dance on Delos, danced in memory of the young men and girls whom Theseus rescued from the Labyrinth on Crete, also took the form of a spiral, leading by a labyrinthine path to the centre, the underground world of the dead, and then reversing and winding out again by a counter-movement. If he is correct the dance repeated the theme of the myth of Ceram—that birth and pro-creation did not occur until death had appeared in the world. Mention has already been made of the rope binding the Geranos dancers together.[2] Kerényi refers to similar dances in ancient Etruria, modern Italy, Corfu, Greyerz (Western Switzerland) and Schwäbisch-Hall. The Munich Schäffler Dances which are still performed at carnival time every seventh year involve a clearly marked spiral, and they reveal the symbolic relation between the spiral and death because, although they are certainly older, the popular tradition is that they were first danced in historical times to mark deliverance from a great plague which had brought death to the city. In these dances the dancers are linked together by hoops to form an endless chain. The Sword Dance of Traunstein in Upper Bavaria follows a similar pattern, and it is also connected with killing, death and new life. It is still danced on the second day after Easter and is associated with horse-riding in honour of St George who, as we know, slew the dragon and rescued the maiden from death. It is also likely that the horse-riding was originally

[1] See above, p. 15.   [2] See p. 77.

part of an horse-sacrifice for it ends with a circuit[1] of a hill chapel and the dedication of the horses.[2]

These customs express the idea which is symbolized by the much older image of the spiral. The centre of the spiral is the ultimate point of the descent into death and, at the same time, the point at which new life is born: new life begins with the reversal of the movement of the spiral and the return from the depths of death. This is exactly the same idea as that contained in the image of apple or seeds as the food linking the living with the dead, since it is only when it is destroyed in the maw of earth that the seed can "unfold" and develop its power to build new life. At the same time the spiral gives form and precision to the idea, and the movement carried by its line conveys a sense of compulsion; the movement inward to the centre and outward to the circumference expresses a sense of inescapable destiny and an unending alternation of Death and Life.

Because of the sense of destiny associated with the rhythm of death and life it is not surprising that the Death-Demon has been associated with the divinities or demons of fate from very early times. Hesiod includes Death among the Children of Night: he calls it Moros, and according to early Greek etymologies *Moros* is cognate with *Moirai*.[3] Among the Teutons Skuld, which means "that which destiny decrees", is the name both of one of the Norns (the Fates) and of a Valkyrie, a Chooser of the Dead. Through this connection of death with destiny the Demon of Death which ravages and abducts is seen to be a being which acts according to the ultimate laws of the world, and this means that when man kills or dies he can recognize that he too is subject to these laws. We must take it that once the connection was made man "knew" it at some level of his psyche, and was able and prepared to accept and experience in life what was

[1] At one time it was three times round.

[2] In some places in Bavaria the ride passed through the church and the horses were dedicated inside.

[3] *Theogony*, 211 ff. The passage is rich in association and part may be quoted: "Night gave birth to Fate, the horrible dark end. She bore Death (Moros), Sleep and the Tribe of Dreams . . . She bore also the Hesperides who guard the sweet apples on fruitful trees beyond the ocean. Moreover she formed the Moirai and the Keres, the Avengers, and the three who fix the weal and woe of every man at birth—Clotho, Lachesis and Atropos. She bore Nemesis as well to the affliction of mortal men . . ."

implicit in the formal, linguistic association. In the Teutonic (and especially the German) realm one can see how the connection between Death and Fate has survived in popular belief or how, when they have been separated, there is a tendency to link them together again.

Frau Holle or *Percht*[1] are still familiar figures today, and they embody the Fate or Norn aspect of Death. The two figures are the same, but the name Percht is more usual in Upper Germany while Frau Holle is more common in Central and Northern Germany. Percht comes from O.H.G. *pergan*, "to hide", Holle is cognate with Holda and Hulda (cf. Nor. *hulda*, Wood Elf, M.Ice. *hulð* and *hulda*) from O.H.G. *holdo* which medieval glosses usually translated as "genius", i.e. "spirit-creature". Holdo is most closely connected with the names of "The Shrouder" which we have already come across—I.G. *kolio*, Teut. *halja*, O.Ice. *hel* and with the West Germanic *Nehalennia* and *Huldana*. Percht and Frau Holle both designate the Shrouder, the Demon of Death, and in these figures there is an echo of the very old belief in the god of the dead and a ghostly train—often called the Hollen or Hollichen.[2]

A widespread custom in Austria shows clearly that Percht has the character of Fate. On "Percht's Night" all those who have eaten together put their spoons into the milk and in the morning they look to see how much cream has set on the spoon: the amount of good luck which each one will have during the following year will be shown by the amount of cream on his spoon. If the spoon of anyone is turned over he will die during the year. Frau Holle leads the Wild Host and according to a common belief this declares Fate for the coming year. Frau Holle knows, spins and foretells Fate, and we should probably think of her as one of the "wise women" of popular belief. The names which have been handed down in Bavaria are "Frau Held" and "Rachel" and Güntert says, "And who can doubt that we have here an echo of our Death-Demon Halja?" Moreover, Frau Holle or Percht is often called "the Spinning Woman" or just "the Spinner". In the Harz district it is said that Frau Holle weaves a net during the twelve nights of Christmas in which those who die during the following year are caught, and in this she is almost identical with Hel,

[1] These are discussed in greater length in Chapter 11.

[2] Both these are plural German forms (*Trans.*).

although, at the same time, there is an echo of the grand but sombre tradition of the Norns.

In Nordic myth the Norns spin Fate. They spin, knot and weave the threads and from this comes their early name, *Urd* (A.S. *wyrd*, O.H.G. *wurd*) which is associated with the German *werden* which originally meant "turn".[1] In the Song of Helgi, the Slayer of Hunding from the *Edda*, it says of the Norns:

> *"Each night they bound the threads of Fate . . .*
> *They spun the golden yarn,*
> *They made it fast in the Hall of the Moon.*
> *At East and West they hid the ends . . .*
> *Northward Neri's daughter cast*
> *One band, unbreakable"*[2]

Like the Greek Moirai the Teutonic Norns are closely connected with the Demon of Death, and at bottom they are identical with it. Like the Valkyries they are represented dressed in feathers as swans swimming on the Well of Urd, and we have already pointed out that one of the Valkyries was named Skuld: it is also said that the Norns rise out of the ground with the spring of living water, knowing both Life and Death.

The Norns are closely associated with Death, but they express a special aspect of the experience of Death. Like Nari's sister, Hel, they descend to the hidden depths at the roots of the World Tree where they learn the Fate of Men. Life rises anew out of Death, and the nets of the Norns weave the Life and Death of man into the fabric of the world. In the labyrinth, the double-spiral, the meander and particularly in the Moirai and the Norns the development of the images associated with Death reaches an extreme point. All these symbolize both the *transcendental distance* of the Killer and the Kingdom of Death from the world of the Living, and also establish it within the rule of world-law—

[1] The original meaning occurs in the word "Spinn*wirtel*"—spinning whorl.
[2] Hel was mentioned as being Nari's *sister* in Chapter 2. Ninck says that Nari is also thought of as Loki's son. Güntert understands "Nari" to mean, "the Fastener"—i.e. in the bands of Death. Other parts of the "Song of Helgi" recall the wolf-form of the Death-Demon, for in preparation for a great battle the wolves ("Odin's Pack") get ready for the prey, and the battle is fought in the "Forest of the Wolves".

for the Fates are the active executives of the over-riding laws which govern all things. Man does not easily become aware of this for it is an idea which lies on the borders of human knowledge, and this fact finds expression in an aspect of the labyrinth which we have not yet mentioned. We have seen that the labyrinth gives expression to the idea of the inevitability of movement inwards and outwards, but it can also have the character of a maze, that is, it can express the danger that one may get lost. This is a well-marked feature of the Cretan legend of the Labyrinth, and also of the remarkable double-spiral of stone on the island of Wier in the Baltic. Here two paths face one on entering: one leads by wider circuits to a blind alley near the entrance, the other narrows until it reaches the centre, where it turns upon itself and leads back in "growing" circles to the place of exit. For the same reason that the labyrinth conceals as well as guides, the Moirai and the Norns are hidden in deep and fearful darkness, they are a hallowed mystery.

Though the Fates are hidden in mystery their power is at work in the lives of all men, so that they are also present at every moment. Although the web of their weaving is hidden from human sight, when their plans ripen their power is felt. Man can only stand in awe before the godhead which is wholly other than himself and yet encompasses all things.

10. The Death-Mother, Marriage with Death and Paternal Aspects

ONCE man had imaged death as an uncanny encounter with an anthropomorphic demon the new aspects of death could become conscious. Certain modes of experiencing death already implicit (but not yet open to consciousness) in the early animal and mixed images of the Death-Demon could crystallize out as actual possibilities when the demon was represented in human form. Three possible modes can be distinguished, each of which is associated with a specific image:

(*a*) Death can be experienced as an encounter with the Death-Mother.
(*b*) Death can be experienced under the image of marriage, as an encounter with an abducting bridegroom or seducing bride.
(*c*) Death can be experienced as an encounter with the Father, although this encounter is not usually direct, more often taking the form of receiving a message from the paternal being.

These three possibilities are all contained in the horrible secret expressed by the devouring jaws of the beast of prey or the gigantic earth, and the first of them to take distinct form and to find expression in terms of a personal encounter would seem to be the idea expressed in the image of a Death-Mother.

Consider the meaning behind the image of Death as the Devouring Earth! The first thing that it brings home to man is the terrifying insecurity of the basis of his life—the ground on which he treads. The firm earth on which all animals move was originally taken for granted and accepted as the pre-existent and enduring background of life, but the awareness of death calls these assumptions into question. The image of the gaping jaws opening in the earth itself gives form to the sense of insecurity which arises when a man realizes that all life stands poised on the brink of death, and at the same time this image makes man consciously aware of the earth for the first time. Man becomes aware of the earth in a way that shatters the blind, unthinking security in which he lived before, and the contrast extends the threat to monstrous size: the ground shakes beneath man's feet, and the "jaws of hell" open on every side: man feels himself to be surrounded by Death, by the Devouring Earth in all places where he had "previously" imagined himself to be secure. Yet when the first paralysing horror has been overcome a new development takes place; turning from the present fear of the engulfing earth man "looks back" and becomes aware of what the earth had meant to him when he was still unconscious of it. As a result of the formation of the image of the earth as a terror man is able to see it as it was before the image took shape—as the firm, secure ground on which he stood. So man becomes conscious, for the first time, of the earth as that which gives life, the provider of fruit and vegetables for men, of grass and leaves for animals.

This picture of a process extending over unimaginably long ages by which man's consciousness of the earth developed is not mere speculation. There are a large number of early traces of images of the Death-Demon which suggest it, and which show that the first terror of death marks the first recognition of the reality of life. When man reflects upon what (for him) the earth was "once upon a time" this is no mere regression to an earlier, unconscious state: in the unconscious state the loveliness and "kindness" of the earth was simply taken for granted, but when they are noticed in contrast to the devouring, dangerous aspect of the earth man becomes aware of them in a new (and relatively conscious) way. The tension between the two aspects of the earth contains the germ of advance to a new synthesis. The dangerous aspect is not forgotten, but the kindly, providing, embracing aspect stands over against it, having equal claim to validity, and just because it must balance the other more sombre picture it must be grasped and realized the more intensely in its concrete reality. The earth stands revealed not only as ground, but also as nourisher of man's being: as she who brings young plants to birth from her body in the spring, and "gives suck" to plants, animals and men from her swelling streams. In a word, the earth is seen as a mother.

The image of Earth as a Maternal Being does not cancel out the other, fearsome aspects, and the Mother Earth that bears and nourishes is the same as that which gapes open with threat of death: the Earth is a Mother with the gaping jaws of the wolf. Earth becomes a symbol of the Maternal, and the Mother becomes a symbol of death, for the ambiguity of the Earth is shared by the Mother. In earliest childhood each individual has to suffer the experience of finding that his own mother, that which he has regarded as the most secure, supporting and embracing foundation of his life, could be unexpectedly and incomprehensively transformed from the closest to the most alien, from the most secure to the most dangerous object angrily threatening death and destruction—while remaining always the mother whose womb offers hiding and refuge, and the highest bliss of rebirth into light. When the image of the Mother is struck by the dark rays emanating from the experience of death, or the image of death is touched by the glow of the maternal, then that which is nearest and that which is most alien, nourishing life and devouring death, are brought together in one image.

There is an ancient bronze sculpture of the Chang Dynasty in China —1400–1122 BC—which expresses these ideas in the most concise way imaginable. Before its wide open jaws a huge tiger holds a mannikin in its paws. Hentze claims that the tiger is a Demon of Darkness and an earth-divinity, and the foetal position of the mannikin shows that he is the son of the demon—that the demon gave him birth, allows him to turn to the light and will ultimately devour him. *Terra Consumptrix!* That this image is not the isolated expression of an aberrant idea and that the interpretation is not arbitrary is shown, for example, by the existence of a very much older stone sculpture of the pre-Hindu megalithic culture from Pageralam in Southern Sumatra. This primitive sculpture is of a pair of copulating tigers from which comes a human child; the female tiger holds the child protectingly between its paws—but for how long? Carl Hentze says that similar representations are also found from the ancient Peruvian culture of Chancai.[1] We have mentioned above the excellent representation of the Death-Mother in the form of the pregnant Toeris, the ancient

---

[1] These images bring vividly to mind the lions, lionesses and griffins holding human figures between their paws in front of their jaws found in Romanesque church sculpture—the Schottentor at Regensburg, the Collegiate Church at Laufen a.d. Salzach, the main gateway of the cathedral of San Rufino at Assisi, the cathedral gateway at Ferrara and elsewhere. Although these figures frequently give form to specifically Christian allegories it is highly probable that the old symbol of the Death-Mother played a part through the unconscious.

Egyptian Mother-Divinity, the "Great One" shaped like a hippopotamus, a crocodile and a lion, standing upright like a human being. We may also recall the statue of Demeter Erinys at Phigalia, which has a horse's head ringed with serpents, and which is shown to represent the Death-Mother by the epithet and the cult.[1]

As the mother robbed of her daughter who grieves over her loss and endures violent impregnation against her will Demeter gives expression to a further connection between death and maternity. The Death-Demon as the Earth-Mother itself suffers motherhood, and this is the working of Fate just as the Demon is the active instrument of Fate in dealing out death; moreover, the fate of maternity is like the fate of death in that both involve suffering, being "robbed and bereaved" and deadly pains. In so far as the Death-Mother herself endures a like fate to death the ancient idea that the Demon of Death is the corpse-like Mistress of the Kingdom of the Dead can be seen in a new light, and it is in this connection that we can understand why at the Athenian Thesmophoria live pigs were thrown into the underground Megaron as a sacrifice to Demeter. The pigs thrown to the snakes in the depths were themselves symbols of fertility and so representatives of the goddess, and after a time their decomposed limbs were mixed with the seed ready for the new sowing: thus in the rite the goddess is both the killer and the killed. The Death-Mother herself suffers the fate of death and becomes a corpse and in this way becomes the bestower of fertility.

It is reported that similar sacrifices of pigs were made in Polynesia. Pieces of the sacrifice were buried in different parts of the tribal territory to ensure fertility. In the myth of Ceram it is said that plants for food grew out of the buried limbs of Hainuwele after she had been slain by men. Surprisingly similar customs are found in German lands. At Salza and other places in the Meininger district and in Hesse special parts of the pig are mixed with the new crops on Shrove Tuesday, Ash Wednesday or February 22nd, and in the German and Slav customs of "driving out death" and (particularly) of killing and dismembering Frau Holle[2] there is a personification of the old Death-Mother who is sacrificed and dismembered to bring fertility. It is clear that when the image of the Death-Demon takes the form of the Death-Mother birth, the other pole of human life is brought into

[1] See Chapter 6, p. 70.   [2] Cf. Chapter 11.

conscious relationship with death. Birth and death are the *limits* of life, and man begins to see himself as one who comes out of the unknown and is finally lost in it again—and yet this frightening "unknown" is also felt to be the containing womb of the mother.

We cannot consider in exact detail the extent to which the protective aspect of the maternal is consciously acknowledged as a feature of the Death-Mother, but this aspect plays such an essential part in the idea of the maternal in general that it can hardly fail to be felt as an undertone, even in this context. One can see this, for example, in the myth of Ceram, which says that in the days of Hainuwele the (other) Death-Mother, Mulua Satene, reigned maternally over men, and that after the murder, although she decreed the fate of Death, she promised that those who accepted it (by passing through the Gate) would eventually be allowed to return home to her and to the security they had forfeited. In this myth the Death-Mother gives expression to an inexorable fate which is hostile to man, and at the same time offers maternal protection. It may be that in the image of the Death-Mother there lies the earliest (unconscious) trace of what we should call a living trust in the divine power.

In summary, we may say that when the Demon of Death takes the form of the Death-Mother it retains its frightening and numinous character, but that the *event of death* loses something of its terrible senselessness. Death remains superhuman, divine and incomprehensible, but it is invested with attributes which bring it near to man and prepare the way for a modicum of understanding and an inward affirmation.[1]

We have now to ask what aspects of the experience of death find expression in the idea of the Death-Bride. A Latvian lament gives a clue:

> "*In their great sorrow*
> *The brothers start to dance.*
> *They have married their little brother*
> *To the daughter of the* Earth Mother".

The implication is that the Death-Bride is a form of the Death-Mother,

[1] The figure of the Death-Mother is closely connected with what Jung calls the "Mother Archetype". Consideration of the Death-Mother illuminates both the transcendental significance of this archetype, and the actual experience of a human mother.

and it would seem to be the case that this figure developed out of that of the Death-Mother. Because the images of the Death-Bride and the Death-Mother are so closely associated the former brings out aspects of her uncanny and fascinating character, and so reveals the almost inextricable complexity of the motifs which centre on man's experience of death. This is well shown by the myth of Ishtar and Tammuz and the legends of Agdestis and Attis, Venus and Adonis and many others. When Attis, for example, is about to marry a young girl his wild mother, the huntress Agdestis, pursues him relentlessly,[1] until in despair he castrates himself and dying he flings the phallus at the feet of the Mother-Beloved (whose desire for him had brought him to his fate) crying, "For you, Agdestis." In this legend Agdestis shows the bestial and aggressive traits of the Death-Mother to the fullest extent, and at the same time she is the Death-Bride. One can see that it is as though man may not act out of his own individual being to create new life in the mistress of his choice, because the Great Mother of Death holds all the power of procreation and guards it jealously that nothing may escape her.[2]

The Babylonian Ishtar stands on the border between images of Death and images of the Death-Bride. By demonic arts she tries to entice Gilgamesh and to seduce him into marriage, and Gilgamesh rejects her, saying, "You have brought death to all whom you have lured in the net of your love!" and to this extent she is a Death-Bride. At the same time she who is the mistress of life, love and fertility is shown to be herself dead and a denizen of the Kingdom of the Dead (where her sister Ereshkigal rules) by the moving epic, *Ishtar's Journey to the Land without Return*. Even in her role of bride she can be seen to be the Mistress of Death as well, for when Gilgamesh rejects her she flies into a fury and threatens gods and men: "Alone I will break down the doors of the underworld! I will bring forth the dead that they may consume the living—the living will depart, and only the dead will remain." These are words of the Death-Mother who lets no man escape, as well as being words of an ensnaring seductress; Love and Death are equally the fate to which man must blindly submit.

[1] According to Jung the "anima" is initially contained in the mother archetype, and its development as an autonomous archetype often takes place only against the strongest resistance from "the Mother".
[2] Cf. Neumann: *Origins and History of Consciousness*.

In the Teutonic myths there are dark hints that Freya has a similar dual role, and it is explicitly said that Hel, Mistress of Death, is also a Death-Bride—at least to V.I.P.s. Saxo Grammaticus[1] reports Baldur's dream with a kind of severe objectivity: "In the night which followed Baldur saw Hel (Proserpina) standing by his couch, and she told him that she would enjoy his embrace the next day."[2] In the song of Gisli Sursson Hel invites the hero to ride with her on her grey steed and shows him the seat prepared for him in her house, and the bed made ready, saying, "Then, generous man, you will have authority over these riches, and over the woman (Hel) herself . . ." Plutarch says that in Attica the dead were called "Demetrioi", and this may point to similar, early ideas about Demeter. Again, when the Greeks said that the dead "climb on to the marriage bed (thalamos) of Persephone,"[3] the image of the Marriage of Death could hardly help being activated to some extent. In Euripides[4] the Keres are called "Brides of the Dead", and the Sirens, who are servants and messengers of Persephone, are clearly connected with the seductive aspect of the Death-Demon. In the figure of the nymph Calypso the bridal and seductive aspect of Death has developed to such an extent that its allure overweighs every other element, and there is little more than the association of the name with *kolįo and the parallels with Hel linking her to the Death-Demon.

Late medieval descendants of Hel, like the enticing Frou Werlte and Frau Vrene or Venus in the mountain of the Tannhäuser legend, have developed in a similar way to Calypso. Frau Vrene's maidens may well be derived from the maidens of Hel or from the Valkyries, the maidens of Odin and also brides of the dead, even though the enticing and seductive element is not so clear. In many more recent figures of legend like the Huldren, the Elves, the Nixies and a variety of enchanted maidens of moor or mountain belonging to the underworld, the seductive aspect is the most emphasized. The distinguishing mark of these figures is their beguiling, unearthly beauty by which they lure

[1] 124, 77.

[2] *Postera nocte eidem Proserpina per quietem astare adspecta, postridie se eius complexu usuram denunciat.*

[3] Similar archaic conceptions occur in an attenuated form in the late collection of dreams made by Artemidorus (AD. 135–200). For example, it is said that if a sick person dreams that he marries a god or goddess this points to his death.

[4] *Heracles*, 481.

men and arouse their love, but like Calypso and the fairy of the Condla legend they also offer magic, elfin food which brings forgetfulness of past life and binds the man to his seductress in a blissful existence in which there is no want and no growing old. Despite the magical allure of these figures it is possible for a *hero* to resist them as, for example, Odysseus broke from the thraldom of Calypso and Gilgamesh rejected Ishtar, and although this possibility gives rise to a development and deepening of the idea of fate this is not our present concern.

When the death-wedding is expressed in the form of a mating with a bridegroom of death it is very rare for there to be any hint of the possibility of resistance. The image of Death as a bridegroom (whether of the soul or of the female as opposed to the male) is usually marked by archaic (i.e. violent) traits—and often takes the form of an abducting beast of prey or dragon. It appears in fairy-tales as an evil magician or murderous robber. Whatever form it may take, the image is not so much associated with the seductive aspect of mating as with ideas of rape and robbery, but we must remember that both these aspects seem to be deeply rooted in the psyche and to be closely related to each other, since they have left traces in customs which are still found even among Europeans, and which even now are emotionally fully comprehensible to us in our present state of conscious development.

Until recent times there were many districts in Germany where boys and girls who died were dressed as bridegroom or bride: until the revolution it was the custom in the villages of Russia to deck the body of a dead girl as though for a wedding with dark ribbons and a garland in its hair, and to put a wedding ring on the finger of both boys and girls when they were buried: the burial service often took the form of a ritual wedding with death. We are told that "When a young girl dies the funeral is held in her parents' house as a wedding feast, and either death or the grave is invoked as a bridegroom in the course of a funeral lament." A Podolian lament goes: "O son-in-law! O green grave-mound! . . . my son-in-law, dark without joy": and another, "Earth, our son-in-law! when shall we see you?" From Poltawa: "My little daughter! My little princess! What is this prince you have chosen? So full of *mystery*! Why did you not tell me before?" In a folk-song from the Ukraine a dying warrior tells his *horse* to give the news to his mother:

"Neigh out loud!
My old mother comes.
Do not tell her, my steed,
That I lie slain,
Say to her, steed
That I have wooed
And taken a little bride—
The grave *in the far clear field."*

From Turkey comes a dead man's answer to his parents: "... I married yesterday, yesterday in the evening very late. *Mother World* is my bride; my mother-in-law the grave." For popular feeling there is a very real parallel between death and marriage. Many Russian marriage songs imply that the young girl experiences the transition to the married state as, among other things, a dying to a life which is dear and well known and an entry into a new life which is mysterious and fearful. Many marriage customs and songs seem to be closely connected with rites and laments for the dead.

Marriage can become a symbol of death and death can be a symbol of the decisive transformation of life which takes place at marriage, especially for the girl. The most beautiful, significant and explicit formulation of this symbolism is the myth of the rape and marriage of the Kore—Persephone. The maiden is abducted and robbed of her maidenhood, but when she receives seed (of the pomegranate) from the man she is transformed: the Kore (maiden) "dies" and in her place rises the Despoina, Queen and Mistress in her own kingdom: the Mother is born from the Virgin-Daughter. It might seem that this is a kind of "reversal" in that a process which is so clearly *vital* (i.e. bound up with life) like marriage is symbolized by death, but this is in fact the point at which an idea already latent in the Death-Demon as an embodiment of Fate breaks through.[1] What is symbolically expressed is that "dying" is not a unique event which brings life to an end but a process which plays its part throughout the whole of life. Young men and maidens are driven by Fate and by their own nature to the consummation of marriage, and marriage brings a death to childhood and youth and the transformation to another state (of life)— and this is only one instance of the universal fate of man. The death of

[1] Cf. Chapter 9.

the past and a dying to the past state coupled with an anxious and painful transformation into a new and previously unknown condition is a constantly recurring process, and the *real event of death* becomes the symbol of the *real event of life,* that is, becoming and transformation.

Becoming and transformation are tasks imposed on man by Fate, working both from within and without him, and this is something which man becomes aware of at the turning points, the crises of his existence. In so far as a man experiences such crises with anxiety and under the image of inescapable death he also experiences himself as one disposed by nature to transcend his existence as it is at any moment and to experience and express previously unknown possibilities. The actual transcendence involves ecstasy as much as anxiety, since ecstasy is a kind of going out, a being extinguished and, at the same time, the shining forth of a new light before which all that existed before fades into shadow. Only a man who can feel his way into an experience of this kind can understand the psychological significance of the demonic and fatefully abducting bridegroom or the demonic and irresistibly seductive bride as forms of the Death-Demon. These images do not arise when the feeling for life fades, and is replaced by a longing for an illusory "better world" (most often pictured in a pretty tawdry way), which is what is likely to be thought by much superficial modern thinking: even though, as we have seen, images of a "better world" occur in the course of the development of the images of the Death-Demon they are not the real root of the Death-Bride or the Death-Bridegroom. According to the myths and sagas it is to the men of most abundant life and power that the nuptial aspect of Death is revealed, and it takes the form of a streaming forth of the man in the intoxication of battle or of the superabundance and transformation of fulfilled love.

In the mythological images of the Death-Wedding there is often a further motif which may appear strange to us. This is the idea that those who live in the underworld or the "Beyond" *need* living human beings, and that this is why they ensnare them. In late legends from Christian times this idea often crops up in the suggestion that the dwellers in the underworld hope to get an "immortal soul" out of their association with living men, and so to share in redemption from their godlessness. This might be regarded as a "reversal" of the idea of a communion of the living with the dead, which we have mentioned above, and it may be noticed that seduction by the dead is often closely allied with the offering of the "Food of the Elves" and of a "finer", everlasting life of joyful companionship. This idea occurs among the African Baja without the bridal aspect, but in the Condla legend the two are brought together, and the Valkyries are abducting brides who carry men to the communion of the dead, the feast of the Einherjer in Odin's Valhalla, although, it must be admitted, the bridal aspect of the Valkyries is given less prominence than their function as messengers of the Val-*Father* and agents of his will.

The Valkyries are sometimes called *Daughters of Odin*, but the Einherjer are called "Oskasynir"—*adopted Sons of Odin*. In this connection several motifs are bound together in a remarkable harmony —the robbery and abduction, the marriage, the community of the ancestors, and the *Death-Father*. Earlier forms of the image of the Death-Father have already cropped up; for example, Moma the Primal Father and God of Death (as well as the creator) of the Witoto Indians; Ouiot, the Primal Father of the Luiseño Indians, who is embodied in the moon which is born, transforms itself and dies; Yama the Primal Father in India, the first man to die, the God of the Dead and he who gathers his children under the beautiful tree that they may enjoy a beautiful, carefree life in union with him and the gods. The frightful messengers of Yama[1] hint at the terrifying, overwhelming character of the Paternal in general, but more often this drops into the background when the demon or god of death is given a paternal form. The Death-Father seems to be a condensed image and personification of that "community of the ancestors" which takes part in the fate of the tribe by advice or guidance even when traces of the wolf or raven form of the Death-Demon (the Hider and the Hidden) can still be detected—as they can, for example, in Odin. The Destroyer, Shiva, has a terrifying aspect: he is the dark murderer, companioned by dogs, jackals and snakes, and it might seem that his only paternal traits are those of horrible immensity, shattering power and arbitrary violence—yet Shiva is "the Gracious One", the God of Fertility and the Preserver, and he begets on the holy maiden Parvati a Son who rescues the world from the tyranny of the Giant and creates order and freedom. Odin is also a Preserver of the World and for his colossal struggle against the gigantic, dark powers which will ultimately destroy the world he *needs* his adopted sons, the Einherjer. The Einherjer live in

[1] Cf. Chapter 8, p. 77.

perpetual communion with the Death-Father *as his helpers*, in order to be ready to endure the struggle to preserve or renew the world, so that psychologically Valhalla represents a fusion of the image of the Death-Demon with that of the community of the ancestors: the earlier idea that the dead ancestors are concerned in the fate of the tribe has been so developed that it has become the idea that the dead are involved in the fate of the world, and the numinous aspect of the mighty Death-Demon has begun to take on that quality which Otto calls "Majestas". As a Father-God Odin is not to be understood as a Death-Demon and nothing more, because the dealing out of death is only one (and not the most characteristic) of his functions. Although he sends out the Valkyries as his messengers of death he does so in order to fulfil and to decree the order of the world and of human existence; in order to form such a conception man must become aware of his own existence as part of a meaningful order which extends beyond its limits.

The formulation of the image of the Father-God brings an extended process of transformation to its culmination, and when the Death-Father becomes the Father-God man has achieved a religious comprehension of the world which is new in every way. This point was reached after a long development but its beginnings can be seen at an early period. Man first experiences death as that which is "wholly other" in that it is the antithesis and negation of life as he knows it: he then gradually comes to see that this apparently "wholly other" actually belongs of necessity to life and that death impinges upon existence at the point where existence extends beyond life. Present existence is felt to take place within a "world" which is largely "hidden", and this "other world" gives meaning and order to the present—a meaning and order which is somehow felt to emanate from the "wholly other". Thus the hidden "other world" becomes something more than a mere negation of life, and neither Life nor Death is any longer felt to be an independent power: taken together they are seen as an activity of the "wholly other", the Godhead.

From a psychological point of view we may say that when this stage has been reached a deeper archetype has manifested itself—the archetype of divinity—which includes Life and Death within itself and rules over them at the same time. The divinity imposes order, and death is only one (but an important one) of the instruments which it uses. Death is thus seen as a spiritual event which is part of "Life" in some higher sense. The synthesis of Death and Life in the Godhead gives expression to the idea of a higher "Life" which includes Death as one of its functions.

What we have just said should not be taken to imply that we imagine that man *thought* his way from the archetype of death to the archetype of God. We are simply trying to use words to illuminate the psychological meaning of the fact that in the early darkness of mythology a shift took place in the images related to death, seeing this as the outward manifestation of a "shift" in the human unconscious. The essential unconsciousness (i.e. non-intellectual character) of the process can be seen from the fact that the image of a paternal God is only one of the ways in which form is given to the ordering and "light" power, painfully developed out of the chthonic realm of death. Although this is the one that points furthest into the future it is not, in fact, the earliest.

The truly primeval image of a divinity uniting life and death, and giving an order of life to all existence is Ishtar. Ishtar is the Mighty, the eternally conceiving and life-giving Womb, and the defeated yet dominating sister of the terrifying Ereshkigal, and she is the source of an order which is largely collective and instinctual. In a somewhat similar way Aphrodite is the sister of the Moirai and has a "dark", chthonic beginning; and the Latin Venus is also known as Lubentia, Goddess of the Grave. Artemis expresses another related aspect of the order of Life and Death, being the playmate of Persephone who both tends and kills the animals which she rules and who, herself a virgin, has power over birth. Again, in Teutonic myth, Freya originates close to the demonic Hel, and yet is goddess of love, birth and the domestic hearth: she gives expression to an order which has significance going beyond birth and death, which are the limits of the life of individual men. We can do no more than mention Zeus (Chthonios!), Apollo, Hermes, Hera and Athene who all show signs of chthonic connections which relate them together, for although it would be fascinating to examine these signs in detail it would require too many separate investigations. We may conclude with a reference to Dionysos. This god unites the dark side of Death with the most radiant aspects of Life, for his ecstatic manifestations eternally recur resplendently, and they are extinguished only to burst out again. It is no accident that he is the Lord of the Underworld and that in Orphic thought he is also the future Lord of the Worlds. When the image of Death is incorporated in that of the Godhead the Death-Demon is no longer thought to have an independent power which is the antithesis of life; he is, rather, included in the exalted Life of the Divine Power which rules over growth and change and all the transformation of life, and which gives to human existence a transcendental meaning and order stretching beyond the life of the individual. When, therefore, the psyche is no longer driven to form an image of death because death has been transcended and incorporated into the image of God we have reason to speak of religious maturity.

If the early images of the Death-Demon develop until they merge into the image of God, in later times in the decay of religion they emerge again in sadly altered form. The modern image is the Cadaver, and though it has the corpse-like quality of ancient Death-Demons its character is dry and intellectual rather than mythical. It is mere lifelessness with no relation to fertility and transformation. It was the same in Imperial Rome when grinning skeletons were set in the mosaics of luxurious dining-rooms. These had little to do with an encounter with the tremendum, but were intended as a sophisticated way of titillating the appetite for life in an utterly "godless" society: they challenged the revellers to enjoy and devour the pleasures of life *"dum vivimus"* (while we yet live). On the other hand the corpse in the "Dances of the Dead" popular in the late medieval and more recent times had more serious import, for it represented death as the messenger and servant of a divine power which was thought of as the true "Life". Yet even this figure was essentially one-sided since it brought nothing but death; it did not so much express a myth as point a moral—and in the end the moral to which it pointed was not very different from that which the Romans dismissed with a laugh and a wry smile. In the same way the corpse today is a bogy from which naïve spirits hide their eyes and flee, or which reminds the more sophisticated of the fact which they acknowledge in their intellect but cannot accept emotionally that this life will inevitably come to an end.

We have now completed our survey of the development of the mythological (more accurately, the pre-mythological) Images of Death, and in the second part we hope to show that analogous images appear spontaneously in modern dreams. Before we do this, however, we propose to present a late, new formulation of the Death-Demon in the figure of Frau Holle of German legend. This figure lived in the "unconscious" of the people during historical time "underneath" official Christianity, and without being cultivated developed from the most primitive forms to a stage at which the first shoots of the mature forms can be seen.

11. Frau Holle and Percht—a Late Return of the Death-Demon

WE regard Frau Holle and Percht as forms of the same figure, and this figure has special significance because it crops up among the German tribes for the first time during the Christian period. It is very remarkable that such a figure, which is essentially a demon of death with extremely primitive traits, should appear during the period when the images of Christianity were directed towards overcoming belief in demons. Frau Holle-Percht is certainly a Death-Demon even though she is never openly acknowledged as such, so that it is only in her two names[1] that her fundamental nature manifests itself and evokes unconscious memories which are not consciously understood. One might say that just as the official spokesmen of the Church refuse to recognize Frau Holle, so the people would not (or could not) admit her real significance into consciousness.

At first sight this figure appears little different from other figures which we meet in legends and which often have purely local or accidental origins, so that it is easy to overlook its significance. It is only when we compare local legends and pick out individual features that we can grasp the unity which binds together the contradictory aspects of Frau Holle, and so recognize her for what she is. In other words, we have to apply to the legends the same principles that we use in understanding those dreams of an individual in which certain patterns recur again and again and belong together, even though the dreamer does not recognize them. When we do this we see clearly that Frau Holle is the "Hidden One" (as her name hiddenly implies), a descendant of the ancient Death-Demon Hel, the Hider. It seems that when the West German people accepted Christianity the existing image of Death was, so to speak, *repressed*, regressed to a more primitive

[1] Cf. Chapter 9, p. 96.

114

state and worked in the deep layers of the psyche where it was unconsciously but continuously developed, however inadequately.

From the point of view of ethnic psychology this process is particularly interesting, because it is not the case (as Grimm and others assumed) that some Teutonic divinity like Freya lingered on despite Christianity, and continued in a disguised and weakened form as Frau Holle-Percht. It is, rather, as though the coming of Christianity created a complete gap, and that an encapsulated vacuum was formed at a particular point: in other words, it seems that one thing was repressed and no adequate substitute provided. The "image of death" which gave expression to the Teutonic attitude to death and the beyond was repressed with considerable violence in the interest of the much more mature Christian doctrine, but the understanding and temper of the people was not sufficiently developed for that doctrine to be accepted in such a way that it could fill the gap.[1]

---

[1] This peculiar process may not be unique, and the author hopes to document it in a separate work, but it may be worth giving a crude outline of the way in which it may be thought to have taken place. The Christian doctrine of death and redemption is only comprehensible when a certain stage of psychological development has been reached, and when Christianity was introduced it is unlikely that the West Teutonic tribes *as a whole* had reached this stage. Psychologically we might say that they were still concerned with the problem of understanding death as part of life, and of comprehending the significance of their connection: the dogmatic Christian doctrine of life after death would seem to "dissolve" death and to devalue earthly life by means of the idea of "eternal life". Since at that time "the Teuton" was engaged in trying to *understand* life and death as the mysterious, dual *fate* of man he could only understand the new doctrine by *evaluating* earthly life and death in terms of *guilt*, and regard both as consequences of the original guilt of man, so that he would feel that he must strive with all his powers to gain the "real" and better life in which there is neither guilt nor death. Understood in the deepest sense the Christian ethic is rooted in the doctrine of death and redemption and it is an ethic of free, loving devotion to God—a believing, trusting devotion which governs all behaviour in relation to others in every situation. The Teuton, however, misunderstood this ethic in terms of a moral legalism, because he could not yet see man in relation to the Divine Trinity nor, more important still, really appreciate the transcendence implicit in the Christian evaluation of life and death, so that he could not relate these things to his own existence. Instead of trusting, emotional faith ("an acceptance-*as-good*" and a "making-it-*dear-and-familiar* to one") the Teuton developed an anxiety-ridden "faith", in that he felt he must hold-*as-true* that which authority seemed to

It may well be a measure of the completeness and depth of the repression that it is not until about AD 1000, two hundred years after the full Christianization of the German tribes, that the *first isolated traces* of Frau Holle and Percht appear. This suggests that all conscious connection with the indigenous image of death had been broken. At the same time there are features which could not be understood at that time, but which we can clearly see as pointing to the mythical character of Frau Holle.

Giperchtennacht—known today in the Salzburg area as *Perchennacht*, the last of the Twelve Nights—is mentioned in a Mondseer glossary of about AD 1000, but there is a much more important reference to Frau Holle in the decrees of Burchard, Bishop of Worms (1001–1024). There are, in fact, two passages which complement each other. The first criticizes women who "through the deception of the devil declare" that they had to ride on certain nights as the attendants of "demons who appear in female form, called Holda by foolish, untutored people": the second passage is almost exactly the same except that it follows the model of romance countries and names the ringleader Diana (goddess of witches), or Herodias. "Frau Berchta" is mentioned

---

demand. Worse, this "faith" was *required* of him under threat of eternal torment in Hell. In other words, the Teuton was faced with a tremendously *excessive* demand, which meant that the one thing he must not allow himself to do was to go on trying to come to terms with the mystery of death in his own way, because if he did he would not be holding as true the authoritative answer of the Church, and would merit the everlasting penalty. From this it would follow that he must eradicate from his mind the autonomous image of death with its own dynamic development, leaving a kind of *gap* which could not then be filled by the Christian doctrine of death. It is a fact that other elements of Christian doctrine were simply assimilated to Teutonic conceptions, for instance, the image of the Son of God in *Heliand*, but when it is a question of the ideas of death and life this kind of assimilation is not possible, in spite of or perhaps because of the primitive forms which they take: the old images are nothing more than a source of tormenting anxiety—compare, for example, passages in the *Muspilli*. We are suggesting, then, that the images of death which belong to the psychological state of the people were forced into the unconscious, where although they remained alive they regressed to the original archaic forms from which they began. At the same time the human psyche secretly sought for them so that they took shape anew and gradually unfolded in the image of Frau Holle-Percht, in an unconscious process which was concealed from the people who knowingly-unknowingly participated in it.

again in a rather late Middle High German poem of the thirteenth century called *Von Berchten Mit der lagen Nas* (or Berchta with the Long Nose), which refers to certain customs still alive today. On the other hand, there is not another explicit reference to Frau Holle until the fifteenth century: Herolt, a Dominican, attacked the beliefs about the Wild Hunt of the Twelve Nights in one of his sermons (Sermon XI) and he says that the leader is "*deam quam quidem* Dianam *vocant, in vulgari: die frawen unhold . . .*" (a goddess whom many called Diana but, in the vernacular, Frau Unhold).[1]

A legend from Virgen and Prägraten in the Pustertal of South Tyrol bears on the name "Herodias" in Burchard von Worms and has survived into modern times: it is that Herod's daughter incited him to kill the Holy Innocents and that as a punishment she has to walk in the world every year on the "Night of the Three Kings" (*sc.* Twelfth Night) from eleven o'clock to midnight, and that she is known as Berachte. It is further said that she is very dangerous, and that if she finds an open window she forces her way into the house—the only protection being three consecrated chalk crosses on the mullion. There is a further story from Virgen that a young man once stood at an open window on "Percht's Night" and that she sprang and clutched him, so that he only managed to escape by slipping out of his coat: the next morning the coat was found in the road, torn to pieces, and the lad himself would have been *torn in pieces* in the same way if he had not escaped.

The connection of Frau Holle-Percht with Diana and Herodias is illuminating. The identification of "*frawe unhold*" (*sc.* Frau Holda or Holle) with Diana makes it clear that she is a *mythical* character, even though she is not consciously associated with Hel, the Death-Demon of Teutonic myth. The association with a Biblical mass-murderess establishes her character *as a killer who comes from distant realms*, at the same time as it incorporates her within the Christian framework. The names Herodias and Berachte point to her character as a cruel and random killer and through Diana, the huntress who roams by night,

---

[1] According to Güntert the confusion between the stems *hulð*—(meaning "pleasing", "friendly") and *huld*—("hidden", "Demon of Death") goes right back to Common Teutonic times. It is easy to understand why it should occur here since the preacher is concerned to make an unequivocal condemnation of the "Un-holden".

she is associated with Artemis who has a mysterious and varied significance.

Luther[1] and his pupil Erasmus Alberus[2] mention *"die fraw Hulda"*, and they do so in a way that shows that she was a well-known figure: at the same time neither Luther nor Alberus has any sense of her mystery and power, and they both regard her as an element in popular superstition, irritating but more silly and ridiculous than anything else. However, among the people a real sense of her power lasted until very recent times. For example, Marie-Andree Eysn gives an account of the processions on Percht's Night in the Salzburg area, and she tells us that until the turn of the century the young men had a very real fear that the Lord of Hell might mingle with the mummers, so that they had to make frequent counts along the route to make sure that there was not "one too many" there. This alone would justify the inference that the feeling of unseen power and danger associated with the chthonic realm of the underworld survived a long time in the unconscious of the people and was related to Holle-Percht, but the inference is supported by a very large number of legendary fragments scattered about Germany. The pictures constructed from these fragments is that of a being which has the characteristics of the primitive Death-Demon or of an uncanny divinity of death.

The many place-names which clearly refer to dwelling-places of this figure (particularly under the name Frau Holle) show how widely these legends are distributed. From Schleswig-Holstein to the Main and Moselle there are "Hollenbergs" where Frau Holle is said to live underground—the entry to the underworld is often said to lie in some particular, dark, uncanny defile; "Höllental" is found in many parts of Germany, and is probably connected far more closely to the kingdom of Hel and Frau Holle than it is with the Christian Hell: in the legend from Rochlitz mentioned above[3] the hound of the underworld appears in a dark valley called Helloch, and in Layen on the Upper Eisack it is said that Berchta lives "in the dark valley": "People do not like to go through that wood . . . She has been seen there by many people; she wanders through the thickets, up and down the valley,

[1] In *Auslegung der Episteln*, Basle 1522.
[2] In his fables.
[3] See Chapter 4, p. 48.

118

with five or six small dogs, especially during the Twelve Nights, and woe to the man who meets her." It is clear that we have to do with a demon like the Ugrian Koljo who dwells in hollow places. There is a tale from Zellerfeld in the Harz Mountains of a miner who met the *"Haulemutter"* (i.e. Frau Holle) in the road. Of giant size she stood with a foot on both banks of the road, and when he boldly passed between her legs she knocked his hat off his head. Güntert relates a similar story from the Böhmerwald.

Although Frau Holle is thought to live in the depths *of the earth* the way to her home is often said to be through a lake, a pond or a well—the kind of places that are often said to be the gateway to the under-world in Greek and Roman legends. The best-known example in the German area is the well in Grimm's fairy-tale of Frau Holle. There is a "Höllbrunnen" near Inzikofen (Hohenzollern) and another near Böhmenkirchen in the Swabian Alps, and there are also a number of "Hellbrunnen" which should be understood in the same way. One of these wells is at Frischborn in Oberhessen which is known as Frau-Holle-Loch, and the tradition is that it is the gateway to Frau Holle's castle under the ground. Of the Hoher Meissner it is said that it is the entrance to Frau Holle's beautiful garden full of fruit trees, which can only be reached through a well or a pool: here too is the Höllental above which "lies a large pool or lake . . . called Frau Hollenbad (Frau Holle's bath). For according to ancient accounts a phantom woman has been seen to bathe in it at midday. . . ."

At the foot of the Hoher Meissner near Kammerbach there is a small lake by a rock in the wood. The water in the lake is clear as crystal with marvellous properties, and this lake is associated with Frau Holle for there is a cave in the rock said to be "the largest in the land of Hesse", known as the Hollstein and referred to in a document as early as 1267. Near Oberseibertenrod there is a "Wilde Holle" who lives at Wildholloch. There is a Holloch which is the seat of Frau Holle near Kranichfeld in Thuringia and it is often the case that Thuringian mountain caves prominent in folk-lore are thought to be the under-ground kingdom of Frau Holle, especially on the Kyffhäuser and Hörselberg Mountains. It is also said that Frau Holle (or Frau Berchta in Orlagau) dwells under the fields with the *Haulemännchen*—the souls of children who have died unbaptized.

In almost all the tales Frau Holle-Percht is said to live in hidden places under the earth, and when these places are identified the association of their names or their generally gloomy character bring up memories of old myths—the underworld kingdom of Hel, Tartarus and the realm of Persephone and Hades. An allusion in a folk-tale from the Pustertal carries further the idea of the underground gardens of Frau Holle. It is said that Percht (Berachte) stole a cow from its stall and a child from its mother and a year later returned them adorned with garlands of strange, unknown flowers and fresh cherry blossom, even though it was long before the time of blossom. The suggestion seems to be that Berachte lives in a far country where the flowers and seasons are not the same as ours, a country reminiscent of the Elysian fields or the distant Isles of the Blest in the Condla legend from Ireland.

The outward appearance of Frau Holle-Percht is liable to change and alter, and has contradictory features. In the Harz Mountains, for instance, it is said that the *Haulemutter* (the Herald of Death) is some-times very short and sometimes immensely tall and bony; sometimes she takes the form of a little white dog which grows and grows until it suddenly vanishes. In districts in which it is the custom to dedicate the last ears of corn to Frau Holle it is said that the Corn Wolf or the Corn-Aunt roams about in the summer grain, and this suggests that Frau Holle might have a wolf form. There are other accounts of her appearance as a dog, and in Thuringia and the Harz Mountains she is said to bark like a dog to announce a death. More often it is that she or Percht is accompanied by dogs (see above), especially when one of them rides as the leader of the Wild Hunt. There are stories from Hesse that Frau Holle changes into a bird after bathing in a fish pond.[1]

Percht (and in isolated instances Frau Holle) and her retinue are represented by human beings wearing masks, and the masks used are instructive. There are wolf- and dragon-masks, and masks of other animals with huge fangs, and sometimes real dogs' teeth set in gaping, mobile jaws are used: at the Percht Races the boys wear black sheep-skins round them, "Percht Caps" of badger's skin on their heads and masks on their faces—even though the masks may be no more than

[1] Percht is also sometimes said to have a duck's foot which suggests a mani-festation in the form of a water-bird, and we may compare the swan-form of the Norns and the Valkyries.

pieces of black material. These things still reveal the original, chthonic character of Percht.

It seems that Frau Holle was always represented in human form but in Hildburghausen she is given horns. She often wears a dark cloak or shroud of dark cloth, but we are told that in a number of places her head and shoulders are covered with a white veil. It is clear enough that she is, essentially, "the Shrouded One". At Veilsdorf (Hildburghausen) the Hullefra is represented with a white head cloth as well as a black cloak and the traditional speeches and behaviour associated with this representation[1] show that the costume expresses both her dark and light aspects, the polar opposites, Death and Life.

Frau Holle is often thought of as a very old, ugly little mother, or as a witch with unkempt, yellow tresses, and Percht as a "grey wizened hag" with torn clothes and dishevelled hair. Luther speaks of "Frau Holle in the straw armour" and this description, which occurs in Thuringia as well, recalls the widespread custom of "Driving out Death", when Death is represented as a straw doll or an old woman clothed in straw. As a complete contrast both Frau Holle and Percht may also be thought of as a wonderfully beautiful and entrancing woman in a white robe.[2] In Vogtland and around Mount Kyffhäuser she is thought of as a queen whose majestic appearance demands allegiance, and the Styrians speak of Percht in the same way. There is a strange emphasis on her outstandingly large nose in many accounts, and when she is thought of as a bogy her great fang-like teeth are often stressed.

The ambivalent character of Frau Holle is brought out in a striking way by the legends of Clausthal. It is said of her that during the Twelve Nights she terrifies by her "red-hot eyes and red mouth filled with fire", but that on Easter Saturday she appears as a white-robed woman with golden hair. Dieter Brenle, a man from Calbach in Hesse, was accused of sorcery in 1630 and in his evidence we come across the ambiguity of Frau Holle in another form: "Frau Holt was like a fine, human woman, in front," he said, "but like a hollow tree with rough bark behind." This, and similar ideas about Frau Percht, recall the medieval poems about Frou Werlte that we mentioned earlier. Frau

[1] See pp. 129–30 below.
[2] She is also described wearing a blue coat under which she hides a troop of small children in order to protect them.

Holle is often said to have a wolf's or fox's tail, or one of tow and straw, like the Huldren in Nordic legends. These traits point to the corpse-like character or the demonic, devouring aspect of the primitive image of death.

The *attributes* of Frau Holle-Percht point to the same thing as the descriptions of her appearance. In Lerbach, in the Harz Mountains, she is said to hold a "chalk-white sheet" (shroud), and this may be connected with the net to catch the dead which we mentioned above. In the Tyrol, Styria, Carinthia and other places her ability to kill (or at least to damage) is brought out by the belief that she has iron teeth, iron claws, iron gloves or iron shoes. Frau Holle-Percht is often represented with a distaff as a spinner, and this is not only connected with her association with household order but also suggests a hidden relationship to the Norns, the Spinners of Fate: at Eisenach she was represented with a spinning wheel or a distaff even on a Christmas cake. According to the fables of Erasmus Alberus she carried a sickle, and she still does so in customs which have survived at Veilsdorf near Hildburghausen in Thuringia. The sickle has a deep mythological significance: it is not only the oldest implement used to harvest the corn but it also appears in myths as a consecrated implement used for killing of which the action goes beyond death to transformation, as in the Greek legends of the castration of Uranus and the murder of Medusa. Moreover, the sickle suggests the sickle form of the moon, and as the moon crops up again in a Percht mask which we shall mention below it may well be that Frau Holle-Percht is connected with the waxing and waning of the self-transforming moon, and if this were so it would involve a further relationship to the primeval, mythical death-figures like Ouiot, Hecate, Artemis-Diana and others.

We also become aware of the close relation between Frau Holle-Percht and these primitive figures when we consider the powers she is supposed to have and the activity which is regarded as typical of her. In Thuringia she is thought of as a malicious old woman who steals children, makes them ill or replaces them with changelings. Up to modern times there was an apotropaic spell for the protection of sick children which assumed that the Hollen were the cause of the sickness: the parents of the child put wool and bread in a juniper tree and each said:

"O Hollen and Hollinnen,
I bring you something to spin
And something to eat.
Spin then and eat
And forget *my sick child."*

By and large Frau Holle-Percht is thought to bring trouble whenever she appears. When she looks at children, breathes on men and treads with her iron foot, then there is distress, sickness and the death of cattle. She is regarded as particularly dangerous in Alpine regions where, for instance, it is said that she slits open the stomachs of lazy girls and stuffs them with sweepings. At Veilsdorf near Hildburghausen the Hullefra is said to come to the children at Christmas. She is said to be dressed in a black cloak, to wear a white head-cloth, to carry a sack of cats on her back and a sickle in her hand. She cries to the children: "Whet! Whet! Slit open belly! Put in cats! Sew up again!" If the children pray the Hullefra gives them *flints*, and these are certainly symbols of new awakenings and new life.[1] This introduces the other, very different aspect of Frau Holle-Percht. As we have said there is a tale in the South Tyrol which tells that Berachte (daughter of Herod) stole a child from its mother's arms, and brought it back a year later garlanded with strange flowers: this seems to suggest a child-*killer* who *brings* a *new child* a year later in exchange for the dead one. Certainly there are many explicit references to Frau Holle as a bringer of fertility, or as one who brings children from her well or pond to human families. In Hesse the Hollen are feared as child-stealers, and in order to protect them a light must be left burning beside unbaptized children until they are nine days old, and yet on the Hoher Meissner it is said that "Frau Hollenbad" makes "healthy and fertile those women who go down to her in her well. New-born children come from her well, and it is she that brings them out of it. At the same time she lures children into her well where she makes the good ones favourites of fortune, and turns the bad into changelings." She gives children wonderful flowers and fruit from

---

[1] In the ritual of Holy Saturday fire is struck from flints to symbolize the light of the Risen Christ. In north Switzerland the author witnessed a wedding custom according to which sweets called "flints" were thrown from the wedding carriage to the children of the village.

her underground garden, and the "Wilde Frau Born"—a spring near Einartshausen in Hesse—is probably a Holle-well, since, ". . . if a woman wants a child she need only drink silently from the spring three times before sunrise; this will have good effect."[1]

The Hollbrunnen at Inzikofen and Böhmmenkirchen in the Swabian Alps, which we have already mentioned as entrances to the underworld, are also thought of as *Kindlesbrunnen* (well of children), like the well by St. Kunibert's Church in Cologne at the bottom of which *Mary* is said to play with unborn children. The assimilation of Frau Holle to Mary as Mother, and of Mary to Frau Holle is a very instructive piece of living myth-formation, and it is not likely that it simply occurred by chance in one place alone. For example, Andree-Eysn says that in Styria Frau Percht is thought of like a mantled Madonna, wearing a blue cloak in which she protects and encompasses many children. Again, there is a strange uncertainty in a Hessian legend, which might well arise if a fusion between Frau Holle and Mary was in process: on the Wintersberg near Einartshausen there is the *Wildenstein* (a name often given to the home of Frau Holle) where there is a depression in a block of rock and the legend has it that once when on a journey Mary put her child to bed in this trough—but a variant of the same legend says that it was Frau Holle who did this. Until 1840 there was music and dancing there on the Feast of St John (June 24th). There are, further, numerous traditions from Alpine regions and from Orlagau presenting Percht, or Berchta or Frau Holle as the terrifying but loving nurse or protectress of the souls of children who have died unbaptized. This image of the Death-Demon surrounded by children almost certainly symbolizes Life, transforming and renewing itself with sorrow. This is the deeper meaning that shines through the legends of Frau Holle-Percht.

The picture of Frau Holle-Percht in the folk-tales is consistent from this point of view. In Vogtland she is said to be "queen of the little crickets under the ground", and in the neighbouring Orlagau crickets are explicitly said to be the souls of dead children. In Hesse as well as in Vogtland she and her people are supposed to watch over the fertility

[1] The same mythological idea in a more primitive form is found among Australian aborigines. The souls of dead ancestors are thought to live in certain water-holes, and if a woman bathes there one of the souls enters her body as the germ of a child, and she becomes pregnant.

of fields and women. She has an even more majestic role in the Kyffhäuser Legend for she is said to live as an exiled queen in the mountains ministering to the Emperor Barbarossa and his many hundred Knights and Squires—much as Hel serves Baldur in her underground dwelling. Frau Holle can even be seen at times sitting spinning at the entrance to the cave, like one of the Norns. A legend from the early nineteenth century shows the tenacity with which the people cling to this mythological and fateful figure. About 1811 or 1812, it is said, an arrogant French marshal set up his camp-bed in the old tower of Mount Kyffhäuser, and during the night Frau Holle appeared and told him that if Napoleon marched on Russia and continued to occupy Germany he would fall in misery and poverty. The marshal is said to have ridden post-haste to Halle to dissuade Napoleon and the other generals from their plan—but all in vain. Frau Holle, the announcer of Fate and Death, had need to weave an enormous net for the dead of that fateful year!

There are many references to Frau Holle as a spinner, and the echo of the idea is heard in the well-known fairy-tale in Grimm. In that story the mythical character of Frau Holle and her Kingdom is clearly visible behind the façade of a fairy-story. As we know the well is the entrance to the Kingdom of Death, and what the girl first finds there (a baking oven and a tree with ripe apples) points symbolically to death as inevitable maturation and transformation. Frau Holle has terrifying teeth which recall, as from a distance, the Death-Demon in the form of a beast of prey. Moreover, the girl actually experiences a transformation in herself as a result of which she becomes mature and radiant. There is also another version of the story according to which she exchanges the role of child and daughter for that of bride, queen and mother—a transformation exactly like that through which Kore-Persephone goes in the Greek myth.

The death and fertility aspects of Frau Holle are expressed less symbolically, and so with greater clarity, in a legend from Andreas-berg in the Harz Mountains. It is said that three betrothed girls met Frau Holle in a wood, and she asked them to scour the place Hahnenk-lee for her during the night, promising that to repay them she would see that they were quickly married. Only one of the three girls did the work, and this girl was married shortly after and received as a wedding present from Frau Holle a silver cradle and a quantity of silver money.

The fiancés of the other two girls were both *killed*—one in a mining accident, the other at the wars—and the girls themselves never married.

In both tales industrious, domestic activity is rewarded, in the Grimm story by the "golden blessing" and in the other with marriage and fertility, but it would be wrong to think of Frau Holle as the judge in some court of morals concerned with industriousness. Frau Holle and Percht are always thought to "keep the women-folk in strict discipline and order" (the phrase comes from the Tyrol), and to supervise spinning, sweeping and scouring. The industrious are rewarded with golden yarn, or a glittering gold piece in their pail of water: Frau Holle or Percht may tangle the threads of the slothful, or wind tow round their arms and set it alight or slit open their stomachs (often with her sickle) and stuff in the sweepings. This last punishment provides a clue to what it is all about: in her supervision of the housework Frau Holle is not so much concerned with the virtue of industrious work as much as she is with *obedience* in relation to *order*. The order of the house is seen as a mirror or index of the order of Life and of the world as a whole, and only where this is maintained is there fertility and new life: where there is no order all is sterile. Frau Holle is a Death-Demon and, at the same time, she gives expression to a world order in which Death cannot exist without Life, nor Life without Death, and which man is required to obey. This is not a matter of morality but of right, meaningful living—and, one may add, of right dying.

It is not surprising that the nights on which Frau Holle-Percht goes about—and it is usually only at night that she is thought to do so—are celebrated all over Germany by popular customs which can hardly be distinguished from *cultic rites*. The time which is most specifically hers is that of the Twelve Nights, from December 25th to January 6th, for this is the time of greatest darkness when the ultimate death of light gives way to its rebirth. In some places Frau Holle-Percht is said to go about in the nights before Shrove Tuesday or, as in the Harz Mountains, at Easter. Of the Twelve Nights the first and the last (and sometimes New Year's Eve as well) are specially set apart, and known by such names as *"Bachlabend" "Perchtennacht"*, *"Frau-Hollen-Nacht"*, and certain customs seem to have been kept up on these nights everywhere from Central Germany to Transylvania from very earliest times. A Latin manuscript of the fifteenth century from Tegernsee contains the condemnation of "the sin and superstition of decorating houses and preparing meals for Frau Percht and her train", showing that at one time Frau Percht was invited to a meal to which the souls of the dead came also—the kind of Souls' Meal which has survived into modern times, the significance of which we discussed in Chapter 8.[1] At Scheibbs in Lower Austria it is the custom to set a table for "Percht and her seven lads" on the evening of January 5th and for members of the household to leave the food alone until the following day, when they eat what is left over. In other places "*Die letzte Richt*"—the remnants of supper—are not to be eaten on that evening, but must be left "for Frau Berchtl". In Upper Bavaria *Kuachln*, small cakes, are set on the table for "Frau Bert" on the Night of the Three Kings. In the Pinzgau there is a special rite associated with supper on "Percht's Eve". At the end of the meal the farmer's wife stays behind alone and in utter silence puts a plate of doughnuts on the table or before the window. If the plate is empty in the morning this means a blessing on the whole house. The author recently received reports of the remains of similar customs from the district of the Inn in Austria. Again the *Bachlkoch*, a gruel of flour covered with honey, was eaten on *Bachlabend* (December 25th) in the Pinzgau, and it was essential that every member of the household should take his share for, "If one were absent Percht would be offended."[2] On the same night flour is scattered in the air ("feeding the wind") or a piece of bread is put on the fence (for Percht). In the Flachgau near Salzburg it is a bundle of ears that is put on the fence on the *Bachlnacht*, and there is little doubt that it was originally intended for Percht. Since in the adjacent Pinzgau the remains of the *Bachlkoch* are smeared on the fruit trees during the night in order to preserve their fruitfulness it is clear that this custom is connected with fertility. At Buttstedt in Thuringia no offering is now made, but an invocation survives and during the Twelve Nights the farmer or his wife shakes the fruit trees in the garden calling, "Do not sleep, little tree! Frau Hulle is coming!" In Thuringia and Hesse it is unequivocally asserted that Frau Holle goes round the fields during the Twelve Nights and makes them fruitful. She is given thanks or an offering, often after the

[1] See above, pp. 91–92.

[2] It is said, "She (Frau Holle or Percht) cuts open the belly of anyone who does not join in the meal." In the M.H.G. poem *Von Berchten mit der langen Nas* it says, "She attacks and tramples on anyone who does not eat properly"— possibly with her deadly iron shoe.

summer harvest. For example, near Göttingen the last bundle of ears is left standing in the field for "Fru Holle". At Teistungen near Nordhausen they say, "Three ears for Frau Holle"; in the Eisenach area they leave one sheaf "for the dear Lady"; at Schleiz in East Thuringia a sheaf "for the poor maiden (*Moosfreili*)"; Bennungen ("*Goldne Aue*") is only a few miles from Teistungen, and there they used to leave three ears in the field "for *Wode*". Both the variety of names given to the power to whom the gift is consecrated and the legend of the Corn Wolf which survives at Bennungen remind one of the indefinite and changeable nature which has been a mark of the Death-Demon from primitive times: its form ranges from the devouring wolf-monster, through Hel and her dark and (sometimes) light manifestations—Norns, Valkyries, Freya—to the Death-Father, Wotan. At the same time the consecration of the last bundles of ears gives impressive expression to that connection between death and fertility which points to new life through transformation. The corn was known as a symbol of transformation in ancient Egypt, where the last ears were left for Osiris, and the revelation of the Holy Ear of Demeter was the climax of the Eleusinian Mysteries.

The processions and masks which still crop up here and there in connection with Percht and Frau Holle are even closer to cultic practices. There is evidence that the Percht Race continues in the Tyrol and the Salzburg area at the present time, and the masks of wild devouring animals which are often very horrible are just like those used by the African Nsei[1] (for example) at night solemnities of the dead and at the great Corn Festival of Nsiä. Just as with African and Indian secret societies men and boys meet at a secret rendezvous for the Percht Race. They run riot through the night over the countryside, ranting behind their masks, swinging pine torches like the members of the Wild Hunt, leaping over ditches and obstacles with long poles and visiting farms and villages. Their muffled shouts and the noise of the huge cowbells they carry spread fear and terror—yet they are welcomed everywhere, because they bring the promise of fertility and a good year.

The double aspect of such customs is clearly symbolized by the masks of "*Schöne Percht*" and "*Schiache Percht*"—the beautiful Percht and the ugly Percht. Karl von Spiess says that the mask of *Schiache*

[1] See Chapter 7, p. 76.

Percht is worn by a boy and that it is a head-piece often more than three metres high, covered with dead owls, great horn owls, birds of ill omen, field-mice and rags, with antlers set directly over the wearer's head, so that he seems to be horned. That of *Schöne Percht* is about the same height, decorated with two squares set diagonally above each other crowned by a silver, luminous *half-moon*: the surface is ornamented with all kinds of bright things, mirrors, silver watches, silver chains and silver coins. These, and animal masks as well, are displayed in the Percht Parade which takes place by day and includes a "*Lapp*" and "*Lappin*"—male and female fools. The fools leap around in the procession in a clownish way, and as they do so they hit the women standing by with a cow's tail filled with sand, or a roll of material stuffed with wool and they may throw to some of them linen dolls dressed like a *Pfetschekind*—swaddled babies. It is obvious enough that the touch of the symbollic phallus and the throwing of the *Pfetschekind* are fertility charms, but what is specially significant is that even today these practices have a solemn, cultic character. According to Andree-Eysn women and girls are only touched with the phallic roll or given a Pfetschekind if they are recognized members of the community: loose women and strangers are passed by. It is in no way absurd to find the Percht Race (by torchlight at night) and the Percht Parade reminiscent of parts of the cult of Demeter, and especially of the δρόμος of the Eleusinian Mysteries which, judging by its name, was once a wild race. The element of wildness can also be seen in what survives of the ceremonies of Frau Holle in Thuringia. At Schnett near Hildburghausen *Wilde Hullefra* appears during the Twelve Nights: she is dressed in straw, wears straw horns on her head and terrifies the women of the village by her ranting. In the end the women suddenly attack her, tear her robe and horns to pieces and seize handfuls of straw to put in the hen-house: those who manage to do this are assured of a bountiful yield of eggs. At Veilsdorf nearby the Hullefrau who comes with sickle, cats and flints is replaced by a straw doll on the last of the Nights and this is thrust into a cask and shot through the bunghole. At Eisfeld she is thrown on the fire and burnt. These customs link Frau Holle to the so-called "Driving out of Death", once carried out all over Germany, usually in February. It is true that in these customs the straw doll was simply called "Death" or "Winter" and not "Frau Holle", but they should be mentioned here because they often included events very like those centring on the "Wilde Hullefra" at Schnett. For example, in the course of "Driving out Death" when the straw doll or masked figure reaches a certain point the doll or the straw robe is torn to pieces by the assembled company in a "wild lynching", and the pieces are scattered over the fields to preserve and increase their fertility. In this there is an echo of ancient, cultic god sacrifices. Another, remoter, echo is found at Eisenach, where ginger-bread stamped with a picture of Frau Holle at her spinning wheel is eaten at Christmas (i.e. during the Twelve Nights), for as the sacrificed god might be incorporated in field or animal it can also be taken into man himself, to work its blessing within him.[1] This symbolism is of deep significance, for what man takes into himself is "Death", and yet it is recognized as the bringer of Order and Life. Although it is improbable that those who take part in such rites are consciously aware of the deep meaning of their symbolic action there is every reason to suppose that the power of the "image" works in the unconscious, and influences their attitude to death and life.

There is a legend from Fulda about a furrowed stone in a wood. There, people said, Frau Holle wept so bitterly over her slain husband that the stone itself was softened. Reporting this legend Güntert refers to the tears of Demeter mourning for the Kore, and of Frigga mourning over the death of Baldur. In this legend Frau Holle has a new relationship with death, for she herself bears its sorrow as every mother weeps for a lost child and every wife for a lost husband. In interpreting this we see that a new aspect of the image of death has been revealed; that is, we become aware of a new way in which man can assimilate the fact of death—and at the same time we see that the wheel has turned full circle. In Chapter 2 we saw how primitive man became a killer in order to assimilate the experience of death by enacting the role of the Death-Demon, and doing as it did in order to comprehend the event of death: we now see that this is the beginning of a circular movement which closes when the Death-Demon takes to itself *man's feeling* when confronted by death. At the same time the feeling itself has changed as a result of repeated encounters with the experience of death, revealing aspects which are ever new. What is finally realized

[1] Purely cultic customs of eating bread stamped with an image are known to us from Aztec Mexico, for example. (In this context one can hardly avoid thinking of Christian Communion wafers stamped with a crucifix. *Trans.*).

is not only that the *fate* of death is the general fate of the world, but also that the *suffering* of death is the general suffering of the world.

Despite the fact that they remain unformed and unsystematized the tales and customs associated with Frau Holle-Percht are infused by a genuine mythological spirit. We can feel behind them the struggle to give expression to that which cannot be expressed, to formulate the insoluble problem of the underlying dichotomy and paradoxical nature of life in this world. The legends of Frau Holle-Percht are crude attempts to comprehend and elucidate her contradictory nature, and as they do so the emotional recognition of a world order of which human life is a part begins to take shape. Such an order is one in which Life and Death are ultimately one and in which our own existence is dimly felt—if not actually understood—as a continual transformation. The reason why the hints and insights in these mythological stories were not brought together into an immense, comprehensive formulation was that (in Otto's words) there was no "man with the gift of prophecy and divination", and this lack was a direct result of the historical situation. It was just those who had a gift for religion and divination who were most deeply influenced by the new religion so that they directed all their energy towards Christianity, in which they found fulfilment and satisfaction. In doing this they turned away from the beliefs of the people, unformed but struggling to find clear expression, and it was precisely those popular beliefs with which they were most unconsciously involved which they attacked and suppressed with greatest violence. The result was that the "soul of the people" was not only out of touch with the only acceptable, conscious model of the world, but that it also lacked any outstanding individual to express its strivings, so that the human psyche was forced to attempt once again to come to terms with the primeval image of the Death-Demon as a split-off complex in the unconscious. It is remarkable that the attempt did not lead to mere regression. The figure of Frau Holle-Percht is evidence that the unconscious initiated a movement of its own which worked upon the experience of actual death (from which the conscious psyche felt cut off), seeking to elucidate its meaning in a new and healing way.

We can see why the legends associated with Frau Holle often have closer connection than the elaborated myths of the great religions with the dream-life of modern people. This is what we should expect when we realize that the conscious attempt to enter into a genuine relation-ship with death has been prohibited in our age—not, this time, by the incomprehensible demands of religious authority but by the fascination of science, since science has implicitly offered endless life and so emptied both death and life of any true significance. The unconscious of modern man is not satisfied, and it often produces primeval dream images, not consciously understood, in the attempt to unearth a satisfying meaning—and so reaches back once more to the primal psychic ground of religious emotion.

Part Two

Introductory Note

So far we have been concerned with the psychological significance of the origin and transformations of the image of death, that is of the conception in popular customs, rites and mythologies of a being which brings about death. We have tried to show that the transformations of this image express the enormous attempt to come to terms with death as a "basic condition of existence", and that in the course of this attempt aspects and stages of the differentiation and growth of the psyche are represented by images expressing complex attitudes. There is no question of intellectual recognition, nor of the development of either consciousness or the unconscious on its own but, rather, of the unfolding of the *whole man*, in whose life both consciousness and the unconscious play their part. We might speak of the religious growth of the soul. The encounter with death and the work which the psyche does on the experience may be the one starting-point of religious development, or it may be one of many points of departure, but in any case it touches on a crucial matter which cannot be evaded today any more than in earlier times. Thus we understand the myth of Ceram to mean that only those who are psychically ready to pass through the ninefold gate and accept contact with death continue as human beings, for the myth itself makes it clear that what is required is not merely the acceptance and affirmation of the bare fact of death, but the inclusion of this fact in life as well. The myth says that when death is included in life man is taken out of his limited existence in the present and confronted with the reality of change and of a complete transformation which, however frightening, is fundamentally fruitful. It hints that what is specifically human is the basic feeling that one exists in past and future as well as in the present: in other words, that although one is the same person that one was, one has been transformed, and is in the midst of further transformation leading forward into the unknown. This is the fate of man which is, at the same time, the order

135

of the world. This specifically human feeling is bound up with the "knowledge" (not necessarily conscious) that death and life belong together, and is impossible without it.

These things stated so long ago in the myth of Ceram are sometimes brought home to us in an impressive way in modern psychotherapeutic practice. Inner crises of transformation are often foreshadowed by dreams in which the patient is confronted by death, either directly or in the form of an archaic image. Such an experience of dying is potentially an expression of the full reality of life in that it symbolizes transformation, but it only bears fruit if the dreamer can go beyond the purely negative aspect of the death-image which does no more than create panic; and this "going beyond" is not a question of intellectual insight, but of sufficient maturity to accept death within life as it is actually lived. A neurotic is sick because he rejects transformation "like death", and because he will not give up his fantasy of security and changelessness even though he may suffer severely as a result, and even though he senses its falsity at a deep level.[1] If, in the course of treatment, the rigid attitude begins to break down the first result is that the patient feels delivered over to death, and this is why dreams involving an encounter with death so often point to the beginning of transformation. What this means is that when the *reality of life* forces transformation upon a man he encounters the *reality of death*, so that he has to come to terms with both together.

It is a fact that many modern people have actually repressed death. Of course they know about it intellectually, but they are dominated by a deep sense of the potential "omnipotence" of science, and regard death as a thing which really *ought not* to happen.[2] Such an attitude

[1] In Künkel's words: "It seems to him that only the psychosclerotic-rigid attitude to life and his fellow men which he accepted on the basis of his training in early childhood guarantees the security of his ego which for him is (unconsciously) the highest, indeed, the only end of life." This is as true of an hysteric who tries to preserve his ego unchanged by "possessing", as for the compulsive neurotic who "avoids" all inner change by rigid legalism. It is equally true of depression, phobia and obsessional or anxiety neurosis in so far as these lead to retreat.

[2] For example, in 1954 an otherwise laudable work was announced under the title, *Via Triumphalis. Nobel Prizewinners in the Struggle against Death*. A series of articles appeared in 1956 on *Der besiegte Tod*—"The Conquest of Death" in the *Frankfurter Illustrierte*: there have been many other publications with equally sensational titles, going as far as *The Nuisance of Dying*.

goes half way to meet the neurotic's unconscious need for assurance, and it is a remarkably close parallel to the earliest attitude of primitive man who "repressed" death by fleeing from a dead man in panic horror.

Contemporary dreams often express the encounter with death in images which, when carefully examined, can be seen to correspond to one or another archaic and mythological image of death, and this leads us to consider whether such dreams, like the mythic images, give expression to specific phases of psychic development. We believe that in the course of a great number of treatments we have been able to see dreams of this kind arise, sometimes with long intervals between, sometimes in series, and that they reveal an autonomous development which has a rough correspondence to the mythological unfolding considered in Part 1. This, however, is only true when the development is not disturbed by the imposition of a restrictive and exclusive interpretation concerned with purely biographical and instinct-determined events. It is true that the therapist should not neglect these things (particularly in the early stages), but he should also be able to allow the feeling of reverence for the numinous which arises in connection with dreams of this kind. At the same time an explicit interpretation or a preoccupation with and stress on the numinous aspect of such dreams is hardly necessary, at any rate not until a stage is reached when therapist and patient together can look back over an extended development. Such a survey can give the patient a strong experience of illumination.

To the extent that they apply, these observations can help the therapist to accompany the patient on his journey to maturity with deeper understanding. If need be he can discover from such dreams (with a certain objectivity) the direction in which the patient's personality is growing. They may also provide criteria for the genuineness of a religious development.

The exposition which we undertook in Part 1 can be regarded as an extended "amplification" (in Jung's sense) of the dreams which we shall discuss, and can be referred to in every case. The examples of dreams are not offered in order to give accounts of treatment; what we wish to illustrate is the heterogeneous character and the obscure way in which the death-dreams of a great number of very different patients interlock when they are related by means of mythical association. Biographical details have to be kept to a minimum, and other archetypal aspects (i.e. those not directly related to the death-image) which will often be very clear to the expert will usually not be mentioned. Naturally both these things (the working through of the patient's life-story and the discussion of symbols other than those connected with death) were taken into account in the actual treatment.

The general arrangement of the dreams is determined by the development of the death-image as that was described in the first part. That is, they are arranged in a sequence which broadly corresponds to that development. At the same time we have also tried to show how the image of death gradually deepened and unfolded in the dreams of an individual, and in order to do this we have sometimes referred from one dream to others which are presented in different parts of the sequence.

It is a fact that the struggle to elucidate and accept the death-image is an essential aspect for many patients, even though they may not be aware of it themselves, and it is part of our purpose to make this more generally known. When one understands the nature of the death-dreams and sets them within the context of the treatment as a whole one sees that they are associated with an ever-increasing courage and an increasing readiness to face crises involving the transformation of the personality. Moreover, one also sees that they express stages of a growth which is fundamentally religious. These "encounters with death" are not merely expressions of infantile anxiety, nor only concerned with the dissolution of petrified "part-egos". These things are involved, but in the end it is a matter of the transformation of the whole man, brought about at the same time as it is expressed by a growing acceptance of death as a condition of life.

What we have in mind was expressed by a thirty-year-old patient most impressively. After a death-dream he said: "I became aware of an entirely new basic feeling, which I can only formulate in the phrase, 'Thy will be done!'—I became aware within me of a perfect assent to the incomprehensible . . ."

12. Dreams 1: Repression of Death, Flight and Initial Acceptance

THE first dream sequence has three parts. The sequence as a whole illustrates death-dreams in general, and the first two parts shows how archaic death-images may be touched on, as it were from a distance, and so often be hard to understand.

The dreamer was about fifty-five. He was educated at a village school and had been employed as a semi-skilled worker in various trades, until he was retired with a pension because of tuberculosis contracted during the war. This was about ten years before the dreams. His condition varied from time to time and sometimes deteriorated, partly because he had an unconscious fear that if he got well he would lose his pension and have to face what would, from any point of view, be a very difficult new start. We shall not discuss the meaning of these dreams for the man himself, nor their significance for his treatment.

The three dreams occurred in the same night and it is only the third that is openly connected with death. Since it is a well-known fact that dreams which follow one another in one night usually deal with the same question (often with increasing distinctness) it is possible to assume that the first two also allude to death. The dreamer's report runs:

Dream 1a. "I am walking with my wife beside a field of ripe corn ... Two masks are lying or half-hanging on corn stalks. I go towards them. I wanted to put on one of the masks, to slip into it ... but it wouldn't stretch and I put it down again ..."

Dream 1b. "I am standing on a platform like that of a goods lift. Near me on my left is a huge, great ... shoulder-high dog with a huge head ... I stroke him, but he doesn't really like it ... he growled a little ... but his master who was on his left does not regard this as being so tragic and says nothing about it. My wife was still next to me, on my right, on firm ground."

Dream 1c. "I am standing in front of a man in medieval clothes (black uniform worn in Napoleon's day) with my wife (who is dressed in black). The man cross-examines us. Then he makes an announcement: six men . . . including me . . . are sentenced to death . . . The man strokes my wife on the neck with his hand and consoles her to some extent . . . Someone else gives an order and the builder's hut in which we are standing falls to pieces, and we find ourselves in the open. Six of us are standing one behind the other, I am among them . . . and so is my friend X . . . Someone shoots a child's water pistol from behind us . . . they all wept because they were shot. I am surprised that despite the fact that I had helped in capturing the criminals I am to be shot too . . . a shot rings out and I feel a stab of pain . . ." (Original record of the dreams.)

One can see a structural likeness between 1b and 1c at first glance. In each one something is "not so tragic": or, one might say, something does not turn out to have results as serious as those that the dreamer expected. The idea of anxiety is expressed, but the feeling of anxiety is not followed up with a full realization of the thing feared. The dog makes the dreamer anxious, but it does not bite; the shooting takes place, but seems to be done with a water pistol. There is also something similar in 1a, for even though there is no clear anxiety the dreamer first picks up the mask and tries to put it on, and then puts it down again.

It is natural to ask if one can find a connection between the dreams 1a and 1b and the death which occurs in 1c. It is not immediately obvious, but in view of our previous discussion we can say that the more-than-life-size and dangerous dog with its huge head (and, by implication, huge mouth) in 1b recalls the numerous occasions in the myths on which the Death-Demon has a dog form. When we turn to the mask and the ripe cornfield of 1a we are again reminded of many cult customs, folk-tales and myths. The mask crops up in the Percht Race and in the cult of Dionysos, and we know that it is related to the Cap of Invisibility which is the mark of the Shades—the "Hidden Ones" who are representatives of the world of Death. Ripe corn and ears of corn are symbols of the unity of Death and Life and of transformation, whether they occur in folk-tales of Frau Holle, Egyptian harvest customs, the Osiris cult or the Eleusinian Mysteries of Demeter.

It can be said, then, that there are features of dreams 1a and 1b which can be recognized as archaic images of death, and that they express the same thing as 1c, but do so in a concealed way at the same time as they provide additional shades of meaning.[1] The first two dreams also show that one can only understand such dreams rightly if one attends to them in a particular way, and has the necessary knowledge. Four other examples are intended to show the various forms in which death-dreams occur to modern people and their meaning for the dreamers.

There are many dreams which are concerned with people who are dead but do not introduce the idea of death at all. They are often so banal and cheerful that it would be easy to think that they had no significance so far as this study is concerned. The following dream of this type recurred (with many variations) during the early stages of the treatment of a woman of fifty-five (cf. Dream 50, pp. 203–4).

Dream 2. "I am having coffee with Aunt B and Uncle A. We are in their old flat. We are sitting at the table, talking. It is very jolly . . . When I wake up I feel surprised because both have been dead for years, but in the dream it was just as if they were alive and I felt no surprise at all."

Dreams of this kind do not necessarily express a neurotic attitude. They often occur with healthy people, and frequently indicate continuing psychic connection with those who have died. If they occur soon after a death they may be compensatory and easy to understand in relation to the real life situation. On the other hand if they occur *repeatedly* during treatment (and, it seems, especially if they do so early on) they should be given special attention. It is just the banal cheerfulness which is frequently found in them which suggests that they are connected with a deep repression of a death complex. The dreamer has, as it were, achieved the attitude of the young man who set out "to learn to shudder". Because he was not yet touched by the tremendum and "not yet a human being" he laughingly greeted the dead man in the castle as his "little cousin" and invited him to play with him. There

---

[1] It should be said that these dreams were made available by a colleague who was not familiar with the ideas put forward in this book. This means that one cannot account for the archaic images of death by supposing that they are due to the therapist's (conscious or unconscious) influence on the patient. They are the autonomous creations of the dreamer's unconscious.

are hints of such an attitude in the dream, and it was in actual fact rooted in an almost convulsive rejection of the idea of death, and especially of the idea of transformation which it includes. The patient suffered from severe depression bringing with it the danger of suicide, which had been touched off by the approach of the climacteric. In such a case one can understand this kind of dream as a regression to that total ignorance of death which comes before the "initial flight" discussed in Chapter 1. The only thing which suggests that the suppression has not been wholly successful is the "surprise" which the patient felt when she woke up: this "surprise" suggests that there was a faint sense that the attitude was "wrong", or in some way incorrect. As the patient associated freely to these dreams and the people and situations in them, so the character of the dreams changed. The surprise was taken into the dream, and in the middle of such a dream she would become aware that the people she was associating with had been dead a long time; this awareness was sometimes accompanied by astonishment, sometimes by horror. It was in this way that she was slowly able to come near to the reality of death.[1]

The next dream was that of a twenty-six-year-old woman barrister of great promise, and one might have thought that her dreams were compensatory rather than regressive if she had not developed severe neurotic symptoms when her father died the year before. Until he died she had had a very close relationship with her father, and each had taken close interest in the other's work. She had been completely healthy before her father's death except for a slight tendency to hoarseness, but afterwards this hoarseness resisted all treatment and she began to have frequent and severe anginal spasms, fits involving suffocation and hysterical constriction of the throat.

The specialist recommended her for psychotherapeutic treatment, and when this began, dreams in which she was with her father as he was when he was alive occurred more frequently than any others: "It was as if he hadn't died at all." This was actually a case of regression to the original condition of "not-knowing", although there was also

[1] This process was particularly impressive for me when I looked back at it, and this was one of the first treatments which (when it was ended) brought home to me the peculiar significance and gradual unfolding of the death-image.

an element of an almost defiant rejection of what she actually did know. As a matter of fact this "not-knowing" is not the same thing as the "pre-human" ignorance: in contrast to this, like all regression, it has a fictitious and illusory character. It is a "not-knowing" which the dreamer always knows ought not to be allowed because it is a denial of reality. This means that it is possible to understand such defiant "not-wanting-to-know" (which contrasts with the purely repressive attitude of the previous dream) as a kind of *flight-reaction*, the "initial flight" described in Chapter 1. This explains the symptoms of suffocation which represent "reality", for through them the patient experiences the ghostly, formless anxiety in *physical terms*. One must add that the experience is also "ego-falsified" (Künkel's phrase) as are all neurotic experiences: the tremendum is divested of its horror, and all that seems to be left is sheer instinctual fear of death.

After a time the dreams changed their character and shudderingly approached the *death* of the father, and only after this had happened the *death-scene* was experienced in a dream, not as it really occurred but with exaggerated horror—

Dream 3. It was in the clinic. My father sat dying in an armchair—not, as actually happened, in bed. He was speaking out loud and saying something which was strange and completely incomprehensible to me. I couldn't understand a word, and I was quite desperate. I felt that whatever the cost he would have to have an operation so that everything in his brain could be jerked back into position. In the end I thought, "No! it probably has to be as it is, and father mustn't be disturbed now."

Strange as it may seem this experience of seeing her father so deranged as to be quite unlike himself (that is, hidden by a strange disguise) came to have a calming effect on the patient. From that moment the restrictions and restraints in her speech and the false attitude to reality which were the symptoms of her trouble cleared up completely. They were no longer needed. In the terms of the myth of Ceram one might say that through her first genuine encounter with death the patient has "become human".

The dreams of a twenty-eight-year-old Jewish woman show the psychological encounter with death in a rather different way. Her parents had been deported to Poland and murdered by the S.S. ten years before, and she herself had only just escaped. Difficulties in her marriage had brought about a serious and chronic illness: in simple terms it could be said that she was unable to accept her destiny as a woman. Medical treatment was supplemented by psychotherapy and in the course of this she dreamt the following four scenes in one night:

Dream 4a. "My mother is lying asleep in bed at home. She is covered up to the neck. She looks young and very beautiful. Yet at the same time I know she is dead."

Dream 4b. "Then my father brings me a lovely blue dress. I know that my father is dead and I am horrified. I refuse the present."

Dream 4c. "Suddenly my father is a ghostly skeleton that wants to embrace me and take me away with him. I know that it is Death."

Dream 4d. "Finally I see a Christian funeral. There are many people at the cemetery. There is a clergyman with a cross and there are the next of kin. The mother is weeping uncontrollably at her daughter's death."

Even in her dreams the patient knows that her parents are really dead. She is already both affirming and denying the fact, and this makes it possible for a change to the realization of the actuality of death to take place so quickly. Yet even so it takes place by stages. Her horrified resistance to the dress the dead man gives her to wear recalls the *motif* of flight and also the idea, which is common in legends and fairy-tales, that if one accepts gifts from the dead one will die oneself. The scene which follows confirms, in a sufficiently gruesome way, that the dreamer feels herself to be as much the victim of death as her parents—something which is true for each one of us! She cannot accept this, is horrified and struggles against it. Yet the fourth scene hints at a first tentative move, still deep in the unconscious, towards assimilating the experience of death, and it also bears witness to the aspect of transformation. In her free associations she said that she had often watched Christian funerals when she was a child at home, and that on one occasion she saw a *mother* who had died when her daughter was born carried by in a glass coffin. The dream was a "complementary inversion" in that there it was the *daughter* who had died, and taken together with the real event it says: "Daughters die and mothers mourn them; mothers die because daughters are born." It contains a distant allusion to something which is given mature and clear form in the Demeter-Kore myth at what, psychologically speaking, is a much later stage.

Without giving full biographical details it can be said that this patient could not accept the life-responsibilities of marriage and love because she unconsciously identified mother and daughter, and had an unconscious fixation on her father. To pass from the status of daughter to that of wife and mother (to make the transition from blossoming to fruit-bearing) would be an open step towards her own death—mothers die, daughters live. She has to make this transition consciously which means that death becomes fully real to her as the destiny of herself and her neighbour and, in the end, of everyone. At the same time she has to recognize that this destiny includes a transforming element.

A thirty-five-year-old literary historian dreamt that he had more or less trivial meetings both with his brother who had been killed in the war and with his parents who had been dead for many years. These dreams went on for months, and in the dreams it was as though brother and parents were still alive. The mystery and horror of death was brought home to him by the next dream, and he was able to see that the meetings in the previous dreams were largely "frivolous", a game played with his eyes shut.

Dream 5. "A young woman was leading my brother (who died in the war), my sister and me along a path through the wood to the Spa-Hotel. We spoke about the strange fact that her mother's death-day coincided with that of our own . . . then she says, 'We will play the little *joke* once more.' Now she leads my sister and my brother to the meadow which was bordered by the wood. She gives a word of command and they run bolt upright to the road; at the same time a tremendous force carries and drives me uphill and down dale along the narrow woodland path. I get to the meeting-place first, and my brother is being driven along beside me. Where the path runs into the town there is an American soldiers' tent: I bump up against the tent and now have to find my way back (alone) crawling painfully on the ground. It is very strenuous."

The "joke" (on the mother's death-day!) suddenly led to the uncanny experience of being driven to an inexorable collision with the reality of life here and now, and at the same time it seems that the dead brother is driven on and away. The following night he had two dreams in which a spontaneous encounter with death brought home to him the fact that it was a reality in his own existence:

Dream 6a. "I am lying in bed. I touch my wife's cheek. It is icy cold, and with mortal terror I know she is dead. I wake up."

Dream 6b. "In the same night, however, I see myself sitting on a round table as a horrible abortion like a gnome, the back of my head is large and bald and my legs are directly connected to it without there being a body. I know that I am at the same time a corpse and a kind of infant —a sort of changeling."

We should note that in the first part death is seen as something that "lies next to me", that is, it is known as the death of "the other": the neighbour. The act of waking from this dream is an actual *flight* which exactly corresponds to the panic flight of the Senoi and Takkui mentioned in Chapter 1. It is only after this (and yet *immediately* after) that the experience of his own death breaks upon the dreamer. He sees his own death before him in a wholly demonic form, and we may remember that we have already come across the changeling as the evil death-child in the Frau Holle-Percht legends and as the divine-demonic death-infant in the Eskimo legend.[1]

The actual problem of the patient is a mother-fixation which has not been resolved by marriage and this note sounds through the three dreams. The regression to childhood is clear enough in Dreams 5 and 6b, but the most important things for us are the uncanny (almost numinous) feeling of being driven and blown away in 5, and the terrifying encounter with himself as the death-infant in 6b. The dreamer is an abandoned infant exposed to death because his second mother (his wife) "is dead". Yet at the same time he is a changeling and so himself a shade and identical with death the killer as the changelings which Percht brought so often were. Yet according to the tales, if one treats the changeling in the right way Percht will change it back for the healthy, living and growing child; and the Eskimo legend says that when the death-child has grown strong enough on the bloody sacrifices of the man he orders him to work and live. Horrible as this dream figure can be it can still be understood as the first moment of transformation.

The following dream of a forty-five-year-old doctor is very different, yet in its own way impressive. He was Medical Superintendent of a

[1] Cf. Chapter 11, p. 122 and Chapter 5, p. 62.

department of a large military hospital and although of high intel-ligence his basic attitude was depressive: this meant that he had always had an (unconscious) need to shield his delicate sensibility from the violent shocks which beset him.

Dream 7. "It is pretty dark. Three men in strange clothes and of strange appearance—archaic, reminding one of the straining figures in Assyrian lion hunts—stand together somewhere in the room. One of them points, half at me and yet at the same time past me to a grave. (Was there a cemetery there?) As he points he says a name which I do not clearly understand . . ."

The strange, mysterious men point to the grave, the "devouring earth" which hides the dead man. The victim is named but at the same time his identity remains hidden. Is it an unknown person? A friend? Or the dreamer himself?

Associating to this dream the patient recalled the name of an early acquaintance, and then the association became blocked. At last a number of friends and acquaintances of his youth occurred to him all of whom had died early and unexpectedly—some, including the first that he recalled, by suicide. At another time he had said that the earliest impression of his life was that of his deceased mother lying on her death-bed. When his mother died he was two so that he had taken in the picture naturally without terror or comprehension, and all he could now remember was a picture of angels hanging over the door and having been told that his mother now lived with them. There was not even the reflection of an emotion (a memory of his grandmother's tears for example) associated with this scene, even though it impressed the child so deeply that it became fixed in his mind at the first conscious impression of his life. This makes all the more impressive the dumb reference of the three archaic men to the grave. As a doctor the patient *knew* well enough about death, but he unconsciously defended himself against the *experience* of it—that is, against the inexorable fact of the incursion of another reality which darkens life in a horrid way. This was because as he awakened to it he could at first only regard that reality as a darkening and as a pre-monition of something strange and hidden.

If they are to succeed in feeling in their own existence something of the greater illumination which is brought by the consciousness of death men have to dare to pass through a long and painful psychological development. A further stage of this development is reflected in the dreams of modern men by a specific class of dreams which are usually understood from a very different point of view.

13. Dreams 2: Killing

DREAMS of killing form a well-defined group that has always attracted the attention of psychotherapists. Even more important, it is usual for them to cause the dreamer himself deep disturbance: what he does in the dream seems dreadful and repulsive to him, and he claims that he can find no traces whatever of any impulse in himself to behave in such a way.

The psychotherapist usually regards such dreams as giving expression to unconscious, dammed-up aggression, "cannibalistic", sadistic, sexual and œdipal urges. Such interpretations are often (but not always) important for recognizing the specific form of the neurosis, understanding the symptoms and, most of all, for working through the patient's problem (the "actual" analysis), and they should not be negelected, especially during the early part of the treatment. On the other hand Harald Schultz-Hencke's warning is of special importance in this connection: the psychotherapist, he says, must always keep the abundance of the possibilities in mind—in this case, specifically, the other ones—and never get stuck with a single one. Many symptoms, and the relationship between dreams of killing and the actual problems of the patient in particular, enable the man who understands to see that the problems are set against the *background* of the patient's "*liability to death*", and that it is really this with which the unconscious is trying to come to terms and assimilate, even though it is still expressed in primitive forms. Dreams of killing play an important role in this connection, and the exposition in Chapter 2 is relevant here.

The three following dreams were dreamt by a thirty-eight-year-old writer whose ability to work was completely crippled at the time, even though his style was acknowledged as outstanding and he had great poetic gifts. These more sharply defined dreams followed a large number of formless anxiety dreams and coincided with the beginning of a change in his psychic attitude.

Dream 8. "I have been summoned before a court-martial—or may it have been not me but a wartime comrade? I am innocent, but am to be shot all the same. Or is it that I am to be in charge of the other man's execution?"

Dream 9. "I am in a court-yard or in front of the entrance to a building. I have a sword and pierce through an American standing in the entrance with it. I was particularly impressed by the way the murdered man reared up as he died."

Dream 10. "Two men are to be sacrificed in a court-yard. I am there and although I am convulsed with fearful horror I do not run away but make myself look on."

At a superficial level these three dreams were bound up with the actual symptoms of the patient, and the treatment had to be concerned with this aspect of them. The continuing influence of "masochistic-sadistic attitudes" in early childhood made it impossible for him to have conscious awareness of certain guilt-complexes and to work through them. In these dreams his rigidity which had resisted all transformation appeared in the centre of the picture. The unconscious forced him to confront the task of accepting his guilt and letting himself be executed by himself. It is probable that he also had to kill his "inner American"—that is, according to his own association, the "success-at-all-costs-man"—who appears to block the way into the *interior* of his house. All this would mean giving up the security provided by his rigidity and surrendering his previous life—"sacrificing" himself and "dying".

At the same time we can detect the basic psychic process lying behind these "real" problems. That is we can see the subtle way in which the dreamer's feeling for existence and attitude to death are changing. At first there is the simple, instinctive fear of death, which is yet no longer *merely* instinctive since the revolt is not simply that of an animal (animals do not revolt in this way) but that of a man who feels that being innocent he must yet suffer the punishment which a "court" imposes on him (cf. here Dream 1c). In a moral sense man is not guilty and deserving of death because he has broken a law, it is simply that he *owes his life to death*.[1] The dreamer's unconscious is dimly aware

---

[1] Cf. Chapter 9 where it is pointed out that "Skuld" is both a Norn (a weaver of life) and a demon of death.

of this, and expresses it by saying in the dream that it might just as well be the fate of "any comrade you like" as his own (these were his own associations)—and it may even be that he himself is the killer, the one who carries out the sentence upon the other. The dream says clearly that the sentence is not brought about by guilt.

Dream 9 does not have the same ambiguity. The dreamer *is* the one who kills, and killing with the sword has something archaic about it for the killer kills directly, with his own hand, and not indirectly as he would by shooting, for example. The victim "rears up" in a way which echoes the dreamer's own "rearing up" (in feeling) against injustice in the previous dream and, like every dead man, he is a sacrifice.[1] It is not said either in this dream or the next to whom the sacrifice is offered, but in Dream 10 it is made clear that the sacrifice is necessary since though "convulsed by horror" the dreamer feels compelled to stay and watch.

Such dream-events can throw light on the *original* psychological meaning of sacrifice. In sacrifice man solemnly executes the decree of a hidden fate which he experiences as absolute and unalterable. In this way killing takes on a new solemnity in that by executing the necessary act of sacrifice man submits his whole being to the tremendum: it is as though he brings himself "into phase" with that which is transcendent and ineluctable. We may notice in passing that when atropaic, petitionary or expiatory ideas become associated with sacrifice it is in danger of going off the rails and sinking back (at least in part) into magic; that is, of becoming the expression of an illusory and futile belief that man is ultimately master of his fate, and so a means of escape from death.

These three dreams can be seen as representing three stages in the identification of the dreamer with the "killing being", as the one who executes the fate of death.[2] The first dream (8) includes a kind of commissioning: "Since you and all men ('any comrade you like') must die, you must also kill." The second dream (9) expresses the execution of this commission: the third (10) defines the killing as a sacrifice and relates it to the larger context of life. It must be admitted that all this is brought out by hints and that it is by no means consciously understood by the dreamer; at the same time it is significant as a token

[1] The German word *Opfer* means both "victim" and "sacrifice." *Trans.*
[2] Cf. the exposition in Chapter 2.

of psychic development and the beginning of a reorientation to the reality of life.

It is likely that sacrifice of some kind is also the subject of three dreams (following closely upon one another) of a thirty-year-old assistant lecturer in philosophy. The patient's neurotic symptoms took the form of a deep-rooted inability to enter into personal relationships, especially with women. This inability was bound up with the fact that the patient had an unresolved fixation on a possessive mother, and did not have a father to provide a pattern of masculinity. In a phase of despair brought about by his inner isolation he plunged violently into a scientific work. In effect he was saying: "I will *sacrifice* myself to *science* and give up life, contact and instinctual satisfaction!" and this fantasy ran counter to his whole yearning for a life which would fulfil his deepest needs.

In order to make clear the manifold relationships of the following dreams we need to say that as a small child the dreamer had once been attacked by a large dog: many years later he was given a little dog as a playmate (he was an only child). His mother took possession of the dog for herself and when it died after some years she behaved as though she were "mad with pain". Moreover, not long before the first dream (11) the patient had read an article giving a sensational presentation of vivisection and of Pavlov's experiments on dogs.

Dream 11a. "I had passed a long window in a passage leading to a dark cellar. It was like the window of an underground workshop. Through the window I saw a kind of laboratory in which it seemed that experiments with dogs were being made. The dogs were suspended on some kind of apparatus and partly cut open. This was loathsome and it repelled me so much that I did not really want to write it down at all. It was like a kind of defilement. Afterwards I was aware of a great loathing—but the loathing was not really directed against myself, it was rather against the general state of affairs, that it is 'like that' in the world."

He also remembered two small dream fragments from the same night:

Dream 11b. "I was in a woody neighbourhood and had a dog with me. I had to kill this dog and it was specified that I must strangle it with my bare hands. I tried as hard as I could but could not do it."

Dream 11c. "I am making up a medicine of which pepsin is the most important ingredient in a kind of cellar-dispensary. There is a friendly elderly nurse nearby: she might be the manageress of the dispensary." The following strange dream came four days later:

Dream 12. "Professor X lay on a platform in a large room like the lobby of the University: he was posed like a memorial figure and gave a lecture. His body was opened up, skin and muscle integuments were exposed and flowed over and round the dais. This was in no sense a demonstration of a lecture on his body, it was rather that he was representing himself as a sacrifice in the cause of science. It seemed pretty theatrical to me."

The motif of digestion introduced by the pepsin in 11c came out clearly in two more dreams which he had within less than a week. This is the second of them:

Dream 13. "I am with a classmate in a hut in the mountains. There are some magazines lying about and in them I found some recent work by Heidegger. One was entitled: 'Digestion as Reciprocal Action'. I wanted to make a climbing tour with a certain friend, but nothing came of it . . . Then I was concerned with the magazines again . . . Then I was climbing upwards in a zig-zag on a perfect motorway—a technical miracle indeed. Heidegger was supposed to be somewhere above. He had gone on ahead . . . a marvellous view over a broad, fantastic landscape. Suddenly as I went up there was a little boy beside me. He stood, without holding on to anything, on a breastwork of the wall of the road and I took it that there was a gentle slope on the other side. Then I saw that the wall dropped precipitately hundreds of feet into empty space. I thought that I should really have to look after the boy, but then I felt: 'One does not have to do that at all, he stands secure in his simplicity.' Then we went on together . . ."

Of these dreams only 11a, 11b and 12 belong to our topic in its narrower sense. Yet if we take them all together they are an excellent example of the unceasing effort with which the unconscious struggles towards clarification and orientation and finally for transformation through the image of death.

It should not be necessary to say that the dream picture in 11a contains a reference to the dreamer's attitude to his analysis, but the other two dreams of the same night show that this is not where the main emphasis lies. The associations which bring up the conflict and the biographical facts point to the "sacrifice" of the libido which is unconsciously directed to the mother and, in all probability, to the *sacrifice of the mother herself* (one could add, of the killing aspect of the mother) which the dreamer still lacks strength to carry out. Deeper yet can be seen, in accordance with the primeval images, the all-embracing and transforming significance of sacrifice itself. In Dream 12 this idea is tested to see if it is genuine, and in 11c and 13 it is brought into relationship with digestion, the thought being that what was experienced as arousing almost physical nausea in dreams 11a and 11b has to be assimilated. In this connection it may be remembered that in the myth of Ceram (and in many other myths) killing appears as the necessary preliminary to the growth of food.

Although it was not at first clear to the dreamer that 11a and 11b were connected with the idea of sacrificial killing the unconscious seemed to know about it, since the word "sacrifice" had turned up as a kind of cue several times shortly before and after the dreams. The peculiar idea that the dreamer has to throttle the dog clearly recalls sacrificial customs among Palaeo-Asiatic tribes and in other places. It is, in fact, often the case that no blood must flow in the sacrifice: for example, among the Gilyaks of Lower Amur strangling is the ritual prescribed for the sacrifice of dogs, and among related tribes like the Koryaks many dogs are killed as sacrifices and hung in the settlements, beside roads and (particularly) in graveyards—a sight to horrify Europeans. The Teutons also sacrifice dogs as well as horses and these dogs were hung round the place of sacrifice, often in great numbers. Some of these sacrifices were made with a knife, some by hanging or strangling. Thus we may surmise that in Dreams 11a and 11b there is a reference to a kind of sacrificial ritual which was not even comprehended by the unconscious—a ritual of coming to terms with death through being a killer oneself.

It is certainly true that the dogs hung up underground at the beginning of the first dream were "victims of science", and that this is the idea of sacrifice in a rational and somewhat shallow form even though such a sacrifice is rejected by the patient in Dream 12: this makes it even more significant that in 11b the dreamer has to go into the wood and, without reference to "science", carry out the primeval sacrifice of the animal of the underworld which is also the animal that was most clearly associated with his mother in his own life. It appears that all this is refused by his stomach or, at least, that he needs assistance from the "magic kitchen" (possibly presided over by the Earth-Mother) to strengthen his "digestive powers". Finally in Dream 13 his philosophical consciousness offers the enigma, "Digestion=Reciprocal Action", and this must mean here: "The living are killed (by us as digestors) and the killed become the living (in us as digestors)." In Dream 13 the wheel comes full circle when the wonderful boy appears as a companion. This boy appears in the course of the climb up the road which is a triumph of technology, and although he has no concern with technology one does not have to fear for him above the giddy abyss. The recognition (digestion) of sacrifice as a necessity of life opens up a completely new perspective and a new possibility of living—the possibility of walking above the abyss without fear. The possibility emerged for the dreamer for the first time in this dream, and was then repeated and formulated in more and more differentiated ways in other dreams. It is true in this as in all other cases that so long as a thing is only worked out in the unconscious it remains no more than a possibility—yet it gives rise to an inner task which demands that the possibility should be actually worked out in conscious doing and living.

The next dream shows particularly well the peculiar sense of a necessity, almost a commission to kill. The dreamer was a married journalist of about twenty-eight: an intellectual who had developed one-sidedly. He came of a family which had been victimized by the Nazis; several relatives had been murdered and his own life threatened, and these experiences had influenced his early development. Later on his natural aggression was diverted to form far-sighted desires for the reform of the world, based on an exalted standpoint of spiritually conceived ethics. This was the result of premature tendencies to sublimation. For a time there had even been a danger that he might lose all contact with reality. Not long before his treatment began he had dreamt that he was concerned to rescue a criminal Nazi boss from a mob that was persecuting him, and this showed how deeply his own aggressive hatred and death-wishes were repressed. This repression led to a repression of death itself rationalized in a peculiar moral way: "Nobody in the world ought to die at all!"

During treatment the formless terror of death came more and more distinctly to his consciousness. As this threat to life took concrete shape in the dreams panic flight was at first the answer. After a while the dreamer struggled with the threat and so learnt both to accept death and also to defend himself. Eventually he had dreams of killing and the two given here are selected from four which followed one another very closely. They are no longer directly concerned with the threat of death for himself, but in relation to his life their topic is release from a possessive Mother-Image through the killing—and finally transformation—of an immature Sister-Anima which was practically identical with it. We should also consider two other things: the explicit reference to the "vital necessity" of death in life in the first dream, and the motif of dismemberment in the second.

Dream 14. "I find myself with many people in the streets somewhere round the Town Hall: there is a Carnival Procession. I intend to appear in the procession as a clown. I am with acquaintances, probably women. Somehow or other it does not seem proper that I should go on playing the clown. With two others I take off my costume again . . . the scene becomes more serious . . . I have a solemn intention . . . I have two male companions and I am inciting them to commit murder. A girl is to be killed . . . it is in an area in front of a castle . . . then I suddenly become conscious of what I have taken on myself—*murder: however necessary it may seem* we may not kill a human being. Full of an ultimate despair I try to make this clear to the two lively[1] lads whom I have just incited to the act. I use all my power of persuasion but cannot influence them. In despair I realize what I have done—the brutal young men insist on committing the murder which they would not have considered if I had not egged them on to do it. One of the two murderers seems to be my old school-mate X." (X had frequently appeared in dreams as the dreamer's primitive shadow.)

The dream was set back two months from the time it occurred to bring it into carnival time, and this may be regarded as a hidden reference to the Dionysiac ecstasy of life under the aspect of death and even of the ecstasy of killing in itself (cf. Chap. 2).[2] In this dream the

[1] "Vital" would be more accurate and carries the right sense but is hardly English (*Trans.*).

[2] The role of clown or fool in which the dreamer appears at first is also revealing. Jung has pointed out many times that the fool often occurs in dreams just before the new insight breaks through. One can compare with this the rope-dancer and the fool in Nietzsche's *Zarathustra*. A similar process was

"vital necessity" of killing appears in a peculiar way. It seems that the necessity was conceptually understood, but that this understanding was permeated by horror at the act itself. The deed is done despite the horror, even if it can only be done by the shadow-figure—the "vital ego" of the dreamer. At the same time the dreamer has to take responsibility for the deed, for the time to dress up as a clown has now passed.

In the dream the following night the dreamer goes with "the girl" over a dangerous dam which crosses a valley:
Dream 15. "The girl fell off the dam. I tried to rescue her and drag her out, but could not. She will probably be sucked into the turbine and dismembered."

That is murder again, even though disguised as an accident. The motif of the dismemberment of the dead comes up again later on—and as is often the case it comes up formulated in a new and more developed way (Dream 29).

A higher official of forty-five reported that at twenty he once dreamt that he murdered his mother with a dagger. This gave him a violent feeling of moral shock. It occurred about the time that he experienced his first love relationship. Some months after his mother died when he was forty-five he dreamt:

recently reported in a nine-year-old boy, although it was not a case of dreams but of a realization in fantasy play and actual behaviour. This child had been kept completely infantile (even in speech) by a widowed mother, and in the course of a play-analysis conducted with the greatest patience and empathy he finally demanded and got from the woman educational counsellor an account of how children originate. His first response was physical, in the form of a very strong need to urinate. After that he painted a remarkable picture: water flowed out from a white oven, and there were fire and flames in a black well. He called this picture, "the upside down world, discovered by X. Y. in . . . 1953". The session ended with an unusual and liberating outburst of tenderness towards the counsellor.

In the next session he addressed all the "darling-bugbear figures" of the Punch and Judy show (particularly Death and the Devil) "foolishly", in the truest sense of the word, as (for example) "Saint-Devil", "Doctor-Death". This phase of the breakthrough of new knowledge of the world soon passed into steady growth and recovery. One may note that in this case the simultaneous encounter with Birth and Death seems to have been the effective central consideration in the boy's development

Dream 16. "I am on a dark plain and I see my mother's coffin in front of me. It is open and she is lying in it. There is a knife in my hand and I cut the corpse into a lot of little pieces. I have an unspeakable feeling of horror, and yet I know that what I am doing is somehow necessary . . ."

The dream of dismemberment brought back the earlier dream to the patient's mind in a vivid way. It appears to represent an enhancement of the killing, which is probably the significance of the second dream of the previous patient as well. On the basis of the total psychic situation it does not seem that in either case an essential part was played by an unconscious sadistic hate component. It is myth, in which this motif occurs very frequently, which can give us a clue to the meaning of this enhancement of killing by dismemberment.

Dismemberment occurs very often in the folk-tales of the South American Indians, for example, and there it is always the prelude to a reawakening of the killed in a reconstituted form to a new life. It is well known that the Osiris myths in Egypt revolve round the same theme,[1] and in the Polynesian myths and cults presented by A. E. Jensen the dismemberment of the first dead and the burial of parts of the corpse is said to be the origin of edible plants, and the cultic repetition of the event is thought to ensure their successful growth: it is as though the execution followed up and made complete by total annihilation was what first made the transformation of the dead into another mode of existence possible, and so transformed death from a mere negation of life to something "fruitful".

A neat supplement to the dreams already cited is provided by one which an elderly married lady once told to a circle of her friends:
Dream 17. "It is silly nonsense and really too horrid to tell. A dream has really persecuted and tormented me the whole week. You see, I always had a specially tender relationship with my long dead mother;

[1] Cf. Jung's exposition in *Symbols of Transformation* para. 354. He says in relation to the dismemberment of Osiris: "We find this motif of dismemberment in numerous sun-myths as a contrast to the putting together of the child in the mother's womb. Actually Isis collected the pieces together again with the help of the jackal-headed Anubis. Here the dogs and jackals, devourers of corpses by night, assist in the . . . reconstruction." "Demeter collected the limb of the dismembered Dionysos and put him together again." Further references in *Psychology and Alchemy*.

and recently I dreamt that, to my horror, I had killed her: somehow or other she had been murdered. Then I went into the kitchen and cut her to pieces: all in little pieces. It was quite clear to me that it was Mummy, but somehow or other I had to do it. Finally I made the pieces into a meal to put on the table. Then *we* ate the meal."

There was nothing more said about the dream, but what was said was enough for it to be a kind of confirmation of the mythical symbol of killing and dismemberment—and that of a Death-Mother (we may compare the exposition on Frau Holle in Chapter 11) in order to provide food. The death of the mother implies the end of the dreamer's life as a daughter (to which she may well have clung for too long) and suggests the need to incorporate her mother into herself as "food" in order to enable her to fulfil her task of transforming herself and becoming a mother-in-herself. The dreamer has been given a hint from her unconscious that she must set herself "to transform death into food"—that is, to accept it and "take it into" herself.

14. Dreams 3: Archaic Forms of the Death-Demon

IN the following dreams we hope to show how the image of death is often formulated as a figure, and frequently a figure with archaic (and hence collective) characteristics. At the same time such figures are entirely individual expressions, since what happens is that the dreams produce the particular "collective" images which are appropriate to the dreamer's own stage of psychic development.[1] It is certainly true that an actual problem in the foreground of the dreamer's life is reflected in many of these dreams, and that the dreamer is concerned with solving it yet, at the same time, it often becomes startlingly clear that such an "actual problem" rises out of hidden depths. The uncanny mystery of human existence itself and the presence of death in life is the ultimate source of disturbance which, distorted by egoistic fears, is given inarticulate expression by the patient's conflicts and symptoms. In contrast to such symptoms the dreams are relatively articulate, and if an onlooker observes them carefully and meditates on them he can

---

[1] The following dream of a fitter and his own associations to it shows that such dreams really do deal with archaic figures of the deep background of the psyche, and it is very probable that they do so more often than one might suppose. The dream: "I encounter a dead woman, thirty-two years old. She has two dogs. The dogs attack me."

Associations: "I am always afraid of dogs. There is a particularly dangerous Alsatian in the village. Not long ago my wife told me that some time back two young lads of our village were said to have seen an uncanny black dog at the window on several occasions. I certainly don't believe in spirits, but surely that has something to do with ghosts."

Naturally the therapist thinks of Hel (or Percht) and her dogs—see Chapter 11 above. It is probably only through such a dream as this that one can see what depths lie beneath such problems and symptoms as those from which this patient of thirty suffered—he had fears of blushing and of physical contact associated with sexual difficulties.

catch a glimpse of the underlying concern. One who can understand the mythological images in such dreams will not regard the patient's regression to the archaic level from a merely reductive point of view, because he will see it as the starting-point of a new development from the "beginning". As the development of myth shows it is a true horror in the face of the tremendum which first gives rise to a real recognition of life.

The following account of a dream-face brings to mind the horrible monstrosity of the prehistoric death-demon Kolio itself. It was given by a foreman of forty or so. He was the son of a rustic craftsman in Emsland and had lived a number of years in Berlin. He awoke from a fearful feeling of being strangled and saw:

Dream 18. "A huge, horrible *mask* in front of my eyes. It has the appearance of a huge head, too big to be human, with giant arms from which bloody muscles hang down in shreds. The hands have powerful claws. The face is framed by a long beard. The upper part of the body is naked . . ."

The dreamer's associations show that he saw this dream-face on the anniversary of his father's death, and that this was the first year that he had not remembered the day. As a matter of fact he had dreamt of the same horrible phantom for many years—the first time not long before his father's death.

The treatment of this patient was carried out along strict Freudian lines (not by the author) and naturally the massive references to an unresolved father-relationship were taken up and worked through by means of a careful biographical analysis. There is no doubt that the results were good and that a far-reaching alteration in the patient set in. Even so we may well ask what may have been happening in the man's psyche. We may wonder if it is only a matter of his becoming aware of the nature of the childishly exaggerated image of his father which still influences him as an adult, and of his discovering what incidents in his life led to the development and fixation of this horrifying image. Is it simply that he has to reduce the image of his father to its proper size and liberate himself from the inhibitions associated with it? Has he to do no more than learn to relate to a father-image on equal terms, as it were? If the analysis does not go further than this it is likely that the real point will only be concealed again. The fact that the patient as a child had formed such a horrible and exaggerated image of his father bears witness to a *real experience*—to an experience of the numinous, the incomprehensible in which our existence is embedded —and we may well think that the child experienced this too early and in too much loneliness so that he could not assimilate it in any way, with the result that it became a burden which made him dumb and rigid.

In our view, the real point of the psychotherapeutic process lies in the fact that the patient again encounters the tremendum in his dreams when he is no longer alone, so that he discovers the possibility of standing firm in face of the horror of existence and (which is the same thing) of death. This happens because of his relationship to the psychotherapist. The patient gets from the therapist the security he missed as a child, and he gets it at the same time as he experiences the most extreme horror. Thus in the next dream he is able to distinguish the experience of death from the horror in itself. In this dream, occurring a few days after, he glimpses death (in a concealed form it is true) as a general fate and so as "worthy of reverence", even while remaining incomprehensible:

Dream 19. "I saw the corpse of President Hindenburg (who had died a few months before) lying in state in civilian clothes—"just somewhere". Many bones lay around the coffin and I asked what they meant. *Then I heard a voice:* 'the dog should eat the bones: then he will be healthy and live till he is very old'. Our dog was there and he ate some of the bones."

The dreamer said that his father had worn a beard like Hindenburg. At that time their dog meant almost as much as a child to the patient and his wife. He really felt that he realized himself in the sprightliness of this living creature, and one could well say that in many respects he identified himself with the animal.

Even at first sight the alteration which has taken place in the father-image suggests that some development has begun in the dreamer's adaptation to reality, but even more can be seen. The numinous character of the dream hints at deep stirrings, and the voice that delivers the peculiar command has a supra-personal[1] aspect—just as Hindenburg himself was a very "mythical" person to the dreamer. We detect a close association with the primal father Ouiot of the Juaneño Indians, for at his lying in state Coyote or the chief of the coyotes appeared and ate a bit of the corpse (cf. Chapter 5, pp. 55 f.) and

[1] This, of course, is quite another thing from the "super-ego".

since then it has been part of the burial rite of every chief that a member of the tribe should disguise himself as a coyote (prairie wolf) and come and eat a shoulder of the corpse raw. We have to understand by this that a member of the tribe plays the part of the Death-Demon in coyote form and ritually eats the corpse. In other words by this rite the process of death is accepted by the tribe as something which belongs to its existence. Moreover, Ouiot was the first man and also the one who declared the fate of death to men, so that we can say that this rite is an affirmation of death as the fate of the tribe. It is further possible that both in the rite and in our dream there is an echo of the idea of eating the god. The image in the dream of the dead, "old, old father" presents death to the dreamer's consciousness in a new form. Death is no longer the senseless murderer who only arouses horror but a power of fate encompassing all mankind. The voice declares that this fate "ought" to be taken into the living which, in this way, will be healed.

Such insight is a long way away from a twenty-nine-year-old woman who suffered from a compulsion neurosis. Her whole being was permeated by the knowledge of death, but this knowledge oppressed her mind: it did not nourish her, but brought about a state of crippling rigidity, inhibiting every expression of life. Her first dream when she began treatment and her explanation of it, which keeps clear of any free movement or development, show this rigidity in a very stark way:
Dream 20. "I had a dream. Yes, it was a fairy-tale. I've forgotten. I think Snow White."
She could offer no associations. When challenged to tell the story of Snow White she would only say, "In the end it was put in a coffin". At the next session she (as it were) continued the sentence, "poisoned by the mother", and next time (having read the story meanwhile) she went on, "*with the apple* and the poison, and she is poisoned over and over again. Then she comes to life in spite of that." After a long pause she added the lapidary phrase: "She must die." This is a fairy-tale which can undoubtedly be set alongside myths and legends, and when we think of it in this way we may say that the image of death takes two forms: first the murdering Death-Mother, secondly the unnamed yet "known" seven dwarfs who, as it were, hide the grain

of seed under the earth and preserve it until it is "transformed" and "coming to life again" the Girl-Child can become Queen and Woman. It seems likely that these images are struggling to become conscious through this dream which is so anxiously restricted in content. The dreamer has a long way to go before she can experience the second (transforming) aspect of death. On the surface she can only take note of death in relation to the murdering mother as negation and cessation, and that is why she ends her statement with the defiant, "She must die!" which contradicts the facts of the fairy-tale. At the same time the unconscious knows more about death, since it has already conceived it in terms of the fairy-tale as a whole and, particularly, in the image of the apple.

A very similar attitude to death is shown by the following dream of a thirty-nine-year-old woman arts and crafts worker, even though there are great external differences from, and an apparent contradiction of, the previous dream:

Dream 21. "In the dream I find myself in a huge house—a hospital or barracks. I am chased up and down stairs and along endless corridors by terrifying creatures. Some are oversized cats with heads at both ends, some are huge and repulsively naked dogs. As I range through the house I eventually come to a 'Private Department'. This is the Superintendent's flat and I stop when I get to it. I hear music coming from a room and a couple is dancing to the beautiful music in a corridor of the 'Private Department'. I think, 'There must be happy and beautiful people there!' but I am harried on by the monsters pursuing me. It is true that the monsters cannot eat me yet, but their breath is poisonous and I feel that I am already poisoned, attacked by blisters and boils, and that I am changing. My body is distorted about the head and shoulders. I become a kind of subterranean, demonic creature . . . Then I woke up."

When she woke from this dream she was suffering from her worst symptom which she described as a "dreadful, crippling cramp". The medical diagnosis of this was "no organic abnormality; psychologically conditioned disturbances".

The dreamer is in a labyrinth from which there is no way out. The fearsome monsters that remorselessly pursue her are like primary images of the Death-Demon! Her unconscious is full of the fear of death. In other dreams she roams through cemeteries where she encounters death everywhere, shakes with horror at it and cannot find a way out: she goes on her knees to beg the cemetery employees to lead her out, but they take no notice of her. In reality she does not dare to look— either at the reminders of death or for the way out: her basic attitude is one of "magic flight"; she refuses to see what "ought not" to be there—but even this breaks down as Dream 21 shows; wherever she goes she meets the uncanny animals which might equally well be the death-demons of a primitive people. When we look close at these figures with an eye on the myths we can see hints as to where the patient might find possibilities of development and differentiation. Like the wolf the dog is not only a devouring demon of death since, for example, he may go into the tent of a girl by night, cast off his skin, and become the procreating father of strong warrior tribes. Again, although the cats embody demonic powers of death we must also take seriously the fact that they have heads at both ends. It is true that like other features of this patient's dreams this may point, in a Freudian sense, to unresolved problems of voyeurism and exhibitionism since they look forward and backward at the same time, but other inter-pretations are also possible.[1] We can understand the cats to mean that the animal of death includes past and future, origin and destiny, birth and death in one image. We may recall that the Teutonic Freya drove a team of cats and that she was a "chooser of corpses" (i.e. goddess of death) and also a goddess of birth at the same time. The Egyptian Sekhmet has two forms: as a lioness she is a cruel, devouring monster, as a cat (sometimes a human figure with the head of a cat, carrying the head of a lioness in her arms) she is called Bastet who brings salvation and healing. As Bastet she is specially celebrated by women with *dancing, music and sistras: her priests are doctors!* In the midst of her persecution by uncanny animals the dreamer is confronted with music and dancing in the (hospital) Superintendent's flat, and this may well be an archetypal image thrown up by the unconscious.

We come across a remarkable form of the Death-Demon in a dream of a thirty-one-year-old unmarried salesgirl who had had the simplest elementary education:

[1] It may perhaps be pointed out that there is no "either . . . or" about the interpretation of dreams: it is always "both . . . and" (*Trans.*).

Dream 22. "I am in a kind of Lilliput town with my friend (a man). The houses are so low that we can touch the roofs. Suddenly a fabulous animal comes along—it is half dog and half horse. It springs hither and thither in an uncanny way. I run into a big house like an Insurance Office. I hope that the animal cannot follow me in there . . . eventually I think, 'What has happened to my friend?' and I want to get out again. Outside I meet my *grandmother* and ask her where my friend is. She only says sarcastically, 'You will soon see for yourself'—then all the houses are burnt, and so is my friend. All I can find are his ashes and I pull a *bone* out from them—I am rigid with horror. Could there have been an explosion there?" (Cf. Dreams 40–42.)

The numinous character of this dream which was felt by the patient marks it off from her other dreams. As so often happens acute and particular problems are closely bound up with the question of her attitude to the decisive and basic facts of Life and Death. In certain features of the dream we can see how the alteration of her attitude and approach to the outward facts of her own life which the unconscious demands would involve and express a deep-rooted transformation in her attitude and relationship to existence itself.

It would be easy to overlook the parable-like quality of the dream. From this point of view it says: "It is no longer appropriate for you to stay in the Lilliputian or toy town with your friend." The playful world must go—and her friend (as he is, or as she experiences him) must go too. Nor will an *Insurance Office* help! On the other hand there are strange, uncanny features of great significance which not only remind us of death-demons in the myths, but also recall certain rites of the dead among primitive peoples. Although the expression is clumsy the demonic character of the dog-horse which persecutes her is perfectly clear. It is the appearance of this creature which causes her panic flight to the Insurance Office and it seems that it is its coming that brings about the destruction of the illusory world and of her friend, although this is not explicit. In Chapter 6 we pointed out that when the image of the Death-Demon is made up of different figures it tends to have a more personal character. The decisive experience is no longer expressed in terms of the arbitrarily devouring dog or the arbitrarily abducting horse, but is seen as having some hidden, dimly guessed meaning and intention. Moreover, the appearance of the Magna Mater (the grandmother) can be understood along the same

166

lines. When she says, "You'll see all right!" (the phrase the dreamer takes as sarcastic) she points to and emphasizes the events which the dreamer does in fact see. When the dreamer draws the bone out of the ashes her action is more than the expression of emotion: she might, for example, have wept helplessly and beseechingly. What she does is a kind of ritual act, for as we know there are widespread ideas that the real and imperishable being of the individual are represented by the parts of the skeleton which remain after the corpse has been burnt or left exposed.

In the short dreams which follow the Death-Demon again appears in mixed forms, this time in that of the bird-woman. The first is the dream of a woman of thirty whose speech was badly inhibited. It was followed by a series of depressive dreams about death and labyrinths which gave rise to great anxiety. Actually it was an anticipatory dream offering possible solutions to the blind anxieties which the dreamer was not yet able to assimilate:

Dream 23. "A bird sat near me, it seemed to have a human head. What struck me was the particularly *large nose*."

A doctor of thirty-five also had a "siren dream", which was more of a half-waking image. It was the appendix to a dream in which a spectral hearse went very swiftly from his birth-place to the home and burial-place of his forebears. Immediately after the dream he saw:

Dream 24. "A mighty being on a throne—half-woman, half-bird. It was a tremendous but fearful being, and yet I felt myself secure with it."

We are justified in interpreting these images as death-symbols because both these last two dreams occurred close in time to other dreams connected with death, and in each of the three cases the patient experienced the image as a specially mysterious one. They must be contrasted with dreams of corpses and labyrinths (particularly with those of the dreamer of Dream 23) in that they must be understood as attempts at creating a synthesis.

Uncertainty about the sex of the Death-Demon crops up in myths and legends and is also reflected in many dreams. Such uncertainty indicates a particular (archaic) stage of development. The next dream is that of an official in his middle fifties, and it marked the beginning of a change in his attitude to his parents (who had been dead for a long time) and so in his attitude to his own life:

Dream 25. "I am with my brother in the cemetery of my home town— a small one. We are actually in the cemetery attendant's living-room. As a student I used to seek out this man and have long conversations with him. He was a book-binder when not working at the cemetery and a very thoughtful and widely-read man. In the dream the living-room was separated from the mortuary by nothing more than a kind of partition which only reached halfway to the ceiling. Over the wall one could see the mourners and other people as well as corpses . . . I was struck by the appearance of a man with a wild look. He had long strands of hair hanging across his face from right to left and the skin showed between the strands. His face was like a mask—yes, really like a mask! This frightful man suddenly came in to us. My brother was frightened and fell back. I was probably concerned not to let my fear show and went up to the man, stretched out my hand and asked him how he was—although I did not know him at all. He said he must now go to Erfurt, and I replied: 'That is most convenient: I am going to Weimar and we can go together'."

This dream had a most uncanny effect on the patient, and it also had a surprising sequel. In the therapist's waiting-room there was a slightly darkened portrait in oils of a young girl of the Biedermeier period. As he was going out the patient suddenly stopped by this picture as though rooted to the ground. He said: "That is what the uncanny fellow looked like":—and then, as though recollecting he went on, "Well, yes, of course, his hair was not so well kept, it was more unkempt and straggly . . ." This contradiction completes the death figure in a perfect way. It is man and woman, fearsome and alluring at the same time. One may recall the "bearded Aphrodite" of Cyprus or, in a wider sense, the contrasting aspects of loveliness and frightfulness in the "Frau Venus" of the Tannhäuser legend.

A very similar uncertainty occurs in an extremely dramatic dream picture of the woman arts and crafts worker who dreamt Dream 21. This dream followed a few days after:

Dream 26. "It is deep night. I am in the open. Suddenly I see a beautiful woman in the sky—a kind of constellation. She has the *face of Stalin*

168

(who, as is well known, had a beard). The picture hangs in the sky like a dreadful demon. Then a blazing cross appeared opposite it but the demon burst out in a horrible, devilish, mocking laugh which rang out over the whole earth, and I woke up in fear and horror . . ."[1]

We know that this figure of indeterminate sex represents the Death-Demon because it cropped up among dreams of labyrinthine mortuaries and corpses horribly mutilated in a railway accident—dreams in which the dreamer flees in horror again and again! In one of these dreams a horrible woman appeared who wanted to seduce her at (or to) the "round dance": this figure has many meanings, but on this occasion it probably represented an aspect of the death mother, recalling the seduction to Death and Life together by the transformed stepmother in *Snow White*. This patient's dreams are specially illuminating from our point of view because they show her fear of Life as a radical fear of Death and this is why they first present a random medley of images. At one time the encounter with death is experienced in realistic and horrible situations set in the present, at another in archaic symbols. The former give shape to fear and fright alone, the latter conceal the beginning of a new formulation deep in the unconscious which we can detect by comparing the images with mythological themes. In this case the realistic dreams gradually became less frequent, and in the others the archaic images of death were enriched with new features as the unconscious sought to work upon it.

The following dreams show further "images of death", but it is not possible to go into the other problems of the dreamer. Like all dreams of this kind they were felt by the patient as having a numinous character. An academic of thirty-five had often dreamt of cosy, social

[1] This dream provides an extremely good example of the way in which the unconscious tests the traditional concepts accepted by an individual to see if they are genuine. This dreamer was a constant church-goer, but *her* image of the cross was too conventional and too little her own to be able to stand up to the demon. Yet if the tremendum is experienced in a dream *only* as evil (as it seems to be here) the shock which results may be enough to initiate a religious development which leads to the acceptance of death and a readiness for transformation through repeated encounters with death images. This would mean that the sacrificial death of Christ would become a personal reality. No doubt it would not have the same superficial shining brilliance but it would be valid, and able to stand its ground in face of the demon.

meetings with dead relatives, and the following dream-picture caused him enormous surprise:

Dream 27. "I am sitting in a room with a young girl. I stroke her hand. The door opens and I hear a voice coming from the figure of a woman, saying: '*She knows everything.*' The woman is like my wife (who was mortally ill at the time) but has a *bird's face*. She wears a black veil over her eyes. As she enters the room I have the impression that it is as though a Norn—fate itself—were coming in. There is a map lying on my knees and I am deeply impressed by this woman figure."

The map may symbolize the attempt to find one's way in unknown regions of the psyche. We have already noticed that a mask or dark band over the eyes often characterizes the Huldren and other subterranean beings. The associations with the Sirens as goddesses of death and with the bird-form of the Norns and Valkyries is explicit. The sense of fate expressed by the designation of the figure as "a Norn" is particularly impressive.

This sense of fate recurs in the following dream of a student of economics, very differently coloured by his own personal problems. It took place just before his final examinations:

Dream 28. "I dreamt that I was going for a walk with my parents. Then I saw *three* uncanny, apparently shrivelled creatures lying in the road. I and my parents were sympathetic to them, helped them to their feet and brought them on to the nearby Negro or Indian village. The chief of the village recognized these female creatures, and gave a horrified scream, and was immediately infected by leprosy and so became a victim of death. His son begs and prays him not to die, because if he did the son could not live any longer either. It is in vain. The chief dies. Then the son seems to grow larger and become a mighty man. He orders the burial ceremonies to take place . . . Now I seem to be the son of the chief conducting my father's corpse to the burial by torchlight in traditionally hallowed style . . . A possible threat to the life of the son becomes visible far away . . ."

The dreamer's leading associations were to the three mysterious figures. From the context in the dream one might expect that these associations would lead to allegories of the plague or some such thing, but this is not the case. What the dreamer recalls are stories, which he heard from his mother many years before, about spirits "which announce death because they already know everything . . ." The number three suggests that these death figures must also be thought of as Norn-like—they announce the death fate of the parents (the father), which is also the life fate of the son—at the end of which death (as fate) waits yet once again.

At one phase in the analysis of a twenty-nine-year-old writer and journalist (cf. Dreams 14, 15) death stands in relationship to the problem of his parents and of the succession of the generations:

Dream 29. "An archaic dream landscape . . . a deep, dark fishpond or lake in a wood with sluices. A tall strange man, like a huge fisher or dweller in the woods, had a kind of mountain hat and apron, and he is fishing dead men out of the water with a long scoop. They are people that have drowned and sunk, and he is, as it were, "raking" over the bottom of the lake to clean it. He flings each cast far out over the surface of the water, and each one brings a corpse to land. Among the bodies are those of my parents . . . I become weighed down with sadness: my parents are dead. Worse still, I am expected to eat my parents, who are made into five puddings, flat like wafers. These puddings are half dark and half light . . . I refuse them."

In this dream the old fisher does not *catch* men but hauls them up from the depths in which he has hidden them: even so he recalls the *Wassermann* (waterman) or *Hakemann* (hookman) and he is so primitive in conception that he even resembles the archaic giant Koljo. In this dream the motif of transformation through the encounter with death stands at the centre even more clearly than it does in the last (28). The last dream was a means by which the dreamer came to the realization that his parents were dead, which realization brought about an actual change in his conception of his own role and function in life. Once the death of his father was accepted as a reality the boy could be seen growing into youth and man. In this dream (29) this aspect is not central, but only hinted in the act of "cleaning" the unconscious (the fishpond) of the corpses of the parents—that is, the continuing influence of the parent-imagos in inappropriate ways in the dreamer's psyche, even though the actual parents were still alive. The dismemberment of the parents implicit[1] at the end of this dream and the need to eat the puddings made from their substance indicates that the

[1] Cf. notes to Dreams 15–17.

171

transformation of the man who no longer has "parents" must take place within him and permeate his whole existence—he is to incorporate the creative, fructifying power of the parents in himself, even if he is still not ready to do it. Finally, the parti-coloured nature of the food shows that the incorporation of Death is also to be seen as the incorporation of Life.[1] We have mentioned again and again that there is an awareness among all the peoples of the world that the food which supports and strengthens men stands in close relationship to death. It is thought to spring from the dead; as the Food-of-the-Dead it plays its part in the abduction of those who eat it into the Realm of the Dead and Oblivion, and it can also mean transformation "through death" to a life of a new kind.

The two dreams which follow were dreamt by the same woman arts and crafts worker who was responsible for Dreams 21 and 26. They were separated by one or two days and when we compare the images in them with those of the monsters in Dream 21 and the demon of Dream 26 we see that they express death in a far richer and more differentiated way—

Dream 30. "I was sitting on a hill: far and wide there was nothing but snow—no path of any kind. A little brown packet was lying near me and I knew that my thoughts were wrapped up in it. Divorced from myself I seemed to sit there alone year after year, for centuries. Suddenly I woke from this state, snatched up the packet and opened it. Inside was nothing but *apples*. Then I felt quite clearly that my brain was filled with thoughts again, and I hurried from the place . . ."

In the continuation of the dream she meets her sister (her "shadow" in Jung's terminology—she did not actually have a sister), wades through a *clear, green* piece of water (a marked contrast to her other dreams) and looks for her home amid some fallen masonry. When she finds it it "was, however, quite new-fitted up . . ."

[1] The eggs in a mystery symbol described by Bachofen have a light and dark part. He says: "Their meaning is clear. The alternation of the light and dark colour expresses the continual transition from darkness to light, from death to life. It reveals the creation of the earth as the result of eternal becoming and passing away—a never-ending movement between opposite poles . . ." *Gräbersymbolik der Alten,* p. 31 in J. J. Bachofen, *Mutterrecht und Urreligion.*

At first sight it might be thought that this dream had nothing to do with the problem of death. Although it is clear that a "transformation" is taking place ("waking up", "wading through" and the newly appointed home all symbolize it), it can be understood in conjunction with the apples in the brown packet in purely Freudian terms as a releasing of a previously contained and inhibited sexuality—and such an interpretation would certainly be correct. At the same time it is extremely probable that an interpretation which stopped here would leave out of account a special element in this dream. The dream-image has a numinous note which only becomes properly intelligible when we remember the universal idea of the Food of the Dead which is also the Food of Life, the apple tree at the entrance to the underworld and the pomegranate which Persephone ate and, eating, not only became the victim of Hades but also developed from Maiden into Woman and mistress (cf. Chapter 8, p. 85). In this dream the paralysing effect of the "Evil Demon" of Dreams 21 and 26, who could only arouse horror, is succeeded by a new "knowledge" and the demon is dissolved. The new "knowledge" is that death actually means transformation and re-birth, fate and the development of a man in preparation for what is to come. It would follow that it would not give a true picture of the psychic process taking place in the dreamer if one were to understand it in terms of instinct alone, or even of the transformation of a "part-ego"—and this is confirmed by the dream which followed a day or two later.[1]

In relation to the following dream it should be said that the dreamer had a natural gift for acting which was generally recognized, and that she often took part in performances by an amateur company—

Dream 31. "A stage play was to be performed at a festival. All the others knew their parts but I had not even seen the play let alone learnt my part. I became anxious. Then I thought to myself: 'Very well, then, simply read it off.' I opened the book which was a large one with a lot of painted pictures, pretty and brightly coloured. On the first page there was the picture of an exquisitely beautiful, well-proportioned girl wearing a tall hat, with brightly coloured, fluttering ribbons, and

[1] It should be made clear that as a result of the pressing everyday problems of this patient the therapist had not had an opportunity of discussing the dreams; he merely listened to them. Nor had the patient studied any psychological or mythical literature. The images appear to have arisen wholly spontaneously.

a timeless, wide, soft, light gown. They called her Annemarie, and the whole book was about her. Other pages were filled with pictures of distant lands . . . One picture was of a huge *cornfield*, full of heavy and laden sheaves. Skulls kept rising up between the sheaves. Suddenly it was as if I was this Annemarie and would have to travel through all those foreign countries, and as if it was there that I was threatened by danger. I shut the book, and the whole festival vanished . . ."

Like Dream 1 this dream brings to our mind the sheaves "in front of Frau Holle"—a transparent image which reveals both Life and Death. We see that the dreamer feels herself in this dream to be, as it were, an actress who has not yet learnt her part—i.e. in life. In the dream she is confronted with her own life as a whole, and her attitude to it *sub specie mortis*. One must admit that the dream contains a worrying omen for the therapist, for in the moment when she has to realize this she shuts the book, and the whole feast (of life) disappears.

The theme of the cornfield, with its mythical and symbolic relationship to Life and Death, is again touched on in the dream of a seventeen-year-old girl. This girl was almost hopelessly ill at the time. She had gone away when she was eleven or twelve when the Saar was evacuated in 1939 with her widowed mother and her younger brother. They lived for more than a year in Hesse in a farmer's house, and they retained a loose, friendly relationship with his family for quite a long time. About five years later the girl fell ill with severe anorexia—that is, wasting. Associated with this were ideas purporting to be religious that food was impure and that as spiritual beings men must learn to be able to do without it. As a matter of fact we are now quite sure that when wasting is psychically caused it must be understood as a specific form of the "refusal" to grow up—particularly in relationship to growing up to be a woman and to take on the woman's task of pro-creation—but we also have to recognize in this as in other forms of neurosis that the acceptance of the procreative function is closely associated with the acceptance of death. After she had been sick for about a year the girl's condition was an extremely dangerous one, and had to be countered by the use of every medical resource. The total condition of the patient was such that psychotherapy could only be used as an ancillary, and even then only with the greatest caution. Her treatment was very unorthodox and during its course she had the following dream which not only showed the immediate cause of her sickness but also revealed its existential depth with startling clarity— *Dream 32.* "I am in the farmer's house at X. The farmer's three daughters are sitting down to a meal and in a most friendly way they invite me to join them. (These girls are grown up: the eldest is married, the second engaged to be married but the third will not marry because her mother will not let her go.) The youngest has piled a great heap of food on her plate—it is dreadful! Then the picture changes. I am going along a narrow path through an enormous cornfield. The tall ears are nodding and I see that they hang heavily from their stalks on very thin necks. A well-trod path leads through the corn on the left to a hut lying rather low in the ground. In the hut a vestibule leads to the main room. The main room is long and rather like a greenhouse; there are a number of grain-testing beds in it, each with grain at different stages of growth. I meet someone working there, exchange a few words and go on through. There is a second vestibule, like the first, at the other end and as I go into it I suddenly meet my mother. It seems she was looking for me. It is very strange that although it is bright sunshine outside she is wearing a dark raincoat and a hood—clothes she has actually got but has never worn. It is most odd."

The patient explains this by saying that the morning before she had been reading the Parable of the Sower in her Bible (Matthew 13): ". . . some (seed) fell by the wayside . . . some fell on stony ground . . . some fell among thorns . . . some fell on good ground and bore fruit, some thirtyfold some sixtyfold and some a hundredfold. He that hath ears to hear let him hear!"

We do not need to say anything about the clear confrontation with the problem of biological growth towards maturity represented by the farmer's three daughters in the first part of the dream: nor about the role played by the mother there. It is the second part of the dream which touches another psychic level, as can be seen from the kind of imagery it uses, and also from the girl's spontaneous association to the biblical parable. One notices, in passing, the remarkable and independent way that the dreamer's unconscious has made use of this excerpt from the previous day. One might well say that the field of corn ripe for the harvest is the most concentrated symbol of the double mystery of life:

175

> *"And shuddering I said as I went by*
> *So far in life is yet too near to death"*.[1]

This is the shudder that always touched man when he was confronted by the Corn Aunt or the Corn Wolf threading its way in the ripe grain, and it is also the shudder out of which there grew the mystic rapture which gripped the devotees when the severed ear of ripe corn was displayed at the climax of the Eleusinian Mysteries. When the dreamer's way leads to the hut half sunk into the earth where there are the testing beds all at different stages of growth, but all on the way to fulfilment through maturation, the symbolism points again to growth and development—something which should be, as it were, tested out by the dreamer. At the same time the final encounter with the mother in the sunken building recalls the image of Nehalennia, who was veiled in a cape as the mother was veiled in cloak and hood despite the bright sunshine outside, or of Demeter who veiled herself to mourn her lost daughter. Demeter also refused to give up Kore-Persephone, and it was only when she could do nothing else that she would accept in her daughter the transformation of the Maiden (Kore) into the Woman and Mother-Mistress (Despoina). The dream does not provide any firm assurance that the dreamer will accept transformation and advance to the noon-day of life: one's feeling is rather that one must withdraw and make reverence as death stands by the bed of this half-child and, as it shrouds itself, also reveals itself to her as that primal power which drives man to grow and develop and to fulfil life by way of continual transformation.

[1] Hebbel, *Des Sommers letzte Rose.*

15. Dreams 4: The Kingdom of the Dead, Death; Procreation and Rebirth

THERE is enormous diversity in the forms through which dreams express the encounter with death, and their concern to express it is not always easily recognized since they inevitably have other themes as well. The encounter with death is closely connected with other motifs, and in a dream it is often hidden behind them. It is most often found associated with the themes of liberation from the parental image, love in all its aspects, procreation and birth and with the mystical idea of rebirth which develops from the others.

The initial dream of a Lithuanian businessman of forty-two who came from a semi-rural area, and was exiled to Germany during the war, seems to involve entry into the land of death itself:

Dream 33. "I was walking in a dark forest with tall fir trees. It is night. I saw glow-worms scattered about—but at the same time they are precious stones which flash and glitter. I heard the barking of furious dogs and I was afraid because it was so dark. In spite of my feeling of being insecure I *had* to collect these very valuable and precious stones. I felt that they were of very great value indeed. I picked them up, and they were icy cold. As I picked up the jewels the thick dry branches of the trees troubled me. All the time I was afraid that one of them would poke into my eye. Meanwhile the barking was getting louder: I heard a dog searching in the bushes. It is getting dangerous but I go on looking for the stones. Suddenly I come upon a human skeleton—and in a flash I realize what is the danger in which I am caught up. The skeleton is that of someone else who was seeking the jewels and who was *murdered by the dog.* A rucksack still lay beside the skeleton. I want to get out of the forest, but the dog is approaching with great leaps. I rush behind a tree to escape, the dog leaps at the tree and his teeth crash against the trunk. He tears large slivers from the tree and I am

177

afraid he will eat right through the wood. Then to save myself I throw all the jewels in my pocket to the dog, and he sniffs at them. I leap from tree to tree. The dog follows and I am sorry that I threw him all the stones at once. I see a high wall and behind it is a tall house with lighted windows. A tree has been felled and the trunk is leaning with its top on the wall. The top of the wall is protected with pieces of broken glass. I am barefoot. I think, 'The dog caught someone here, too, and cut down the tree with his teeth.' I climb to the top of the trunk and fall to earth on the other side of the wall with a crash. As I lie on the ground I calm down, and hear little bells faintly tinkling. I think, 'Death looks like this.' An old gentleman with a white beard and a stick in his hand comes up. He looks like St Peter but has no halo. The tip of his stick is like a needle and he stabs me three times in the side with it. I feel no pain and think, 'Am I really dead?' Yet I feel something flowing from me in three places: perhaps it is my blood. Then I notice that I am lying in a little water-channel. The old man says something incomprehensible (castellan?) and goes away. I could not get up although I wanted to. I hear the barking again, and before I can rise the dog is standing over me with its eyes glowing and glittering like a tiger! I am so terrified that I wake up."

We have given this dream in full with only a very little grammatical correction because the naïve character of the dreamer who is still so close to collective experience comes out so clearly.

This dream certainly reflects an important aspect of the patient's life—the sense of insecurity of a man who has been uprooted from his home and finds himself in a labyrinthine environment. Not only this, but the sense of a mortal threat is also directly related to his actual life, since he was seriously ill some years before, and he had had a long treatment involving injections (with a needle!), and he was still not completely recovered at the time of the dream. We shall not be further concerned with the individual motifs (which were, of course, most important from the point of view of the treatment) like the dried branches which disturbed him as he hunted for treasure, the felled tree and the three stabs in the side: our interest is in the way in which the dream expresses the dreamer's feelings—for instance, in the picture of a nocturnal jungle-labyrinth in which he is hunted by an inescapable death-bringing, primeval demon. The forest is a place of death and might well be the Kingdom of the Dead itself—an idea suggested by the fearsome hound, the discovery of the skeleton and the figure of St Peter.

As we know the Kingdom of the Dead or the dwelling-place of the Death-Demon is represented by an enormous variety of images in the mythologies of the world. There are the Greek Kingdom of Hades, the subterranean Hall of Hel and the Kingdom of the Babylonian Ereschkigal (the dark sister of Ishtar) for examples. It would seem that the image of the labyrinth hidden in the belly of the earth, like the uncannily coiled entrails of an animal, was developed first (or, at any rate most impressively) in Babylon, and there the *wild cedar jungle*, the home of the frightful Humbaba whose face is said to be formed of entrails, is regarded as a symbol of the labyrinth. It is said that no one (except, perhaps Humbaba himself) may attack and fell the trees in that jungle, and our dream has echoes of just such a place. According to the Gilgamesh epic: "Whoever thrusts into the forest is overtaken by disaster", "None can overcome him (Humbaba), all are brought to ruin." The spiral or meander gradually developed from the labyrinth of entrails in Babylonia, and so, by devious ways, something new is brought to light, because the centre of the spiral hides the invaluable dynamism of the *return*—rebirth from the depths of death (cf. Chap. 9). It seems possible that our dream contains a premonition, however indeterminate, that such a treasure is to be found in the Labyrinth of Death, even though the dreamer is certainly a long way from understanding its meaning: this treasure is not to gratify the thief's greed, nor will it serve to pacify the monster.

One might also suggest that the fallen tree is a mother symbol guiding the dreamer to St Peter, into the forecourt of Heaven, as though he were again in his childhood. If this were correct one would have to interpret the dream along lines similar to those which we applied to Dream 26: we said that the cross offered no protection against the hideous demon in the sky because that symbol had only been conventionally experienced by the dreamer; here we might say that the image of Heaven or of the Saints failed for the same reason. Certainly the religiously determined figure of St Peter—the Doorkeeper of Heaven—gives numinous character to the whole dream and by being associated with the inexorable sequence of events in the dream the childish conception of Heaven presents the motif of transformation and rebirth as a distant image: "Except ye become as little children, you shall not enter into the Kingdom of Heaven." It is possible that the shock which the horror of death gave the patient might serve to re-awaken the original *fulness* of his childhood faith (covered over as it was by the hard realities of everyday life) which might then develop and mature. If this were so such a transformation might be the *real* "treasure" which the dreamer could bring out of the "labyrinth" to his waking life—a precious stone which would one day start to shine for him.

A twenty-year-old girl kept dreaming of persecution, flight and hopeless wandering through huge, ancient buildings which recalled her convent school in the Rhineland. She was a music student who was highly gifted but whose personality was cramped. She had ghastly fears in association with these dreams and although she found the one below quite as horrible as the rest it actually shows certain essential changes which clearly reveal the breakthrough of a new attitude— *Dream 34.* "I am wandering through passages and corridors in an enormous building. I can find no way out nor a place to which I am going. At last there is an open door leading into a room! There is no one in the room. I go into the next room where a woman is waiting for me who wants to give me an audition . . . I start to sing all right, when the woman suddenly changes—her features are distorted by terrifying malice. Suddenly this demonic creature hurls herself at me, seizes hold of me, throws me to the ground and tears my legs apart— this causes me to feel a frightful pain. I defend myself and finally overcome her after a terrible struggle. I kill her with a knife. But now, what to do with the corpse? I simply must get out! In the end I carry the corpse of the old woman over my arm. As I go to the exit she hangs over my arm like an empty dress, a husk or a mask. I get quietly through the door without being stopped . . .

"The picture changes now. I am sitting in a fairly empty tram. I am travelling somewhere or other, and suddenly notice that a 'spectre' is sitting behind me. I know it is the dead woman . . ."

The dreamer herself had scarcely noticed that the scene of this "labyrinth" was different from that in her other dreams. The building was no longer like the old convent school but seemed more like some old administrative building, and this time she was not pursued but wandered about seeking an exit or some kind of goal. As in the last dream (33) the labyrinthine aspect can still be easily recognized, but in this dream the demon is represented as awaiting the dreamer in the innermost cell—this is not a matter of flight, but of being put to the test.

The dreamer designated the woman a "female demon", and she had something to do with the mother whom she both loved and hated. Her account of herself had shown that in actual life she had endured a continuous state of yearning towards and anxious fear of her mother existing at the same time, and when, as the dream progressed, the "mother-imago" was killed this probably represented an unconscious preparation for liberation from her ambivalent mother-fixation. Nevertheless, the real-life relationship to the mother certainly does not exhaust the meaning of this "mother archetype". It is the *mythical Death-Mother* who is encountered in this dream, a demonic figure which symbolizes concealment in the innermost chamber, the maternal womb of the earth, but which does not permit such concealment to be nothing more than a return to foetal life—a testing is involved. In real life the dreamer played an instrument, but this test involves her voice, which is the immediate expression of her intimate self, and it is like a deeply serious question asked by death,[1] "to what extent have you realized *yourself*?" Does not the dreadful attack in the course of which her legs are wrenched apart symbolically represent the human fate which involves conception and childbirth? And in the dream this fate is imposed "by death". On the one hand the virgin (and the "daughter") come to death through conception and childbirth, and this is also death for the individual as she was before; but on the other it is also victory over death, the climax of life, for it is the transformation of existence from that of the daughter to that of the mother, and also the birth of new life. This is why when these things have been realized (even though only symbolically) the Death-Mother herself can be killed. The spiral has been reversed, and turns back towards life—but the dream makes a further, impressive statement: As we return we take Death with us. Death remains by our side as by that of every man as our fate and companion, even in public transport which carries men to their working life.

The seventeen-year-old girl who dreamt Dream 32 had a dream in

[1] The dreamer was in actual danger of suicide at the time.

which the spiral concept associated with the labyrinth was connected with the idea of the narrow, inner room (the Temenos—the Temple Precinct). This was the girl about whom the doctors and the psychotherapist were seriously concerned, anxiously hoping that she would succeed in turning back to life. The penetration into the interior of the "labyrinth" in this dream is a kind of compensation to her actual situation at the brink of death, for in the first place it points to a *return* to life: it might well be that the "holy precinct" of her own life-figure is there delineated in faint outline. This dream occurred fourteen days after Dream 32. It begins in deep darkness:

Dream 35. "I am riding on a he-goat or a ram on a grassy path in the dark. There is a fence of meshed wire on the left. Behind the fence I see two points of light, like wells of light. I imagine that these are quite close and I try to grasp them by reaching through the meshes. I cannot reach them. I ride round the corner trying to find an entrance. On the other side of the square, roughly in the middle, I find·a gate through which I go into the area. Once inside I see that there are two fires burning in the middle of the ground. One can actually take hold of the rays, which are not at all hot, and I use them to pull myself along to the fires. I am by the fire (apparently only one now) and several students are standing there . . ."

(The following dream fragment occurred the next day, and may be inserted here:

Dream 36. ". . . by a dog . . ."

The dreamer associated this with Sigrid Lagerlöf's story *Karr und Graufell*[1] and the phrase, "He must be shot as unfit; then he helps Graufell to get back into the forest, into his element." This fragment seems to contain a hint that the encounter (conversation) with the "death-animal" actually helps to bring the imprisoned "young game" into its own element and the freedom of its proper life.

At first the dream of the he-goat could not be related to the dreamer's conscious awareness at all. There was a fleeting memory of the garden of her childhood by association with the fence of meshed wire, but after that there were only negative associations defending the dreamer against any conscious acceptance of either the he-goat or the students. It is obvious that the specification of the animal as male and the presence of the students had great significance to the actual living of

[1] Karr is a dog and Graufell an elk.

the dreamer at her stage of life, and also that it was relevant to the analysis of her attitude that at this point in the treatment she was quite openly "obstinate as a goat";[1] but when all this had been taken into account the therapist needed to become aware of the chthonic aspect of the dream which is expressed both by the unexpected mount and by the hint of a meander or spiral in the path traced out. He-goat and ram both give expression to the union between procreation and death; for instance Hermes the psychopomp (conductor of souls) is commonly represented as ithyphallic (with erect phallus) and often appears in the form of a ram.

It will be recalled that this patient was in a most dangerous condition, and because of this it was very important that the therapist should recognize the way in which she was coming to terms with images of Death and Life in her dreams as her medical treatment progressed. It was further considered that the psychotherapist's primary task was to co-operate with the extremely careful physical treatment which was being carried out by cautiously opening up the mythological motifs in her dreams to encourage and help the unconscious continue the development of the images which it spontaneously presented. Thus at this stage the patient was told, in the course of an apparently speculative discussion, that ram sacrifices and the skin of a ram played an important part in the cult of Aesculapius and Trophonios,[2] gods who live in darkness holding both healing and death in their hands, and who reveal his true salvation to the man who sleeps in the temple seeking a dream oracle and pays devout attention to it. It was also possible to speak of Hermes, the Ram, who was born in a dark cave of the rock but is closely bound to life and its transformations—so much so that in many statues he is represented with the child Dionysos as a careful tender of growth and life. The patient found these associations perfectly intelligible, as well as the memory of the he-goat team of Donar, the friend of growth and agriculture.

It was also possible to compare the way in which the patient made a

[1] *Bockig* (=obstinate) is derived from *Bock* (=he-goat), cf. our "mulish" (*Trans.*).

[2] The he-goat (like the dog) also belongs to the chthonic Delphic Apollo, and both the fertilizing and death-dealing aspects of the thunderstorm can be felt in the he-goat team of the Nordic Thor-Donar. In more recent times, as is commonly known, the he-goat was connected with the devil, the Lord of Hell.

(partial) circumambulation of the enclosed area in her dream with archaic rites of circumambulation at the laying of the foundations of house or city. Such rites were carried out, for example, in connection with the oldest Roman city foundations, and they have continued from Teutonic times to the present day in certain rural areas of Germany in the form of circular rides round the holy precinct of a chapel —for example, the Leonhardi and Georgi Rides in Tölz, Traunstein and other places. As in the girl's dream such circular rides lead to the centre (often taking a spiral form) where both the rider and the animal on which he rides are consecrated to a new life. One could approach the patient through this world of symbols, whereas she stubbornly and uncompromisingly rejected the least suggestion that the students round the fire might mean something to her: it was as though her unconscious would not tolerate any disturbance of its autonomous development. The cautious amplifications which were offered were a strong stimulation which did not result in a mere imitation and repetition, but in the independent production of new symbols which helped to open up further vistas and to carry the development forward. In the dream which followed the laconic fragment about the dog the motif of fruit trees was introduced—

Dream 37. "A fruit-bearing pear tree stands by the door of an old, half-ruined house or hut. I want to pick the fruit for myself but an old woman, like a witch, comes out and prevents me. Even so I take a few pears which, I must say, were pretty wretched ones."

There may well be a connection between this old woman and the Mother-Figure in Dream 32 who would not let her daughter leave the house (i.e. to marry), and who finally revealed herself in the figure of the Death-Mother shrouded in her Capa. One might have had cause for alarm if the old woman had herself offered the fruit to the girl. As we know, the Elves' food is ambivalent, but when the apple tree—or pear tree, as in this dream—stands, as it were, beside the "entrance to the underworld", it is likely enough that the independent picking of the fruit by the dreamer points to transformation and the new life which grows out of death. If this were the case the pears would mean the same as Freya's apples, the apple or quince of Aphrodite, and the pomegranate of Persephone.

The young student of twenty-three who had the dream about the son of the chief (Dream 28) produced some drawings a little while afterwards. They came out of the unconscious and showed a *nightmare* and a *Wassermann*, both with terrifying hooked claws, and a dwarf dragging a huge sack out of a deep cave. The dreamer's own, spontaneous associations made it seem that these were Death-Demons, and he suddenly remembered a dream of a few days before which he had completely forgotten—

Dream 38. "I am strolling through a strange, thick, dark wood with my cousin, who is the same age but more pushful than I. In a clearing I meet my beloved, who does not exist in real life. She comes down a narrow path through the wood riding a horse, and is like a princess or a fairy. She slips off her horse and after a long search the three of us find a place to settle in a kind of stone quarry in the middle of a rather inhospitable area. Our talk is suddenly disturbed by an ugly dwarf who is hiding behind a heap of stones opposite us, and who throws large stones at us. I am full of indignation and will not stand for this, and throw stones back. The dwarf disappears, but is suddenly behind us and throws stones from the back."

Both the drawings and the dream seemed completely strange to the patient, until he was able to see the sexual symbolism of the disturbing and serious intervention of the "strong Tom Thumb," and that this Tom Thumb "wants to be there" at the otherwise ethereal and tender meeting. At that time fear of women was one of the patient's actual problems. Nevertheless the unconscious of this very sensitive patient seems to be giving expression to a premonition of the deeper demands of existence behind the pressures of Eros and sexuality. The dream itself reveals something dark and uncanny comparable with the fantasy drawings behind the "disturbed idyll of love". The disturbing dwarf—an earth-spirit in a pointed Hel cap—is obviously a double of the terrible nightmare and the *Wassermann*, both of whom we have already come across as popular representations of the Death-Demon, and we may take note of the name "*Walriderske*" ("Maid of Hel") used for the nightmare in Oldenburg. From this point of view the strange wood in the dream is seen to have a particular meaning in addition to its general symbolic reference to the maternal, protecting world of the unconscious, so that it becomes a symbol for the Realm of Death and the underworld as well. The Frau Venus of Tannhäuser, as well as Frau Holle and Percht—all three of whom are attractive and dangerous at the same time—are very much at home in a wood, and in the dream the fantasy beloved who lures the dreamer like a seductive fairy or Huldr also belongs to the wood. It is as though "with the help of the dwarf" she lures him to the highest fulfilment of life and, therefore, to the awareness of mortality.

This "Virgin in the Wood" has a remote relationship to the very, very old spiral labyrinths of stone in Finland which the Swedish peasants call "Jungfrudans".[1] In these, it will be remembered, the turning point for the young men in their symbolic journey into the "Realm of Death" was sometimes a virgin and sometimes a stone coffin through which they had to creep. Virgin and coffin both symbolize death in that they receive the seed from which a new, transformed life is to be born. This rite is still dimly remembered by the peasants and suggests a hint (for us and the patient as well) about the deeper meaning of the dreamer's fear of love-relationships. The fear to which this hint points is one which cannot be overcome by determined activity, but one which can only be dissolved by a genuine transformation (new birth), so that it is quite logical that the active and pushful cousin should remain completely passive and inactive throughout the dream.

In his earlier dream as the "son of the chief" this patient became aware of the death of the father as an inevitable fate (signified by the three spectral "Norns"), and now he is confronted by his own death in the double image of fairy and dwarf—which both hides it from and reveals it to consciousness at the same time, in true fairy-tale fashion. The dream marks the moment when he prepares himself to take his place in the circle of fate (which includes both Life and Death) as a lover—for the lover creates birth, and with it his own death.

There should be no suggestion that strange and deeply significant symbols of rebirth only occur in the dreams of exceptional people who have some special disposition for this kind of thing. For example, there is an unmistakable allusion to re-birth in the dream of a very sober wholesaler of forty-five, the only son of an equally sober family of manufacturers. After several relatively superficial elaborations of

[1] See p. 94 above.

day-remnants and the like in his dreams, he reported the following (showing clear signs of disturbance as he did so)—

Dream 39. "Now I have had a nonsensical dream. I had to bring my mother (who in real life had been dead a long time) into the Clinic where she was to have a child—i.e. she was to be confined."

A few days later he had another dream which (as he explicitly said) did not arouse any particular emotion, in which his mother was dead, and he then had to fit his car into the right place in a hall which was half a garage, half a repair workshop.

It was obvious that for this man the problem was that of "release from the mother", and to judge from all kinds of indications this was a problem that he had previously understood in a most superficial way. In these dreams the unconscious acted quite independently and pointed to the archetypal progress of rebirth, that is, to the idea of a change which involves the production of something wholly new. Such a change would seem to be both an expression of and a prerequisite for the final separation from the mother, after which he could fit his car —his drive and motive power—into its right place.

There was a far richer abundance of symbols in the dreams of another businessman. At the time of treatment he was the office manager of a large firm concerned, among other things, with the building up of a new undertaking. He was thirty-eight and had reached an important position in the business world by his own efforts. He was "happily married", the contented father of several children and a conscientious and practising Roman Catholic. He had suddenly developed certain physical complaints about which he was hypo-chondriacal, and to which no corresponding organic disturbances had been found. It was clear that these complaints were symptoms of difficulties that he had encountered in the inner building-up of his own life. At first it seemed that it was a matter of tackling the task of the second half of life, that is of self-discovery and "individuation", but it soon became clear that there was still a need to deal with im-portant problems connected with the first half of life, particularly the problems of release from the parents and of making a fully affirmative relationship to woman (in this case to his wife).

At one stage in the treatment his dreams could be seen to concentrate on these two problems, and they made almost exclusive use of images which (as we know from popular beliefs and from myths) are images of Death. This series of dreams reached a provisional conclusion in a dream of Death and Rebirth. His unconscious worked at high pressure and in one month produced fourteen dreams, of which only three were primarily concerned with the elaboration of day-remnants, the rest circling about the problems we have just mentioned.

There is not space to reproduce all these dreams here, and we content ourselves by describing the most important symbols:

> The Serpent (occurring twice).
> A huge fish with dangerous, devouring mouth.
> An uncanny crocodile with magic powers.
> The Turtle which burrows underground to pass the winter.
> A horse (twice).

These animals were all experienced as ambivalent—beautiful or attractive and dangerous at the same time. In the context of the treatment (which cannot be given here) the phallic symbolism of the serpent and the relationship of the devouring and magical animals to the mother-imago were both clear. The horses can easily be understood as the embodiment of the mighty power of the "animal sphere of instinct". Five of the dreams, scattered through the series, place the emphasis clearly and unequivocally—some, almost exclusively—on the encounter with Death,[1] and this justifies us in thinking that the death motif is at work in the other dreams of the series in which it is not specifically stressed. Death is probably concealed in and revealed by the chthonic animals, which are to be understood as forms of the Death-Demon precisely to the extent that they include the double idea of procreation and birth. The concluding dream of rebirth is a kind of summary in which the various motifs are condensed. The text of the dream is abbreviated—

Dream 40a. "It is known that an old woman of over eighty has died, but her death was not noticed at first. It is now high time to bury her.

---

[1] One of them was a remarkable dream of a church which the dreamer had to build partly below, partly above ground. It was to take the form of one (or two) interconnected auricles—and the dreamer described it as "two labyrinths". There was also a dream of a kind of blood poisoning threatening the heart from the inguinal glands and one in which his mother made an accusation of murder.

I must somehow be related to her or connected with her because I am to bury her in the grave in which her husband was buried a few years ago. I get the spade and boards ready for digging the grave. It seems that my mother and brother are somewhere near. As I dig I shall have to pick out of the earth parts of the corpse of the husband, which are probably still not completely decayed, as well as his skeleton, and lay them all aside. (These thoughts arouse strong feelings in the dreamer but he says, 'It is assumed that I have the aptitude, or at least that it is possible for me to do this.') When I have lifted a layer of earth from the hollowed out grave there is a child of about two, nested in clean, white linen, lying roughly on the belly of the corpse. The child comes to life at once and I am both astonished and moved. It looks at me with beautiful, blue eyes and says, 'I am now here again!' My feelings are disturbed by the fact that my mother is standing beside me, but I still follow my first impulse and make the sign of the cross on the child's forehead saying, 'In the name of Jesus Christ.' That is the most lovely moment! Now my mother calls out joyfully, 'That's Martin!' (the dreamer's Christian name) . . . I'm now inclined to think this too but the child is far better looking than I was at that age, and may actually be a girl (the dreamer's daughter) . . .''

The same night he dreamt:

Dream 40b. "I have missed my way while climbing on a wall of rock in the high mountains with my brother-in-law. An old miner and his young companion help me on to an alpine meadow, pulling me up to it. The younger has something mysterious about him, he is like an 'understanding giant' something like St Christopher. This man has me led across the meadows by children and we come to a farmhouse with a strange, medieval gatetower. On the thick walls of this, under the roof in a kind of glass pulpit, there is a *wheel* which *continually revolves* in a horizontal plane. Things something like *lanterns* are fixed at the end of the spokes of the wheel. It is said that this is for rescuing those who are in peril on the mountain, and I understand this quite clearly. It is true that the light is beamed on to *only one sector* of the mountains—that from which I have come—but in that sector the light can be clearly seen . . . The apparatus is peculiar in that the wheel turns and the lanterns burn of themselves. It is clear that they do not need any attention."

In this dream the image of climbing too high on the "rock wall above deep clefts and abysses" seems to evoke an idea connected with the labyrinth which threatens with death. One aspect of St Christopher is the same as that of Hermes: he is the preserver of the lives of travellers and a "guide of souls" into the world of the dead.[1] The motif of the way into death and the return to life is taken with the utmost seriousness in this dream, and it culminates in the symbolic image of the wheel and lanterns. We should take it that the light from the lanterns only shines on the sector of the mountains from which the dreamer comes for a brief period, but since the wheel turns ceaselessly the light which has darkened and disappeared from that sector will "rise" again; like a star, it will be born anew . . .

The following dream of a fifty-year-old university woman is concerned with a "journey of the dead". The dream is abridged—
Dream 41. "I am hunting on my father's behalf in a wild wood, cut by water channels. Two dogs are with me. I start my journey in a primitive skiff made of three boards and two little planks. When I have killed many animals I rest in a solitary clearing, and then I know that I am really travelling for myself, and not for my father. The whole sequence occurs twice in the same night, as though on two successive days. On the evening of the first day I come to an antiquated Old People's Home, like the ones you see in North German cities like Lübeck, and go in to the low-lying ground floor. It is probably the subterranean dwelling of the old people.[2] On the second day the ending is different, as I come back from hunting I find myself at a festively spread table in a comfortable country hotel. Some old people, like dead relatives, are waiting for me. I recognize my dead mother among them and also my (still living, but very old) father. It is impossible to reach an understanding with my father who is strangely altered and whose words are utterly confused—it is as though he speaks with tongues."
One can deduce that the journey in this dream is a "journey of the

[1] A fairly recent memorial stone set up to the victim of an accident near Munich has an image of St Christopher and the inscription: "St Christopher brought him to the other shore".
[2] Primitive races often call their dead ancestors "the Old Ones", so that this journey led to community and connectedness with the ancestors, to the knowledge of individual origins.

dead" from the peculiar boat made of "three boards and two little planks", and when we take into account the mythic themes embedded in it we see that the goal of the journey is the recognition of Life in its relatedness to Death—that is, living more rightly and maturely in the presence of Death, and this, in turn, means living more independently. The dreamer had a deep love of animals and at first she is sent hunting by her father. This means she must *kill* animals, and here one might cite the stories of the Luiseño Indians about the dying, primal father Ouiot:[1] these stories are particularly relevant in that the dreamer soon realizes that she is really hunting for herself and not for her father. When we think of her roaming through the woods alone with her dogs (who are, surely, psychopomps as well) we are reminded of Frau Holle or Percht with her "little dogs", and also of Artemis keeper and killer of game who watched over birth as well. At its end the journey leads to the home of the "Old Ones", half under the ground, and in the second edition (the repetition of the dream) the significance of this is made even clearer. The huntress comes to the "table of the ancestors" and is expected to feel herself united to them in the *communio* of a meal—and just at this point there is a further indication that she herself must shape her own life. Her father speaks to her, but she cannot understand him. It may well be that his "speaking with tongues" suggests that what he says is wisdom which can only be understood by those already in the Beyond. The nearness of her father links her to the dead, but she is excluded at the same time by the strangeness of his speech, and this throws her back on herself and her own life. It is highly probable that there is a remote allusion here to what we have met before as "re-birth", but further allusions give the idea a new emphasis. It is significant that the dreamer has to visit the ancestors before she is, as it were, sent back to life by them for this sequence touches on the feeling of the continuity of life through the generations, which gives rise to the idea that the individual is responsible for his own life *in the sight of the Community of the Ancestors:*[2] though it must be admitted that these ideas only appear as germs in the dream. As is well known it is a leading Christian motif that man's responsibility for the life he leads becomes visible in relation to Death and Mortality, but this idea only appears late in the mythological formulations of the experience of death, and even then is only seen

[1] See Chapter 2, p. 30.   [2] Cf. p. 88 ff. above.

as a faint intuition—and what is true of myths is true of dreams as well.

The motif of individual accountability and responsibility before the ancestors associated with the awareness of death, is indicated with relative clarity in the dream of a jurist of about fifty-two:

Dream 42a. "I am about to hand an important document to the Highest Authority. When I reach the central crossing of the town a *rope* is suddenly thrown in a circle round (or under) the people. Those inside the circle are to be investigated by the police, and none is allowed to go away. I am one of those enclosed. It is evening and pretty dark. I make two attempts to escape, but each time I am recaptured. I object, saying that after all I am a judge and have nothing on my conscience, but I am pushed back with the words: 'Oh, with judges, too, all kinds of things crop up'."

There was a second dream the same night:

Dream 42b. "It was *All Souls' Day*. I was to join in a procession and *prayers for the dead* in my home town. I thought: 'Just leave me in peace, I already do that by myself when I choose.' Then I was suddenly like a schoolboy playing truant, and I went to do an errand for my mother."

These dreams occurred in May, nearly six months from All Souls' Day. The dreamer brought up the association that it was near to Corpus Christi, and this shows that the subject of his dream was not so much the result of working up a "day-remnant" in the ordinary sense as to a process of inner development.[1] As so often happens when two dreams are dreamt on the same night these two supplement and help to explain each other. The second dream shows that we are concerned with a "confrontation" by Death, which confirms the suspicion that the strange rope which captures the dreamer and others in the first dream symbolizes death—that it is the Noose of Death, the rope of the messengers of Yama, the Rope of Hel and the net of Frau Holle.

It may be that Death is evoked because the dreamer is still turning away from the Ancestors, like a man childishly bound to his mother. He will not think of the dead and present himself before them for

[1] It may be noted that Corpus Christi is the feast on which the idea of the provision of food out of the slain god is stressed (*Trans.*).

the others. The dream says that in the presence of death there is no judgement, and that is why he is trapped in the Rope of Death with distinction of persons, and each individual is asked as an individual *who he really is*. The dreamer has to answer for himself in his own right —he cannot claim the protection of the "persona" of his office, but must speak out of his own true being and life. The judge stands before the Judge.

16. Dreams 5: Dreams of Death as an Expression of the Process of Development

IN this concluding chapter we give some further dreams in which expression is given to the "encounter with death" to show how such dreams reflect or accompany the development or maturation of the personality. The selection of the dreams has been made from a great deal of material, and we have chosen those in which mythological and related motifs appear relatively clearly. It should be noted, however, that such "collective" motifs are only one aspect of these dreams and that each dream has an individual character of its own determined by the personality and life-situation of the dreamer. In order to enable the reader to enter into the feeling of these dreams and to understand something about them it is necessary to give a brief account of the dreamer's character and history in each case.

The first three dreams were dreamt by a thirty-year-old girl who was a salesgirl in a beauty salon, and they show to what an extent the encounter with Death in the unconscious can awaken or transform consciousness. She was psychologically immature and even infantile, and some ten years before had developed very severe compulsive symptoms. The psychic emptiness of her existence was appalling, and among other ways it showed itself in completely passive relationships with a succession of men. After a lot of treatment she dreamt the following three dreams in the course of a month, and these dreams marked a decisive turning point in her development:

Dream 43. "I am going through a wondrous avenue of trees with my friend. We are both quite naked and we hold each other's hands. Blue sky is shining between the tops of the trees, and I see a broad, sunny landscape to right and left. We are relaxed and happy. Suddenly a coal-black Negro comes behind us. He is coming to fetch me! But I say to my friend, 'Don't look! he can't do anything to us', and in spite of him we go on untroubled. All at once we are no longer in the avenue, but in the middle of the town. We are dressed normally, the black man is still coming up behind us and we run away from him. Eventually we manage to hide in the town gate and so, in the end, we get rid of the persecuting Negro." (The town gate was at the biggest traffic crossing, and the girl passed it every day on her way to the shop.)

The second dream occurred a few days later:

Dream 44. "I dream of four black dogs. It is known that they are precursors of the Russians. I find myself with other people in the power of the enemy. I have to carry out some reconnaissance work for them and part from my friend. It is a painful yet beautiful parting because we know that even though we are separated we belong together!"[1]

Naturally one's first idea is that the Negro of the first dream is a primitive "animus" figure which gives expression to the dreamer's unconscious instinctuality, and this was how the dreams were first understood. There are also pointers to the repressed "voyeur and exhibitionist instinct" (Freud) in the stress on the couple's nakedness, the exclamation "Don't look!" and the commission to spy something out which is given, characteristically enough, by the "enemies" represented by the black dogs. Interpretation along these lines fitted well with the fact that the "voyeur and exhibitionist" motif frequently cropped up in her other dreams, and was an element in her compulsive symptoms as well. Nevertheless such interpretation leaves out of account the atmosphere of the dreams, which struck the dreamer as being quite unusual. It takes no account of the relaxed happiness of the two people in their devotion to each other, the entirely new discovery of the experience of nature and the warmth attaching to the sense of mutual belonging between the dreamer and her friend.

The third dream, which followed soon after, seems to show the background of the psychic transformation which was revealing itself in the first two:

Dream 45. "I come home and open the door of my flat. As I come in

---

[1] In the German this dream (except for the last line) is given by the author in the third person. It is transposed to the first person here for the sake of consistency; Dream 28 (p. 170) has also been put into the first person. (Trans.)

I feel as though someone is there. I look into the corridor, and then into the kitchen. There is no one. Then I see into my living-room and there is an old man inside who is over sixty and looks like death. (I have actually seen this old man many times on the tram.) He has broken in as a burglar. I am full of horror and run out of the flat, but I cannot bar the door from the outside. I ring my neighbours' bells and shout for help, but there is no one to be seen and no door is opened. I am quite alone—and I go back into my flat and into the room where the uncanny man is."

The meaning of this dream-picture is unmistakable, and it belongs to us all. We suddenly know and acknowledge that Death has thrust his way into our living-room and become visible to us there. We can neither bar him in nor out: nobody will nor can help us drive him away. We must not only accept his presence in our home, we must actually go in to him. This dream is not to be treated in isolation but must be taken in connection with the other two with which it is closely connected: it helps to give a fuller understanding of them, and they in their turn illuminate it. The four black dogs which were precursors of the Russians were not experienced as particularly terrible, but even so they recall the dog form of the Death-Demon (as in the "little dogs" of Percht, for example), and give expression to the patient's hidden fear of destruction—so that the warm feeling of love and belongingness is a "deeply human" *reply* to the unconscious "encounter with Death".

These considerations also illuminate the background of the first dream (43). The Negro symbolizes more than the primitive, instinctual side of the dreamer. He is explicitly described as "coal-black" and has something of the character of the "Black Man", the children's bogey who is related to the Lord of the dark, underground Hel or Hades, the Lord of the Underworld and Death. Thus this dream also is concerned with the encounter with Death which comes to clear expression in Dream 45, and one cannot really enter into the dream situation unless one recognized this. It is just the realization that the "Black Man" is coming to fetch her that enables the dreamer to discover the blooming richness of life and so experience her companionship with her friend in terms of mutual self-giving—something which she had never done before. Again the injunction "Don't look!" might well be understood as an echo of the Greek feeling that the gods of the underworld were to be worshipped with averted head:

the feeling that the presence of Death is to be endured but that one has no need to wish to lay bare his secrets. It is only when sheer horror and the urge to escape break through again in the further course of the dream that the world becomes once more the grey place that it was for her on her (always harassed) journeys to her work in the town. In this respect the second dream represents an advance, since this time when the "Messengers of Death" decree that she must part from her friend the effect is to awaken that sense of unity which transcends separation. Finally, the third dream brings Death into her living-room, that is close to her consciousness.

The transformation which had taken place in this patient showed itself in a warmth of feeling that was quite new to her, but which was only likely to last if she was able to dare a full encounter with Death —that is, to become consciously aware of it. This would mean that death was no longer merely the "burglar" who strikes her with panic fear, but that she was reconciled to the fact that he "lives" with her at all times.

After a fairly long pause in the treatment this girl dreamt Dream 22, the dream of the Lilliput town, which shows the dreamer coming to terms with death (and life) through differentiation—a significant step towards maturity for such a hopelessly undeveloped psyche.

A thirty-five-year-old doctor had dreams which were no less primitive but which, in conformity with his whole personality, were much richer in their motifs. Rather more detailed introductory remarks are necessary. The patient had turned to his present vocation after completing a course in theology. He had mastered the study of both subjects with quite primitive vital energy, and had put a great deal of his strongly developed ambition into each. His change of profession was a result of a growing understanding about his true vocation; it was not a case of a superficial extrication from pressing problems but an attempt to grapple with ultimate questions at a deeper level. He had had an unusual accident during the war which made it impossible for him ever to think conscientiously of marriage. He was employed in a Westphalian base hospital and lived with his sister who was slightly older than he was. In the course of treatment the following dream occurred:

Dream 46. "In my former hospital a young nursing Sister[1] was lying

[1] The German is literally "deaconess-sister".

as a patient (this was an actual memory). She was very ill. A lion was lying opposite her in the bed, and its teeth were like the *teeth of a corpse*. It is known that the Sister is waiting for a pre-arranged moment when the lion will crush and devour her with its teeth . . . She has a tubercular fistula on her seat, and speaks about it quite openly in front of her fellow patients in the ward who are horrified and amazed . . . It is also known that the Sister has to go into the lions jaws because, as a Christian martyr put it, the body must be crushed in the teeth of the beast of prey like a grain of wheat that the bread, which is the Body of Christ, may be prepared."

Some time later he dreamt:

Dream 47. "I am in the garden of our home. The head physician, with whom I have recently made friends, suddenly appears. All at once a large square stone appears out of the earth. At that moment an apocryphal *logion* of Christ comes into my mind: '*Qui juxta me est, juxta ignem est*' ('He that is near me, is near the fire').[1] On the stone another text appears: '*Ecce venio*' ('Behold! I come'). Then a black-haired woman appears. She says 'This is the thalamos . . .' (bridal chamber) and she writes on the stone: '*Ut hunc thalamum benedicere, sanctificare et consecrare digneris*' ('Mayest thou graciously bless, sanctify and consecrate this thalamos')."

This was followed by the dream of the lime-cart or hearse and the enthroned bird-woman given above as Dream 24, and nine days later he dreamt—

Dream 48. "I am in my workroom. There is an indistinct figure sitting in my chair: it looks like me but also, perhaps, like my friend (and colleague). My sister comes towards me from beside my writing table and I rise to dance a Spirit-Dance-of-the-Dead with her. I have an inner feeling of triumph and am compelled to dance a waltz of the dead, beginning with a shriek that makes the others' blood stand still in their veins. My sister comes to me casting one more glance at the figure at the writing desk which has by now changed into my father (who was actually dead). She gives a rather sexual slant to the dance and this annoys me, destroying the uncanny character of the dance and so making me sad."

Mythical images appear in these dreams with impressive power. The lion, the devouring beast of prey, is the Death-Demon, and this can

[1] This was handed down by Origen.

be recognized by a very old sign—as the comment on his teeth shows, he is himself corpse-like. This interpretation is explicitly confirmed by the quotation from the martyr. The demon's victim is the nursing sister, who is waiting for the moment when he will devour her: it is said that he will actually crush her in his teeth. The very old Christian image is strangely mixed up with the demonic one, and also linked with widespread ideas about the grain of corn which is thought either to die in the earth in order to be transformed and spring to new life, or else to be crushed and transformed into food for the building up of life or for bringing the living into communion with the dead.[1] It is clear that in this dream the motif of crushing and transformation through death is given a Christian interpretation centring upon the idea of a mystical[2] union with Christ brought about by eating His sacramental[2] Body. We should notice that it is not the dreamer who has to encounter the devouring demon and experience transformation, but the nursing *sister*. This, surely, is a plastic representation of the patient's struggle to sublimate his "anima": she is to be sacrificed, as it were, to the demon or transformed into the substance of Christ.[3] But as well as this there is an encounter between the dreamer and the Death-Demon which is so concealed and shut away that it can hardly reach consciousness at all. In relation to the dreamer himself it is the *nurse* who is the Death-Demon—the nurse about whom the dream stresses the peculiar fact that she has a tubercular fistula on her seat. This sore is clearly felt to be painful, and even nauseating, by her fellow-patients and it suggests to us a characteristic which is often that of the feminine form of the Death-Demon. As we have said, there are a large number of accounts in which it is said of the Huldren, Frau Holle and Frou Werlte that their backs are hollow or rotten, or full

[1] Compare, *inter alia*, the discussion of meals for the dead made from seeds, in Chapter 8.

[2] These qualifiers of Christian theology were never, of course, intended to suggest any lack of reality in either the union or the body—they implied a "higher" and a more enduring level of reality than mere "physical reality". Ideas have been turned upside down in the last two hundred years or so, and it is often hard for modern men and women to enter into a way of thinking for which the physical is "accidental", transient and, as it were, "only just real" (*Trans.*).

[3] One might put it that the dreamer does not intend to enter into the transformation with his whole being, but only with a part of himself.

of worms and snakes and putrefaction. Accordingly the nurse would represent the seductive aspect of death, and there may well be an allusion to the medieval, theological significance of Frou Werlte. In fact the patient's next dreams (which we do not give) centre upon an uncanny, female death-figure and in one of them she has a dead person's face. This dream, however, shows an enormous inner tension, for it is as though the nurse were the victim who must be offered (and sublimated) to save the dreamer from becoming the victim of his own Death-Demon.

The second dream in which the thalamos occurs involves an even deeper fusion of the primeval, mythic experience of death with the Christian spiritual attitude. We note particularly the great square stone which rises out of the earth, because the square has been the image of an earthly order from ancient times. At the time the word "thala-mos" and the idea of a bridal chamber seemed wholly alien to the dreamer. His first associations were connected with "a pagan sacrificial stone, a Hun's grave or a Dragon Stone". Then: "Fire is struck from a stone at the beginning of the Catholic service on Holy Saturday. The stone is the grave, the fire is Christ's rising again." It was not until some time later that he discovered the idea of the thalamos again in Psalm 45, "A song of praise for God's Anointed and his Bride." In the Latin of verse 7 the throne of the Anointed is called "thalamus" and the Bride is said to stand at the right side in verse 10. Following these associations of the dreamer we get a chain of ideas leading from the pagan sacrificial stone and the Hun's grave through the grave of Christ to the Throne of the Anointed (and his Bride). We may then remember that when a young Athenian was snatched away by death he was said to "mount the thalamos (bridal bed) of Persephone," and recall the passage in Saxo Grammaticus[1] in which Hel prepares the bridal bed for Baldur, and see that we have come upon that very old mythic symbol according to which a dead man is thought of as the bridegroom of the goddess of Death, and the grave seen as the bridal chamber. It is as though with this dream Persephone herself comes saying, "This is the bridal chamber!" The figure of the dark woman in the dream has very uncanny traits, and the dreamer says that there is "something seductive and almost harlot-like" about her. "The same woman" occurred in dreams of the same period once with

[1] Cited in Chapter 10, p. 105.

a face like that of a harlot and another time with the face of a dead person. Yet the stone of the thalamos also represents the grave of Christ and His Resurrection, which is also declared by the solemn words, "*Ecce venio*". Moreover, the woman whom we have brought into association with Persephone and who is probably connected with the nursing sister of the previous dream (a female "descendant of Hel") writes upon the thalamos a text which seems based on the most holy liturgy for the Consecration of Catholic Priests, "that Thou mayest graciously bless, sanctify and consecrate this thalamos".

We do have here a true encounter with death, and death is first presented in its seductive, female form; but a very different aspect appears at the same time. The dreamer is presented with the possibility of taking a share in the authority and responsibility towards the living of those "under the earth"[1] (the ancestors), and this possibility arises out of a genuinely religious perturbation. Even so death still comes to the dreamer in the form of the "anima", and it may well be asked if he has understood that the warning "*qui juxta me est, juxta ignem est*" is undoubtedly directed at him as well. It is not clear whether it is really time for the thalamos to be consecrated with the Holy Liturgy, and the observer is not yet in a position to tell whether the dreamer himself is ready to share the thalamos (the stone as Throne of the Risen One) with the "Lord's Anointed".

A negative answer to these questions is given in Dream 48, even though the intervening dream of the primitive hearse driving swiftly to the place of the Ancestors and the "enthroned bird-woman" (Dream 24) leads us to expect something more positive. That dream seems to point to an acceptance of fate which would bring with it a sense of security, for it suggests that he who was to mount the thalamos is, as it were, on his way to the Community of the Ancestors and that life could grow and be blessed in communion with them. In view of this the development revealed in Dream 48 is somewhat unexpected.

In Dream 48 it seems that the dreamer has been stirred to the depths of his being and, as it were, intoxicated by the mighty images which he has encountered. We saw that Dream 47 left open the question whether he had really responded to the process expressed in the images with the necessary, deep-seated reverence, and now a definite answer is given—for the dreamer can be seen to regress from the inner

[1] Cf. Chapter 8, pp. 86 f., and Chapter 10, pp. 109 f.

maturity which he might have been expected to reach to a far more primitive attitude. The attitude expressed in Dream 48 is comparable with that of those who kill and in doing so identify themselves with the Death Demon,[1] but there is an important difference. With primitive people the identification involves the idea of *service*, in that the killer feels himself to be the servant or agent of the mysterious killing power, but in this dream it is much more a case of *possession* by that power. It is as though the dreamer *is* the Death-Demon itself, arousing horror and terror and disposing of the fate of men. In the dream he *wills* to prove himself Master of Death—first in his own eyes, then in those of his friend and, finally, before his father, the representative of the Ancestors—by the marrow-freezing shriek and the horrible dance of Death. Nevertheless the observer (and no doubt the dreamer himself, however faintly) can hear the question, "Who is really dancing with whom?" since it is "the sister" who actually determines the character of the dance. Though he does not realize it the sister with her "sexual" dance appeals to him as the seductive Demon of Death—not, this time, in the character of the august Persephone but in that of one of the Huldren—and this provides the dreamer with an opportunity to see that he himself is not truly "immortal Death" but a man who, in spite of everything, is condemned to the fate of procreation and of dissolution in Death. Instead of seeing this he becomes annoyed.

Dream 48 expresses a state of hybrid inflation, and it is most important that the possibility of this and the special danger implicit in it should be pointed out.

The dreams of a married woman about forty-five years old seem far simpler. The images in them have grown out of deep suffering and a careful attention to her fate into which she was continually penetrating more and more deeply.

Her youth was overshadowed and oppressed by the fact that her mother developed a chronic sickness early on. When she grew up she married a man with whom she lived in human and friendly fashion, although her marriage never wholly fulfilled or satisfied her. Her mother had become completely dependent upon her and lived with her and her husband until she died. This meant that the patient had had no real opportunity to develop her own character. The death of

[1] Cf. Chapter 2.

her mother (a year before treatment began) and climacteric disturbances had intensified her depressive attitude to a dangerous extent. During her youth and afterwards (so far as external difficulties allowed) she had at least tried to cultivate her considerable musical talent, but after her mother's death even this field of activity contracted away to nothing. The following dreams occurred within a single month, and introduced a deep change in both her inner and outer attitude:

Dream 49. "The mother of the choirmaster at our church had suddenly died. (This was a real memory.) A funeral service was held for her. I was kneeling in a pew when suddenly there was a very tall—taller than life-size—old woman beside or behind me. She looked like an animal. As I left the church she followed close behind me. I was horribly afraid, but could not run away. The old woman had great big ears and a frightful mouth—she made me think of the wolf: 'All the better to *eat* you with!' "

The patient woke in terror, openly afraid, and this made it possible for her to *glimpse* the Demon of Death—which had been a continual source of worry in the unconscious—even though it did not yet confront her directly. However dimly the dream brings the connection between the patient's depression and her mother close to consciousness: the dead mother is not only loved but feared as the Devouring One at the same time. The figure in the dream makes the patient think of Red Riding Hood's grandmother who is "transformed" into the devouring wolf, and is thus a form of the wolf-shaped Hel. One can feel the brutal menace which comes from her and understand the patient's crippling fear of the ineluctable fate to which she, like Red Riding Hood, is helplessly exposed. The dream at least showed that her unconscious fears had taken some kind of dynamic form within her.

A few days later a very different kind of image presented itself:

Dream 50. "A number of musicians were to go on a star tour. I joined them. It was somewhere high up on a mountain plateau. They had some wine. A young man offered me a glass of wine, but I declined it with thanks, saying, 'Of course I'm not working with you, I'm not entitled to this.' Then each of the participants had to leap from a balcony into the abyss: this was a condition of being allowed to take part. A little girl of six turned back with determination; 'No! I won't take part in that!' she said. She was afraid of the jump into the abyss. Nobody forced her to do it, either. Then another rather taller girl wanted to go with them or make the leap. The first girl was dressed in grey, but the second had to get a little red coat from her for the journey or the leap. The taller girl got the cloak and the little grey child (the shorter one) dissolved, leaving the taller girl looking forward to the journey."

This dream is intelligible enough if we regard it, in contrast to the previous dream, as one which gives expression to a transformation through which the dreamer's feeling for life is passing. In her neurotically entangled condition it is a big step that the dreamer should be able to recover any contact at all with the world of music, and to experience the offering of the Dionysiac, solvent element—even if this is only presented as a modest glass of wine. Even so, she refuses to enter into any real connection, any *communio* with the company because she feels unworthy. After this the course of the dream is remarkable, for we must regard the events which centre on the leap into the abyss as something more than an allegory of the leap into life which has to be dared. The dreamer thought of the leap as a kind of solemn rite, and felt that both girls represented herself—from which it is immediately clear that the sequence "younger-older child" represents an actual growth of the dreamer. The little red cloak is not only a symbol of childhood yearning but also of full-blooded life and it is connected, by association through "little Red Riding Hood", with the previous dream. This symbolic cloak has to be worn by the child when it dares the leap into the abyss, and all these considerations suggest that something of central importance is taking place which is an inversion of the events in the previous dream. In the previous dream the encounter with the wolf-faced "Death-Mother" was only half-dared, and even then it produced a paralysing horror; in this dream the behaviour of the younger girl is a close parallel, but the question is posed as to whether the growing girl will dare the "Death-Leap" into the abyss. The maturer part of the dreamer answers, "Yes!" and to this extent the dream is rightly included among the "death-dreams".

In addition to what we have just said there are parallels in cults from ancient times. In *Labyrinthstudien* Kerényi tells us that among other motifs the cultic death-flight occurs again and again in Greek mythological stories. For example, a priest is said to have performed this rite in the Temple of Apollo Leukates by throwing himself into the sea from the high rocks on which the temple was situated, and in historical times criminals were hurled into the sea from the same place—first being dressed in a *cloak* embellished with bird's feathers. If the criminals came up alive it was thought that they had expiated their crime and they were then regarded as reborn and transformed. They were pulled out of the water and discharged unmolested. It is also said that the death-flight is represented with a similar meaning in Etruscan grave pictures. It is undoubtedly a fearsome act of *daring* but the dream and the cultic legends indicate that it is the *condition* necessary to the start of a new life.[1] The legend also makes it seem that the cloak in the dream has a specific meaning—the leap into the transforming or devouring depths must not occur blindly and purposelessly but only after a deliberate inner and outer preparation.

This patient's next dream also touches on the motif of Death, although at first she was not at all conscious of the fact:

Dream 51a. "I am coming from my therapist, and find myself at the Circus[2] with the obelisk in the middle (in the town where she lived). A tram is going round the Circus which of course it does not do in reality. I see this with astonishment. The tram completes the circle, and as it passes me the second time I get on and travel in it."

Dream 51b. "Then I see an *apple-tree* which has always borne lots of fruit. One of its branches is propped up."

We can make no more than a passing reference to the *Mandala* character[3] of the first part of the dream, which is suggested by the circle

---

[1] Dreams of this kind often occur, though most of them are more rudimentary. Some time ago the author was sent an equally impressive dream by a thirty-year-old Reader at a University. Connected with powerful symbols which came first the following sequence occurred:

At the beginning the dreamer finds himself standing up to his chest in the basin of a clear spring, and this is like a baptism to him. He then finds himself with a leader-figure on a high bridge where two boys on skis are leaping over the edge into deep water, as though from a ski-shoot. At first they do it badly but each time the leap is done better. Now his companion challenges him to do this leap too, and wants to help by pushing him off. The dreamer wakes up half wanting to dare the leap, half afraid of it.

This dream occurred at a time when the treatment was concerned with the critical question as to whether the dreamer could muster the determination and strength to consummate the encounter with death in a transformation.

[2] "Round Place", "Square" is the natural English word, but "round square" will hardly do! (*Trans.*).

[3] See works of C. G. Jung, *passim*. (*Trans.*).

with its clearly marked centre. The circle is actually given very special emphasis, once by the reference to the central obelisk, and then by the importance attached to the completion of the circuit. These things point to the constellation of the personality about a centre of phallic (i.e. creative) character, and to the attainment of a bounded life. The circle which is walked (or, as here, driven) round is a very old symbol of the Temenos (Holy Precinct of the Temple) and the sacred living area of a city, and the dream may be understood on the subjective level along these lines as the reflection of an inner event. But it is the apple tree in the second part (which does not, in itself, belong in the neighbourhood of the Circus in the city) which establishes the dream's place in this sequence of dreams.

It is certainly true that the dream as a whole can easily be understood as a sexual transference dream, in a Freudian sense; particularly as the therapist lived in a "round-place". From this point of view we should first notice the circling about the phallus and then the emphatic appearance of the feminine, symbolized by the apple tree. Yet in making an interpretation in terms of an exclusively sexual transference we should, surely, miss the essential feature in the dreamer's development. It is not for nothing that the phallus has cultic importance in many religions, nor that it was set up as a symbol on *graves* in Asia Minor, for example. That reveals a knowledge of the fertility of death which brings about transformation, and this same knowledge glimmers through in the dream, reinforced by the image of the apple tree, which also symbolizes Life-transformed-through-Death—as we know from many myths and some of our dreams. It is only in the foreground that the therapeutic encounter is concerned with repressed sexual desires directed upon the therapist, and if no more is done than dissolve them by making them conscious then the patient is left alone in her deepest concern—the "really human" need to understand the continuing process of her life in a meaningful way. It is when we consider the images in this present dream as continuations of the preceding dreams that they aid such an understanding and help to clarify it.

Within the dreamer the (unconscious) knowledge of Death is being transformed. As a result of the encounter with the wolf-like Death-Mother there comes the possibility of daring the leap into the abyss in faith: now the phallic obelisk and (more distinctly) the apple tree express the demand for a total transformation (corresponding to her growth) through the encounter with Death. The shrinking back when confronted by the leap into the abyss is hardly surprising, and neither is a shivering in the depths of the psyche when confronted by a possible transformation into something new and unknown. The leap which "ought" to be made is surely madness! and so is transformation, and it is even madder when the result remains hidden and uncertain. We can well see why it is that when the patient's unconscious becomes aware of the touch of death, and before she is really aware of its transforming power, she has two dreams which terrify her to the roots of her being:

Dream 52. "As I go into the therapist's consulting room I meet two other patients who have just said 'goodbye'. They are supposed to be insane, and as they go away the therapist looks anxiously after them through the window."

Dream 53. "I am at the therapist's and have to sign something. As my signature I write, 'Maria (this was her Christian name), Eternal Father, All-merciful One.' I was terrified about this. I no longer knew my own name."[1]

A man's name is widely thought to express his inner being, and among many peoples adolescents receive a new name after passing through the rites of initiation. We may compare the giving of a new name in Baptism and Marriage, both of which mean a change of being. It seems that the dreamer was to confirm the fact that she had entered a new process of becoming by the signature—"Maria . . .": she is still herself, and yet has also become another. These two dreams spring from a final fear that besets her at this point, and they marked the climax of the crisis, the resolution of which was expressed in the next two dreams:

Dream 54. "In a year's time I am to have a child. I am looking forward to it very much."

Dream 55. "I have an etching in front of me. The Conductor X had given it to me some years earlier, shortly before he died (this was a fact in external reality—he was one of Germany's most distinguished conductors, whom the patient held in high esteem). Now, in the dream, the picture is quite pale. One can only see it as a kind of shadow

---

[1] The idea of "being mad" has continually cropped up in connection with the experience of Death (cf. Dreams 3, 41). It corresponds to the "Dionysiac" aspect, that of the "Mad God" in whom the intoxication of death and the highest ecstasy of life are united.

on the white paper. It is only within that it is really present to me and I seem to trace it over line by line, but I am very sad that it has disappeared. Can I, perhaps, reproduce it again? The etching bears the signature, 'Tchaikowski, 5th Symphony'. Above is Death the Fiddler, large and fine. Right at the bottom is the earth, and bottom left Russian peasants are being subjugated by cruel lords with knouts. A proud, haughty troika is driving in the middle, and on the right freed human souls are rising from (or, rather, out of) the earth up to Death the Fiddler."

A beautiful picture of "Die and Become!" If the patient dares to look at it squarely and sketch it in from her own inner vision, then the surface of her own existence, so far only slightly marked, will come to life and a new beginning will unfold in her soul. As the previous dream lapidarily put it she will "bear a child"—that is, of course, experience a new birth of herself.

The last dream leaves the mythological realm behind, and the image which the unconscious produces is markedly personal to the dreamer. This shows how the idea of transformation has risen up out of the deep layers of the collective unconscious and now "wills" to become the wholly personal concern of the dreamer—it approaches consciousness and "wills" to express itself in the patient's life.

Finally we present the dream of a woman of unusually rich personality, vital, powerful and deeply mature. At nearly fifty she had a leading position in political life. In this dream the motif "Die and Become" has taken form with power and pith:

Dream 56. "I was in the Kingdom of Death. It was pitch black night. I knew that I was to die. The atmosphere was calm and collected. Someone whom I did not see led me (more than once?) round a square (of water?). As we went I had to stretch out my hand several times, and when I did it came into contact with an electric field. It was as though iron balls were held above it and I felt the current in the palms of my hands quite distinctly; there was a soft luminosity on my palms. This was a kind of test. Then I was to climb down into the square and sink into the mud. I understood that it was vital not to defend myself, and to be completely relaxed. We sank quite slowly. On each side, to right and left of me, was an unknown man sharing the same fate. When we had sunk pretty deep the man on my left said, 'Sickness means being the *second person in the third person. This (i.e. death) means being the fourth person in the first person.*' Then came the moment when the mud closed over us completely. It was the end. And I was willing for it. All at once I noticed that I was coming up again, and immediately afterwards I was standing with my two companions in the open, on a kind of nocturnal meadow or terrace. I recognized Pastor X on my left (a leading Pastor, a friend of mine, who was murdered in a concentration camp). He stood sunk into himself, pale but alive. 'Now for some strong coffee!' I cried, gripped by a sudden enthusiastic, defiant joy in life."

In this dream we again come across the image of the devouring earth as the Kingdom of the Dead, and the idea of mud (marsh, rotten earth) may possibly be the unconscious's symbol for the Devouring Earth-Mother. By means of the *circumambulatio*—the perambulation which marks off the area—the Devouring One is, as it were, taken from the external world and included in one's own, interior realm; the Fate of Death (as transformation) is no longer an outer threat but an entirely inner happening. This change is only possible after contact with the electrical sphere of the spirit, after the hands have become luminous.

By this interiorizing of the event the dream is distinguished from the collective and mythical, and one doubts if one should dare even to try to interpret the words which are spoken. It is just possible that they mean that through sickness a man is in danger of losing his "thouness" and becoming an impersonal "patient", and that death, on the other hand, signifies fulfilment in totality as the ego (the first person) is extended to the whole, since four is commonly a symbol of wholeness or totality. A mystical perception seems to lie behind the spoken words which no one, not even the therapist, ought to touch: but the therapist may *allow himself to be touched* by the dream's deep resonance with the experience of death as transformation, as also by the elemental power of enthusiastic joy in life. Here we see once more how light shines out of Death upon Life, and that only the man who is prepared in his soul to pass through the Gate of Death "becomes a living human being."

Bibliography

Bachofen, J. J.: *Mutterrecht und Urreligion*, Stuttgart.
Boas, F.: *Sagen aus Britisch-Kolumbien, Zeitschrift für Ethnologie*, Berlin, 1894.
Budge, E. A. Wallis: *The Book of the Dead*, London, 1910.
Bühler, J.: *Deutsches Geistesleben im Mittelalter*, Leipzig, 1927.
Buschan, G.: *Illustrierte Völkerkunde II*, Stuttgart, 1923.
Buschor, E.: *Medusa Rondandini*, Stuttgart.
Campbell, J.: *The Hero with a Thousand Faces*, New York, 1949.
Chantepie de la Saussaye, D.: *Lehrbuch der Religiongeschichte*, 1928.
Cod. Lat. Tegerns., No. 18434 in Munich State Library.
Danzel, Th. W.: *Mexiko*, Hagen, 1922.
Deubner, L.: *Attische Feste*, 1932.
Dieterich, A.: *Nekyia*, Leipzig, 1893.
Dobrizhoffer, H.: *An Account of the Abipones*.
Dürck, J.: *Die Existenzformen von Bemächtigung und Vermeidung*.
Dührssen, A.: *Psychogene Erkrankungen bei Kindern und Jugendlichen*, Göttingen.
— *Zum Problem der psychogenen Eszstörung*, in *Psyche* 1950/51.
Eliade, M.: *Ewige Bilder und Sinnbilder*, Olten-Freiburg, 1958.
Erck, L. and Böhme, F.: *Deutscher Liederhort*.
Erman, E.: *Die Literatur der Ägypter*, Leipzig, 1923.
— *Die Religion der Ägypter*, Leipzig, 1934.
Frazer, Sir James: *The Golden Bough*.
Frobenius, L.: *Atlantis*, Jena, 1928.
Gebsattel, V. E. von: *Prolegomena einer medizinischen Anthropologie*.
Genzmer, F.: *Die Edda*, Jena, 1922.
Gercke, A. and Norden, E.: *Einführung in die Altertumswissenschaften*, 1933.
Glasenapp, H. von: *Die Religionen Indiens*, Stuttgart, 1943.
Graber, G.: *Sagen aus Kärnten*, Graz, 1944.
Grimm, J.: *Deutsche Mythologie*.
Gruppe, O. F.: *Griechische Mythologie*.
Güntert, H.: *Kalypso . . .*, Halle/S, 1919.
Hedin, S.: *Meine Hunde in Ostasian*, Wiesbaden, 1953.
Hentig, H. von: *Vom Ursprung der Henkersmahlzeit*, Tubingen, 1958.
Hentze, C.: *Mythos und Ritus um Geburt und Tod—Zur Symbolik chinesischer Kultbronzen*.
— *Sakralbronzen*.
Herrmann, P.: *Nordische Mythologie*, 1903.
Herzog-Dürck, J.: *Die Behandlung der Neurose als existentielles Problem*, in *Psyche* I. 1 1947.

Herzog-Dürck, J.: *Zwischen Angst und Vertrauen—Probleme und Bilder aus der psychotherapeutischen Praxis*, Nuremberg, 1955.

Heyl, J. A.: *Volksagen, Bräuche und Meinungen aus Tirol*, Brixen, 1897.

Hindringer, R.: *Weiheross und Rossweihe*, Munich, 1932.

Indianermärchen, published by W. Krickeberg, Jena.

Jensen, A. E.: *Hainuwele—Volkserzählungen von der Molukkeninsel Ceram*, Frankfurt/M, 1939.

— *Das Religiöse Weltbild einer frühen Kultur*.

Jeremias, J.: *Unbekannte Jesusworte*, Gütersloh, 1951.

Jordan, F.: *In den Tagen des Tammuz*, Munich, 1950.

Jung, C. G.: Collected Works (various).

Jung and Kerényi: *Einführung in des Wesen der Mythologie*, Zurich, 1951.

Kerényi, K.: *Labyrinthstudien, Albae Vigiliae* x, xv, Amsterdam/Basle.

— *Die Mythologie der Griechen*, Zurich, 1951.

Köhler, W.: *Volksbrauch im Vogtlande*, 1867.

Königer, A. M.: *Das Rätsel des Pfarrhoftores zu Remagen*, Munich, 1947.

Koty, J.: *Die Behandlung der Alten und Kranken bei den Naturvölkern*, Stuttgart, 1938.

Kretschmar, F.: *Hundestammvater und Kerberos*, Stuttgart, 1938.

Künkel, F.: *Einführung in die Charakterkunde*, Leipzig, 1928.

Lévy-Bruhl, L.: *Die geistige Welt der Primitiven*, Munich, 1927.

— *Die Seele der Primitiven*, Leipzig/Vienna, 1930.

Maass, E.: *Orpheus*, Munich, 1895.

Mahler, E.: *Altrussische Volkslieder aus dem Pecoryland*, Basle, 1951.

— *Die russische Totenklage: ihre Rituelle und dichterische Deutung* (published by the Slavonic Institute, University of Berlin), Leipzig, 1935.

Mannhardt, W.: *Mythologische Forschungen*, Strasbourg, 1884.

— *Wald -und Feldkulte*.

Maringer, J.: *Vorgeschichtliche Religion*, Einsiedeln, 1956.

Mead, M.: *Sex and Temperament in Three Primitive Societies*, New York, 1935.

Meiche, A.: *Sagenbuch des Königreichs Sachsen*, Leipzig, 1903.

Meier, C. A.: *Antike Inkubation und moderne Psychthoerapie*, Zurich, 1949. (*Studien aus dem C. G. Jung—Institut*, Zurich, I).

Mitscherlich, A.: *Vom Ursprung der Sucht*, Stuttgart, 1947.

Neckel, G.: *Walhall: Studien über germanischen Jenseitsglauben*, 1931.

Neumann, E.: *Die Grosse Mutter*.

— *Ursprungsgeschichte des Bewusstseins*, Zurich, 1949.

Nilsson, M.: *Griechische Feste von religiöser Bedeutung*, new ed., Darmstadt, 1957.

Ninck, M.: *Die Bedeutung des Wassers in Kult und Leben der Alten*, Leipzig, 1921.

— *Wodan und germanischer Schicksalsglaube*, Jena, 1935.

Otto, R.: *Das Heilige*, Munich, 1936.

Otto, W. F.: *Dionysos*, Frankfurt/M, 1933.

Panzer, F.: *Bayrische Sagen*.

Pauls, H.: *Grundriss der germanischen Philologie*.

Plischke, H.: *Die Sage vom Wilden Heere in Deutschen Volke*, Leipzig, 1914.

Preuss, K. Th.: *Religion und Mythologie der Uitoto*, Göttingen, 1923.

Quensel, P.: *Thüringer Sagen*, Jena, 1926.

Rademacher, L.: *Das Jenseits im Mythos der Hellenen*, Bonn, 1903.

Rasmussen, K.: *Die Gabe des Adlers: Eskimoische Märchen aus Alaska*, German translation Frankfurt/M.

Reinhardt, L.: *Kulturgeschichte der Nutzpflanen*, 1911.

Rhode, E.: *Psyche, Seelencult und Unsterblichkeitsglaube der Griechen*, Tübingen, 1925.

— *Urkunden zur Religion des alten Ägyptens*, Jena, 1923.

Rocholz, L. E.: *Deutscher Glaube und Brauch*, Berlin, 1867.

Rühmann, H.: *Opfersagen des Hausgeist- und Zwergenkultus*, Frankfurt, 1939.

Scharff, A.: *Die Götter Ägyptens*, Berlin, 1924.

Schmidt, A.: *Das Kornfest Nsiä, Archiv für Kultergeschichte* XXVIII, Brunswick, 1934.

— *Tontengebräuche in Nsei im Grasland von Kamerun, Wiener Beiträge zur Kulturgeschichte und Linguistik*, Vienna, 1943.

Schell, O.: *Bergische Sagen*, Elberfeld, 1922.

Schmaltz, G.: *Komplexe Psychologie und körperliches Symptom*, Stuttgart, 1954.

Schultz-Hencke, H.: *Lehrbuch der analytischen Psychotherapie*, Stuttgart, 1951.

Seler, E. G.: *Einige Kapitel aus dem (astekischen) Geschichtswerk des Fray Bernardino de Sahagun*, Stuttgart, 1927.

Setälä, E. N.: *Finnischugrische Forschungen*.

Sieber, F.: *Harzlandsagen*, Jena, 1928.

Tesman, G.: *Die Baja*.

Thurneysen, R.: *Sagen aus dem alten Irland*.

Uhland, L.: *Volkslieder*.

Vatter, E.: *Religiöse Plastik der Naturvölker*, Frankfurt/M, 1926.

Vetter, A.: *Natur und Person*, Stuttgart, 1949.

Wähler, M.: *Thüringische Volkskunde*, Jena, 1940.

Waschnitius, V.: *Percht, Holda und verwandte Gestalten*, Sitzungsberichte der Akademie, Vienna, 1914.

Wiesner, J.: *Grab und Jenseits: Untersuchungen im ägäischen Raum zur Bronze- und frühen Eisenzeit*, 1938.

Wilhelm II, Kaiser: *Studien zur Gorgo*.

Wirbel, R.: *Das Schottentor*, Augsburg.

Witzschel, A.: *Sagen aus Thüringen*, Vienna, 1866.

Wundt, W.: *Elemente der Völkerpsychologie*, Leipzig, 1913.

Wuttke, A.: *Der deutsche Volksaberglaube der Gegenwart*, Berlin, 1900.

Zaunert, P.: *Hessen-nassauische Sagen*, Jena, 1929.

Zimmer, H.: *Maya. Der indische Mythos*, Stuttgart/Berlin, 1936.

Index of Authors

Adler, A., 9
Andree-Eysn, M., 118, 129
Aeschylus, 62
Apollonius Rhodius, 61, 62
Artenidorus, 105

Bachofen, 172
Burchard of Worms, 116

Campbell, J., 52

Dobrizhoffer, H., 33

Edda, 48, 97
Eitrem, S., 31
Erasmus Alberus, 118
Euripides, 61, 105

Frazer, J. G., 29, 31, 69
Freud, S., 9
Frobenius, L., 31

Grimm, Brothers, 21, 115, 119, 125
Güntert, H., 39, 44, 52, 73, 79, 96, 97, 117, 119
Guotaere, Der, 81

Hedin, S., 47
Heliand, 78, 116
Hentig, H. v., 37
Herodotus, 47
Herzog-Dürek, J., 10
Hesiod, 40, 44, 57, 61, 62, 95
Homer, see Iliad: Odyssey
Honorius Augustodunensis, 82

Iliad, 61, 78

Jensen, A. E., 30, 33, 158
Jung, C. G., 1, 9, 11, 17, 34, 45, 47, 56, 64 f., 70, 75, 103, 104, 145, 156 f., 158, 172, 205

Kalewala, 48
Kalidasa, 52
Kerényi, K., 10, 62, 77, 94, 145, 204
Koty, J., 35
Kretschmar, Fr., 47
Künkel, Fr., 9, 136, 143

Lagerlöf, S., 182

Luther, M., 118

Mahabharata, 52
Mannhardt, W., 69
Maringer, J., 26
Mead, M., 37
Muspilli, 116

Neumann, E., 57, 71, 104
Nietzsche, Fr., 156
Nilsson, M., 31, 90
Ninck, M., 97

Odyssey, 40, 61 f., 67
Otto, R., 10, 24, 110, 131
Otto, W. F., 10

Pausanias, 58
Plutarch, 105
Pretakalpa, 77
Prschewalski, 46

Rasmussen, K., 62
Reinhardt, L., 85
Rhode, E., 68 f.
Rocholz, L. E., 32

Saxo Grammaticus, 105, 200
Schell, O., 34
Schmaltz, G., 9, 36
Schmidt, A., 89
Schultz-Hencke, H., 149
Sophocles, 61
Storm, Th., 68

Tacitus, 52
Tesman, G., 89

Uhland, L., 87

Vetter, A., 66, 72

Walther v. d. Vogelweide, 87
Wide, S., 90
Wirbel, R., 82
Wundt, W., 10, 23
Wuttke, A., 32

Zend Avesta, 44, 47, 60

Index of Proper Names

Abipones Indians, 33
Adonis, Agdestis, Attis, 104
Aegean culture, 89
Ainus, 31
Alberich, 78
Allgäu, 67
Amam (Am-mit), 71
American, 150
Amphìaraos, 58
Andreasberg, 125
Anthisteria, the, 90
Anubis, 51, 158
Aphrodite, 77, 83, 85, 86, 111, 168, 184
Apollo, 111, 183, 204
Argonauts, 61
Artemis, 44, 111, 122, 136, 191
Aesculapius, 58, 183
Assisi, 101
Assyrian, 147
Athenian, 102, 200
Athene, 78, 111
Attica, 90, 105
Austria, 96, 127
Australian, 92, 93, 124
Avernus (Lake), 40
Aztecs, 49, 51

Babylon, 51
Babylonian, 104, 179
Bachlabend, 126
Baldur, 81, 105, 125, 130
Baja, 86, 89, 109
Barbarossa, 125
Bastet, 165
Baxbakualanu Xsiwae, 63
Bavaria, 91, 94 f., 96, 127
Bavarian, 87
Bena Lulua, 31 f., 35
Benares, 52
Bennungen, 128
Boecklin, 69
Bouphonia, 31
Buryats, 34, 36
Bushmen, Bush Negroes, 25, 26

Campus Martius, 69
Camtschatka, 31
Ceram, 15 ff., 28, 64, 94, 102 f., 135, 143, 154
Cerberus, 44, 53, 55, 57
Calypso, 39, 85, 105 f.
Cameroon, 59, 80
Carinthia, 80, 122
China, Chinese, 47, 101

Christian, Christianity, 113, 114, 131, 144, 191, 198 ff.
Christ, 169, 199, 201
Chukchee, 32, 46, 76
Chrysaor, 64
Cologne (St Kunibert Church), 124
Corjaks, 31
Courlanders, 48
Crete, 98
Croats (Slovenes), 48

Danish, 68, 84, 86
Delos, 77
Demeter, 40, 43, 64, 58 f., 102, 105, 128, 130, 140, 144, 176
Demetrios, 105
Devil, 78, 80
Diana, 116 f.
Dionysiac, 204, 207
Donar, 183
Dürer, 69
Dungans, 25
Durgha, 52, 77

Echidna, 44, 57
Eden, Garden of, 28, 85
Egypt, Egyptian, 51, 55, 70 f., 102, 128, 140, 158
Einherjer, 109
Eisack, 118
Eisenach, 128, 130
Eleusinion Mysteries, 128 f., 140, 176
Elves, 84, 105
Elysium, Elysian Fields, 87 f., 120
England, 69, 94
Enkidu, 59
Ereshkigal, 104, 111, 179
Eris, 85
Erinys, Erinyes, 57, 102
Eskimo, 31, 62, 148
Estonians, 43
Etruria, Etruscan, 94, 205

Finno-Ugrian, 42 f.
Fenris-Wolf, 44, 56 f.
Ferrara, 101
Fidi Mukullu, 32
Finland, Finnish, Finns, 43, 48, 94, 186
France, 69
Freiberg (Saxony), 49
Freya, 62, 83, 85, 111, 115, 165, 184
Freyr, 85
Frisia, Frisian, 52, 74, 88

Gaia, 57, 61
Garmr, 44, 53
George, St, 94
Geranos Dance, 77, 94
Germanic-Teutonic, German, Germanic,
22, 34, 40, 43, 48, 76–78, 85, 87, 91, 96 f.,
102, 114 f.
Germany, 69, 78, 106, 118, 126
Gilgamesh, 59, 64, 104, 179
Gilyaks, 31, 154
Greyerz, 94
Greece, 80
Greek(s), 39 ff., 57 f., 60, 67 f., 70, 78 ff.,
85, 87, 95, 97, 105, 119, 122, 125, 196,
204
Grimhildr, 79
Gula, 51

Hades, 40, 43, 61, 68, 78, 120, 173, 196
Hainuwele, 15 f., 28, 102 f.
Hakeman, 76, 171
Hamatsa Dance, etc., 50, 63
Harpies, 60 f., 67, 76, 81
Harz Mountains, etc., 96, 120, 122, 125
Hathor, 71
Haulemännchen, 119
Haulemutter, 119 f.
Heidegger, 153
Hecate, 40, 43 f., 57, 80, 122
Hel, 40 ff., 52, 57, 68, 73 f., 77, 81 ff., 84,
96 f., 105, 111, 114, 118, 120, 128, 192,
200, 203
Hell, 87, 118
Held, Frau, 96
Helloch, 48, 118
Hellbrunnen, 119
Hera, 111
Hermes, 90, 111, 183, 190
Herodias, 116 f.
Herolt, 117
Hesse, 102, 119 ff.
Hesperides, 40, 85, 95
Hildburghausen, 122, 129
Hindenburg, 162
Hloðyn, 52
Hludana, 52
Hörselberg, 119
Hoher Meissner, 119, 123
Höllbrunnen, Holloch, Hollstein, Hollen-
berge, 118 f.
Holda, Holde, Hulda, 73, 78, 91, 96, 116 f.
Holle, Frau, 76, 80, 91, 96 f., 113 ff., 140,
146, 191, 192, 199 f.
Holy Saturday, 123
Huldren, 78, 80, 105, 170, 186, 199
Hungary, 48
Hydra, 57

Idun, 55
India, 29, 44, 51, 69, 77, 81 f., 109 f.
Indo-Germanic, 39 ff., 67 f., 79
Inn district, 127

Iranian, 44, 47
Ireland, 84 f.
Ishtar, 104, 111, 179
Isis, 51, 52
Israel, children of, 58
Italmens, 46

Jakutis, 34
John, St (feast of), 124
Juaneño Indians, 55, 162
Jungfrudans, 94, 186

Kali, 77
Kalmüchs, 25, 34
Koljo (finn. ugr.), 43 ff., 66, 83, 119, 161,
171
Kolio (Hider), 46, 77, 83, 96, 105
Ke'let, 43, 47
Keres, 105
Kirkises, 25, 34
Korjakes, 43, 47, 154
Ku-Kul (death-demon of the Jukaghires),
43
Kwakiutl Indians, 50, 62 f.
Kyffhäuser, 119, 121, 125

Labartu, 51
Lapps, 48
Lares, 79
Lato, Latona, 79
Latvian, 103
Laufen a.d. Salzbach, 101
Lavrin, 79
Leto, 79
Livonians, 48
Lohengrin, 79
Loki, 44
Lorelei, 79
Lüneburg, 85
Luiseño Indians, 29 f., 76, 80, 109, 191

Managarmr, 57
Mangyan, 24 f.
Maro Dance, 15, 94
Mary, the Virgin, 124
Medes, 47
Medusa, 57, 64, 122
Mexican, 55
Mexico, 49 f., 59, 63, 71
Midgard Serpent, 56 f.
Miktlantekutli, 49
Moirai, 95, 97, 111
Moma, 29, 109
Mongolians, 46
Moros, 95
Munich, 10 f., 94, 190

Napoleon, 123, 140
Nari, 97
Nazi(s), 155
Nehaennia, 52 f., 78, 85
Neri, 97

New Year's Eve, 126
Ninib, 51
Nobiskrug, 87, 90, 120
Norns, 95, 97 f., 120, 122, 150, 170 f., 186
Nsei, 76, 80, 88 f., 128
Nutka, 50

Odysseus, 62, 66
Odin, 44, 62, 64 f., 68, 78 f., 105, 109 f.
Ogygia, 40
Oldenburg, 73
Origen, 198
Orlagau, 91, 119, 124
Orphic, 111
Orthros 44, 55
Osiria, 29, 71, 140, 158
Ouiot, 29 f., 80, 109, 122, 162 f., 191

Palaeo-Asiatics, 43, 154
Pangwe, 59
Parsees, 41
Pavlov, 152
Pegasus, 64, 67
Percht, 91, 96, 114 ff., 140, 146, 191
Persephone, 40, 61 f., 68, 83, 85, 105, 107,
   111, 120, 125, 173, 176, 200 f.
Perseus, 64
Peruvian, 101
Phigalia, 58, 70, 102
Pinzgau, 127
Podarge, 61, 67
Podargos, 67
Poltava, 106
Polynesia, 102
Polynesian(s), 80, 158
Pustertal, 117

Quetzalcoatl, 59

Ran, 76
Red Riding Hood, 203 f.
Rochlitz in Saxony, 48, 118
Roman, 184
Romanesque, 82
Roman-Teutonic, 52
Rome, 69
Rosswoderer, 67
Russian-Rusinian, 80
Russia, 106 f., 125
Russian, 195
Rye-Wolf, Rye-Aunt, 69, 128 f.

St Christopher, 190
St George, 94
St Michael's Horse, 64
St Peter, 178 f.
Salza, 102
Salzburg, 118, 127 f.
Samojeds, 48
Satene, Mulua, 15, 103
Schäffter Dances, 94
Schembartlauf, 80

Schladern, 49
Schottentor, 57, 82
Schwabisch-Hall, 94
Seklmet, 165
Senoi, 23, 25
Shakti Durgha, 51 f.
Shiva, 51 f., 109
Shrove Tuesday, 126
Sibyl, 83
Sirens, 61 f., 64, 66, 77, 80, 83, 105, 167,
   170
Skuld, 95, 97, 150
Skylla, 44
Slav, 102
Sleipnir, 68
Snow White, 85, 163, 169
Solon, 86
Soma, 29, 69
South Tyrol, 49
Stalin, 168
Styria, 122
Styrian, 80
Sword Dance, 94

Takku, 23, 25
Tammuz, 104
Tannhäuser, 82, 105, 168, 185
Tartarus, 57, 120
Terlan, 49
Teuton(ic), 52, 62, 67, 73, 80, 95, 105,
   115 f., 154, 184
Theseus, 77, 94
Thesmophonia, 58, 102
Thrace, 93
Thugs, 77
Thuringia, 91, 119, 127, 129
Tibet, 47
Tibetans, 35
Tlocoa'la, 50 f.
Toer's, 71, 101
Transylvania, 126
Traunstein, 94
Trinity, 115
Trophonios, 58, 183
Turkey, 107
Twelve Nights, 76, 116 ff., 121, 126 f.,
   129 f. (see 91)
Tyrol, 122, 126, 128
Typhon, 57

Ukraine, 106
Unhold, Frau, 117
Ur and Uruk, 57, 59
Uranus, 122
Urd, 97
Urga, 47, 52, 60
Uroborus, 57

Valhalla, 87, 89, 91, 110
Valkyries, 62, 64, 68, 74, 95, 105, 109
Val-Father, 109

Wahawut, 29, 80
Walriderske, 74, 85
Wasserman, 76 f., 171, 185
Werlte, Frou, 105, 199
Westphalia, 74
Wier, 98
Wild Hunt, 48, 51, 61, 67, 73, 84, 117, 120, 128
Wild Hunter, Wild Huntsman, 67, 77, 84
Wildenstein, 124

Wildholloch, 119
Witoto, 29, 58, 76, 109

Xolotl, 51

Yama, 17, 86, 88, 109

Zellerfeld, 119
Zeus, 58, 111
Zips, 91

Index of Subjects

Abandoning, Abandonment: of dying, etc., 23, 25, cf. 34 f.
Actuality: of death (see reality), 144
Aggression, 149, 155
Agricultural: peoples, etc., 23, 33
Alders, 40
Alluring: element, etc. (see "luring", "seduction"), 64
Ambivalent: character (of Frau Holle), 121; mother fixation, 181
Amplification(s), 137, 184
Ancestors, 89, 110, 191 f., 201 f.
Anima, 104, 156, 199, 201
Animals, 120, 128 (see "masks")
Animistic, 88
Animus, 195
Announcer, Announcing: of death, 120, 124, cf. 49, 96, 105
Anorexia, 174
Antlers, 129
Anxiety, 34, 37, 81, 108, 136, 138, 149
Apotropaic, 151
Apple(s), 53, 84 f., 91 f., 95, 164, 172, 184, 205 f.
Archaic, 136, 139, 147, 151, 160 f., 169, 171, 184
Archetype(s), 8, 45, 103, 110, 181
Archetypal, 187
Assimilation: of Frau Holle to Mary, 124
Assurance, 137
Avoiding, 136

Back (without flesh), 29 (see "hollow")
Band (over eyes), 79, 170
Baptism, 88, 205
Bat, 64
Bird(s), 55, 59 f., 62, 65 f., 75, 167; bird-characteristics, 59; bird-demon, 64; bird-dragon, 59; bird's face, 170; bird's feathers, 205; bird-form, 61, 65 f., 70; bird-like (death-demons), 64; bird-woman, 167, 198, 201
Biography, biographical, 137, 161

Birth, 19, 28, 52, 63, 70, 92 f., 157, 165, 186, 191, 208
Black (of death, etc.), 51, 77, 140, 170, 195 f.
Blindness, 79
Blossom, 120
Bone(s), 47, 51, 162; bone-chambers, 89
Book: of the dead (Egyptian), 71; with pictures, 173 f.
Boy (Divine Child), 153, 155
Brazen: serpent, 58
Bread, 91, 127, 198; stamped with image, 130
Bride (death as), 99, 103 ff., 107 f., 200
Bridegroom (death as), 99, 106, 108
Brother(s), 103, 145, 168, 171
Brother-in-law, 189
Burglar, 194
Burial, burying, etc., 23, 25, 39, 41 f., 46 f., 82, 167, 188 f.

Cake: Christmas (with image of Frau Holle), 122, cf. 130
Cap: of invisibility, 78, 140
Capa, 53
Cape, 176
Carrion-eating: ravens, etc., 60
Cat(s), 123, 129, 164 f.
Cemeter(y) (ies), 147, 165, 168
Centre, 93 ff., 184, 205 f. (see "middle")
Changeling(s), 123, 146
Changing, 50 f., 198 (see "transformation")
Chariot: race, 69
Chasing, 164 (see "following", "persecution", "pursuing")
Child(ren) (and Frau Holle, etc.), 22, 123, 204, 207
Child: Dionysos, 183
Child (Divine), 189, 207
Childbirth, 181
Churingas, 93
Circle, 192, 205; circular: course, ride, etc., 69, 93, 184

Circuit, 95
Circumambulatio(n), 184, 209
Circus, 205 f.
Climacteric, 142, 203
Cloak, 53, 78, 121, 123 f., 204
Clown, 156
Collective: images, motifs, etc., 17 f., 160, 194; unconscious, 208
Communio(n): with ancestors, of living with dead, 84, 92, 108 f., 191, 204
Community: of dead, of ancestors, 88 ff., 109 f., 191
Compensation, compensatory: dreams, 182; 142
Composite: god-figures, 71 (see "mixed images")
Compulsion: neurosis, 163; compulsive: neurotic, 136; symptoms, 194
Comrade, 150
Corn, 69, 139, 175 f., 199; Festival, 80, 128; Corn-Aunt, Corn Wolf, 120, 128, 176 (see "Rye-Wolf")
Cornfield, 140, 174 f.
Corpse, 112, 189; corpse-devouring: wolf, 46; corpse-devourer, 43; corpse-eating: dogs, 47, cf. 162 f.; corpse-ritual, 47
Court, 126, 150; court-martial, 150
Coyote, 49 f., 55, 163
Cradle, 125
Creator: god, 29, 109
Cris(is)(es), 136, 138, 207; critical: question, 205
Crocodile, 81, 102, 188
Crops, 102
Cross, 169, 179; sign of, 189
Crow(s), 60, 62, 66
Cult(s): Osiris, 140; Polynesian, 158; ceremonies, 59; customs, 140
Cultic: rites, 126; customs, 130; death-flight, 204
Cypress, 40

Dance(s), dancing, 15, 50, 63, 94, 112, 164 f., 169, 198, 202
Daring, 204 f., 209
Dark, raincoat, 175
Daughter(s), 70, 102, 106 f., 144 f., 175 f., 181, 189
Dead: Dances of, 112, 198, 202; food of, 86, 91, 172 (cf. Ch. 8 passim); journey of, 16, 190 f.; Kingdom of, 87, 104, 177, 179, 209 (see "Death, Kingdom of"); prayers for, 192; tribunal of, 71, cf. 192 f.
Death: passim; bonds of, 77; driving out of, 121, 129; Kingdom of, 208 (see "Dead, Kingdom of"); modern attitude to, 9 f., 112, 136; sentence of, 140, 150 f.
Death-Bride, 103 f.
Death-Demon, 24, 40, 43 f., 46, 48 f., 51 f., 55 ff., 66 ff., 75 ff., 93, 95 ff., 99 f., 102 f.,

105, 108, 110, 112 f., 114, 117 f., 126, 130 f., 140, 165 ff., 169, 173, 198
Death-infant, 146, cf. 62
Death-Father, 109 f., 128
Death-flight, 204
Death-hounds, 48
Death-Mother, 99, 101 ff., 159, 163, 169, 181, 184
Death-wishes, 155
Decayed: corpse, 189
Decision, 20
Decomposed: body, 41
Demon: see "Death-Demon"
Depression, 136, 142; depressive, 147, 167, 203
Deranged: condition of father, 143 (see "insane")
Descent: into Hell (Mexican), 63
Destiny, 25, 69 f., 71, 81, 95, 145 (see "fate")
Development(s), 17–20, 106, 135, 176, 194, 206 (see "growth" and "maturation")
Devouring: Death, etc., 43, 53 ff., 99, 100 f., 165 (see "voracious")
Digestion, 153 ff.
Dismembering, dismemberment, 15, 64, 76, 102, 157 ff., 171 (see "tearing to pieces" and 189)
Dispensary, 152
Distaff, 122
Doctor, 146, 165
Dog(s), 41, 44, 46 ff., 51 ff., 55, 78, 109, 120, 139 f., 152, 154, 160, 162, 177 f., 182, 190, 195 f.
Doll: straw, 121, 129
Double spiral, 93, 97 f.
Dragon, 56 f., 59, 94, 106, 120, 200
Dream(s), 10, 75, 105, 114, 132, 136–209; of one night, 139, 144, 152, 167, 192
Drowned: people, 171
Duck's foot (of Percht), 120
Dwarf(s), 78, 185 f.
Dwelling-places (of Frau Holle), 118

Eagle, 60, 64
Ear(s): of corn, 69, 120, 127, 140, 175
Earth, 39, 41 ff., 44 ff., 52 f., 63, 99 ff.; earth-goddess, 71; Earth-Mother, 102 f., 155, 209 (see Mother-earth); Earth-Woman, 63
Easter, 94, 121, 126
Ecstacy, 28, 32, 108, 156, 207; ecstatic, 36, 37, 70, 111
Eggs, 129, 172
Elf, elves, 84, 86, 88, 91, 93
Eternal: life (Christian), 115
Ethic(s), 115, 155 (see "moral")
Excessive: demand, 116
Execution, 150 f.
Exhibitionism, 165; exhibitionist instinct, 195
Exposing: of dying, 34 f., cf. 25

Fairy-tale(s), 62, 106, 119, 125, 158, 163; fairy-story, 85

Fate(s), 93, 95–98, 103, 106–109, 115, 122, 125, 131, 135, 151, 162 f., 202, 208 (*see* "destiny"); fateful: character (of Frau Holle), 125

Father, 15, 21, 88, 109, 142 ff., 152, 161 ff., 170 f., 190 f., 198, 202; Fathers: World of the, 88, cf. 109

Father-God, 110

Father-image, 161 f.

Favourites: of fortune (children), 123

Fear(s), 22, 32, 118, 139, 150, 155, 160, 168 f., 197, 185 f.

Feathers: as raiment, etc., 62, 76, 97, 205

Felling: trees (= killing). 178, cf. 32

Fertility: rites, etc., 69, 102, 109, 123, 127 ff, 206

Fire, 41, 63, 129, 198

Fish(es), 22, 188

Fixation: father, 145; mother, 146, 152, 181

Flight, 23 f., 26, 66, 143 f., 156, 165, 180

Flints, 123

Following, 178 (*see* "chasing", "persecution", "pursuing")

Food, 15, 84 ff., 88, 91 f., 95, 102, 127, 154, 159, 172, 175

Food-gathering: people, 23

Fool(s), 129, 156

Forest, 177 ff., 182 (*see* "wood", "jungle")

Friend(s), 147, 166, 194 f., 198, 202; friendly: fashion (of married life), 202

Fruit-trees, 85, 127 (*see* "apple", "tree")

Future, 165

Garden: of death, 40; of Frau Holle, 119, 124

Genuine(ness), 137, 154, 169

Ghostly: skeleton, 144

Gingerbread (with picture of Frau Holle), 124, cf. 122

Girl(s), 58, 94, 106, 125 f., 129, 157, 170, 173, 184, 189, 203 f.; Girl-Child, 164

Goat, 83

God: sacrifices, 130

Goddess: of love, 71, 77, 111

Grain, 163, 175; grain-testing beds, 175

Grave(s), 68, 94, 107, 189, 200, 206; grave chambers, 98; grave pictures (Etruscan), 205

Greenhouse, 175

Growth, growing, 19, 135, 138, 174 ff. (*see* "development" and "maturation")

Guilt, 115; guilt-complexes, 150

Half-moon, 129

Halo, 178

Harvest, 128

Hat: of Hel, 78

Hate, 158; hatred, 155

Healer (Gula), 51; healing significance (of snake), 58

He-goat, 78

Hell, 40; jaws of, 42, 100; Lord of, 118; torment in, 116

Hell-hound, 44

Hellish: mouth, 56

Herb: of life, 59

Hidden, the, etc., 38, 60, 64, 72, 83, 98, 109, 114, 140, 160

Hiding: in the earth, etc., 39 f., 41, 78, 96

Hider: Goddess, etc., 38, 42, 45 f., 60, 66, 77, 109

Hippopotamus, 71, 102

History: feeling for, 89

Hollow: back, 80 ff., 199 (cf. 121 and *see* "back"); places, 119

Hood, 175, cf. 53

Horns, 129

Horror, 21 ff., 36, 66, 72, 89, 162 f., 169, 202, 204

Horse(s), 66–70, 75, 95, 106, 154, 166, 185, 188; horse's head, 102 (*see* "steed(s)")

Hospitable, "hospitable one", 86 f.

Host: the Nobis, etc., 87

Hound: of death, 48; of hell, 44

Human: form(s) (of Death-Demon), 66, 72 f., 99

Hun's grave, 200

Hunting, 30, 190 f.; dog, 49; peoples, 30 f.

Huntress, 117, 191

Hyena, 55

Hysteric, 136

Identify, identification, 21, 145, 151, 162, 202

Illusory: belief, etc., 36, 108, 143, 151, 166

Image(s), 19, 38, 41 f., 44 f., 58 ff., 70, 72, 109 ff., 115 f., 130, 135 ff., 156, 177, 209

Impregnation, 69 f., 102

Incorporating, 130, 159, 172

Ineluctable: fate, 151

Inescapable: destiny, etc., 95, 108

Inevitability, 98

Inexorable: fact (of death), 147

Inflation, 202

Initiation: rites, 19, 207

Inn (of Hell), 87 (*see* "tavern")

Insane: patients, 207 (*see* "deranged")

Instinct, 69, 188, 195; instinct-determined: events, 137

Instinctual: satisfaction, etc., 152, 196; instinctuality, 195

Insurance: Office, 166

Intoxicated: dreamer, 201; intoxicating: drink, 69

Inversion: complementary, 144

Invisibility: cap of, 78, 140

Iron: claw, shoe, hook, teeth, gloves, 76, 122

Irresistibility: seductive bride, 108

Ithyphallic: Hermes, 183

Ivy, 40

Jackal(s), 52, 109
Jaguar, 49, 55
Jaws, 42, 44, 46, 99 f., 120, 198
Journey: of dead, 16, 190 f.
Jump (into abyss), 203
Jungle, 179; jungle-labyrinth, 178 (see "wood", "forest")
Juniper tree, 122

Kitchen, 159; magic, 155
Knife, 76, 158

Labyrinth(s), 98, 164, 167, 179, 182, 190; labyrinthine: path, 94; mortuaries, 169; environment, 178
Labyrinthstudien (Kerényi's), 204
Lady, 83, 158
Lament(s), 103, 107
Larve (etymol.), 79
Law(s), 91, 98, 150
Legalism, 115
Leopard, 55
Leprosy, 170
"Letzte Richt", 127
Light, 189
Liturgy, the Holy, 201
Love (goddess of), 71, 77, 111
Loving: devotion, 115
Luring, 84, 86, 186 (see "alluring", "seduction")

Mad: God, etc., 207, cf. 143, 190
Madonna (mantled), 124
Magic, 26, 51, 151; magic(al) practices, attitude, etc., 31, 34, 36, 50, 165
Magna Mater, 166
Maid: of Hel, 185
Maiden(s), 15, 58, 105, 107, 109, 128, 173
Mandala, 75, 205
Man-eater, 55
Manifestations, 111
Mares, 73 f.
Mantled: Madonna, 124
Marriage: rite, 86; with Death, 99, 105
Marrying (and death), 104, 125, 175
Mask(s), 63, 79 f., 120, 128, 139 f., 161, 168, 170, 180
Maturing, maturation, 17, 125, 176, 194 (see "development" and "growth")
Maturity, 175, 202
Maternal: Being, etc., 100 f., 103, 185
Maternity, 70, 102
Meander (-band), 93, 97, 179, 183
Megalithic: culture (pre-Hindu), 101
Megaron, 102
Meteor, 55
Middle, mid-point, 94, 182 (see "centre")
Mixed: images, 70, 99 (see "composite")
Moon, 30, 64, 122
Moor: maiden(s), 105, 128

Moral, 112, 115, 150, 155; morals, 126
Mors (etymol.), 74
Mother, 71, 85, 100 f., 104, 107, 120, 124 f., 130, 144 f., 152, 154, 157 ff., 169, 174 ff., 179, 187, 189, 192, 203; archtype, 181; Terrible, the, 71 (see "Death-Mother")
Mother-Beloved, 104
Mother-Divinity, 102 (see "Mother-goddess")
Mother-earth, 53, 100 (see "Earth-Mother")
Mother-Figure, 184
Mother-fixation, 146, 162, 181
Mother-goddess, 71, 93 (see "Mother-Divinity")
Motherhood, 102
Mother-image, 156; Mother-Imago, 181, 188
Mountain: maidens, 105
Mourners, 168
Music, 164 f., 204; musical: talent, 203; musicians, 203
Mystery, 26, 58, 98

Naked: body, dogs, etc., 161, 164, 194
Name, 207
Natural: science, 27
Nature (experience of), 195
Nausea, 154
Necessary: sacrifice, 151; necessity (of sacrifice, etc.), 155 f.
Negation (death as), 164; negative: aspect (of death-image), 136
Negro: village, man, 170, 194 ff.
Net(s), 76 ff., 96, 122, 125
Neuros(is)(es), 10, 19, 149; neurotic: sickness, attitude, etc., 18, 141 f., 152; neurotic, 9, 136
Night(s), 95, 116 ff., 125–130
Nixies, 105
Noose (of death), 77, 192
Nose, 121, 127, 167
Nuisance: of dying, 136

October-Horse, 69
Oedipal: urges, 149
Offering, 127
Omnipotence: of science, 136
One-eyedness, 79
Oracle, 183
Order, 26 f., 109 ff., 126, 130, 135, 200

Pallor, 78
Panic, panic flight, etc., 22 ff., 66, 136, 146, 156, 197
Paradise, 28, 58
Parents (murder of), 30, 34
Part-ego, 138
Persecution, 165, 180 (see "chasing", "following", "pursuing")
Persona, 193

Personal: character (of Death-Demon), 166
(see "human form"); image (of death),
208
Pestilence, 73
Phallic: symbol(s), symbolism, 58, 183,
188, 206; phallus, 52, 104, 129, 206
Phantom: woman, 119
Phobia, 136
Physician, 198
Pig(s), 58, 102
Plague, 48, 94
Play-analysis, 157
Plumed: serpent, 59
Poles (opposite), 172; polar: opposites,
121; polarity, 83
Pomegranate, 85, 91, 107, 173, 184
Poplars, 40
Poppy-seed: cake, 91
Prey: beast, birds of, 44, 46, 55, 106
Priests (as doctors), 165
Princess, 185
Psychopomp, 51, 183, 191
Psychosclerotic-rigid: attitude, 136
Pursuing, 180 (see "chasing", "following",
"persecution")

Quince, 85, 184

Ram, 182
Raven(s), 60, 62 f., 65, 109
Real (death as fully), 145; experience (of
numinous), 162
Reality: of death, life, change, etc., 12, 49,
100, 135 f., 142 f., 147
Re-birth, 92, 173, 177, 179, 186 ff., 191,
cf. 208
Reconstruction, 158
Redemption, 108, 115
Regressing, regression, 100, 114, 116, 131,
142, 146, 161, 201; regressive: dreams,
142
Repressed: Death-Image, etc., 114, 136,
155, 195, 206; repression, 155 (see
"suppression")
Reproduction, 93
Responsibility, 89, 191, 201
Return, 179, 181 (see "reversal")
Reversal, reversing (of spiral, etc.), 94 f.,
107 f., 181 (see "return")
Reverence, 137, 162
Rewarding (and punishment), 126
Rider, 68, 72
Rite(s), 17, 22, 34, 53, 163, 165, 184, 204
Ritual (n.): of the dead, 47; of Holy
Saturday, 123; sacrificial, 154
Ritual (a.): act, 167
Robber, robbery, 106
Rope, 77 f., 193
Rope-dancer (Nietzsche's), 156
Round: dance, 169
Rye-Wolf, 69 (see "Corn Wolf", "Corn
Aunt")

Sacrifice(s), 31, 48, 69, 130, 151 ff.; sacri-
ficing, 58, 150
Sacrificial: animal, death, etc., 31, 69, 154,
169, 200
Sadistic: urges, hate, 149, 155, 158
Science, 27, 132, 136
Sea-serpent, 55
Secret: societ(y)(ies), 50, 128
Security, 136, 150
Seduction, 169; seductive, seductress, 80,
83, 99, 104, 108, 186, 200 f., 202 (see
"alluring", "luring")
Seed(s), 90 ff., 93, 95, 186, 199
Serpent(s), 57, 75, 102, 188 (see "snake(s)")
Sexual: urges, difficulties, etc., 149, 160,
198, 202, 206
Sexuality, 19, 22, 173
Shades, 84
Shadow, the, 156, 172
Ship, 84
Shooting, 129, 140, 150 f.
Sickle, 122 f., 129
Sickness, 43, 51, 76
Sinking: into mud, 208
Silver: cradle, watches, etc., 125, 129
Sister, 86, 104, 145, 172, 197 ff., Sister-
Anima, 156
Skeleton(s), 52, 79, 112, 144, 167, 177, 189
Skiff, 190
Skulls, 52, 174
Snake(s), 52, 55–62, 64, 66, 83, 109; snake-
shaped: Demon of Death, 85 (see
"serpent(s)")
Son, 170 f., 186; of God, 116; son-in-law,
106
Soul(s): Land of, feasts of, etc., 86, 90 f.,
108, 124, 127
Sower: parable of, 175
Spectre(s), 48, 180
Spinner(s), 96, 122, 125
Spinning, 96 f., 123, 125; spinning wheel,
122, 130; spinning whorl, 97; Spinning
Woman, 96
Spiral(s), 59, 93 ff., 97 f., 179, 181, 183 f.,
186
Spiritual: development, character, etc., 65,
73, 174
Spiritualization, 65
Square, 182, 200, 208; square: stone, 198
Stage: play, 173
Steed(s), 67 ff., 72, 107 (see "horse(s)")
Stepmother, 169
Stones, 93 ff.; stone: coffer grave, 94
Strange, strangeness (of speech of the dead),
143, 191
Strangling, 152
Straw: doll, etc., 121, 129
Sublimating, sublimation, 155, 199
Subterranean: Hel, etc., 82
Suffering, 102
Suffocating, 33, 69

Sunk: into earth, sunken, 176 (*see* "underground", etc.)
Super-ego, 162
Superintendent, 164
Suppression, 142 (*see* "repression")
Swans, 97
Sword, 150 ff.; Sword Dance, 94
Symbol(s), 22, 56 f., 64 f., 68, 70, 91 f., 93, 100 ff., 107, 128, 140, 158, 169, 175, 184 f., 187 f., 204, 206
Symbolic: meanings, etc., 76, 90 f., 94, 130, 185, 204
Symbolism, symbolizing, 58, 63, 69, 95, 97, 173, 185, 192, 196
Symptom(s), 149 f., 160, 187, 194 f.

Tavern: of Helle, 81; the heavenly, 87
Tearing to pieces, 117, 129 f. (*see* "dismembering")
Teeth: corpse, dogs', etc., 78, 120, 125, 177, 198
Temenos, 182, 206
Temple: dream, 183
Terror, 24, 55, 203
Test(ing), 181
Thalamos, 105, 198, 200 f.
Thief, 55, 179
Throttling, 154
Tiger, 101, 178
Torchlight, 129, 205
Towers: of Silence, 41
Tram, 180, 205
Transformation, 9, 51, 64, 70, 92, 107 f., 125, 128, 131, 135, 144, 146, 153, 166, 171 ff., 176, 179, 184, 197, 199, 206 f.; transforming, 16, 19, 26, 51 f., 154, 159, 164, 186 (*see* "changing")
Tree: apple, or with apples, 125, 184, 205 f. (*see* "fruit trees")
Tremendum, the, 24 ff., 35, 37, 40, 55, 112, 141, 151, 162
Tribunal: of dead, 71
Trident, 76
Turning point(s), 108, 186 (*see* "return", "reversal")

Turtle, 188

Unalterable (fate), 151 (*see* "ineluctable", etc.)
Uncanny (effect, etc.), 24, 26, 168, 200
Underground, under the ground (castle, workshop, etc.), 118 ff., 124, 152, 196

Victim(s), 68
Violets, 40
Virgin, 181, 186
Vivisection, 152
Voracious: animals, 56 (*see* "devouring")
Voyeurism, 165; voyeurist: instinct, 195

Wasting, 174
Water, 29, 32, 97, 119, 157, 171 f., 205, 208
Water-bird, 120
Water-channel(s), 178, 190
Water-holes, 124
Waterman, 171
Wedding: carriage, 123
Well, 97, 119, 123
West (Land of Dead), 43, 85
Wheel, 189 f.
White: horse (and rider), 68
Wife, 146, 170
Wine, 203 f.
Witch, 184
Wolf, wolves, 41, 43 f., 46 ff., 50, 52 f., 55 f., 66, 75, 109, 120, 165, 203; wolf-faced: Shakti-Durgha, 52; wolf-figure, 56; wolf form, 120; wolf-hound, 54; wolf-masks, 80, 120; wolf-monster, 128; wolf-skins, 80
Woman, women, 29, 32, 63, 81, 85 f., 96, 105, 119, 123 f., 126, 129, 141 ff., 145, 152, 156 f., 160, 163 f., 167 f., 170, 172, 174, 176, 180 f., 184 f., 188, 190, 198, 200 ff., 208; Women of the Woods, 80
Wood(s), 118, 125, 130, 185 f., 190; Women of the Woods, 80 (*see* "forest", "jungle")
World-law, 97